Excellence
Without a Soul

Excellence Without a Soul

How a Great University
Forgot Education

HARRY R. LEWIS

PublicAffairs
A Member of the Perseus Books Group
New York

The caricature of President Eliot (page 36) originally appeared in the *Harvard Lampoon* of March 1, 1877. The chart showing the percentage of students on Dean's List (page 110) was compiled by the author and first appeared in the *Harvard Crimson* on April 23, 2001. President Lowell's curve of grades from A to E (page 113) originally appeared in an article by Robert C. Brooks in the journal *School and Society,* January 2, 1915. The 1830 table of the Scale of Rank (page 128) is reproduced courtesy of the Harvard University Archives (Corporation Papers, 2d Series, UAI 5.130, Box 2, 1830). The Thomas Nast cartoon "Education: Is There No Middle Course?" (page 233) originally appeared in *Harper's Weekly,* August 30, 1879.

Copyright © 2006 by Harry R. Lewis

Published in the United States by PublicAffairs™, a member of the Perseus Books Group.

Book Design by Brent Wilcox

Library of Congress Cataloging-in-Publication Data
Lewis, Harry R.
    Excellence without a soul : how a great university forgot education /
Harry R. Lewis.
        p.   cm.
    Includes bibliographical references and index.
    ISBN-13: 978-1-58648-393-7 (alk. paper)
    ISBN-10: 1-58648-393-5 (alk. paper)
    1. Education, Higher—Aims and objectives—United States.   2.
Universities and colleges—United States.   3. Academic achievement—
United States.   4. Harvard University.   I. Title.
    LA227.4.L49   2006
    378.73—dc22

                                                                2006002732

First Edition

10 9 8 7 6 5 4 3 2 1

To the memory of my parents and Marlyn's
for what they gave us

Remember that our University was founded for the public good and that it has a great history—that steady progress is essential to its moral and intellectual health and that the health and true welfare of our University and our country go hand in hand. Thus have they been made and thus only shall they endure.

—Henry Lee Higginson,
presenting the Harvard Union to
the University, October 15, 1901.

[T]he test of a civilization based on liberty is the use men make of the liberty they enjoy, and it is a failure not only if men use it to do wrong, but also if they use it to do nothing, or as little as is possible to maintain themselves in personal comfort. This is true of our institutions as a whole and of the American college in particular. . . . the warfare of civilization is waged not more upon the battlefield than in the workshop, at the desk, in the laboratory, and the library. . . . the crucial matter in civilization is the preparedness of young men for the work of the world; not only an ample supply of the best material, but a product moulded on the best pattern, tempered and finished to the highest point of perfection.

—A. Lawrence Lowell,
in a speech to Yale freshmen, 1916.

Contents

Acknowledgments

This book is a culmination of a three-year project. I am grateful to Boston University and to the Massachusetts Institute of Technology (MIT) for harboring me while I was at work, and in particular to my hosts at those institutions, Azer Bestavros and Hal Abelson. The kindness of the theory group at MIT's CSAIL, where I did the most intense writing, kept me stimulated, connected, and cheerful.

As detailed in the endnotes, I consulted a great many sources in the course of my research. The Harvard University Archives assisted me by easing access to many original documents. The Harvard Presidents' reports, available online through the Archives' website, were a rich source, expanding the view of Harvard's history gained from secondary sources, especially the several works of Samuel Eliot Morison and Frederick Rudolph's *Curriculum*. For my views on the history and present condition of college athletics, I found much to ponder in Ronald A. Smith's *Sports and Freedom*, David C. Young's *The Olympic Myth of Greek Amateur Athletics*, and Paul Weiss's *Sport: A Philosophic Inquiry*. Most quotations from *The Harvard Crimson*, *The Boston Globe*, *The New York Times*, *The Harvard University Gazette*, and other newspapers and newsletters are from their online archives. I extend special gratitude to the *Harvard Crimson* for its openly accessible archives and for the decades of student journalism they record. The *Crimson* has always provided the best documentation of student life at Harvard. With the end of the publication of the president's reports, it also provides the only easily accessible documentary record of many faculty events.

The quotations that open the book and each chapter are the words of figures who have had roles at Harvard. I note their connection to the university if it is not obvious.

I know nothing about being dean that I did not learn from someone else. To all the assistant and associate deans, Senior Tutors, Proctors, and Tutors who worked with me at Harvard over the years, I am deeply grateful for what they taught me. They are the ones who see Harvard and its students as they really are. A special salute goes to the memory of the greatest of them all, the late John Marquand.

Many people read drafts of part or all of this book and suggested improvements. In particular I want to thank Fred Abernathy, Karen Avery, Charles Ducey, James Engell, Vasugi Ganeshananthan, Anne Greene, F. Washington Jarvis, Karan Lodha, James McCarthy, John McGrath, Michael Mitzenmacher, Elizabeth Studley Nathans, Jeff Orleans, Georges Peter, Leo Reyzin, Peter Roby, Hal Scott, Harvey Silverglate, John Stauffer, Susannah Tobin, and Dean K. Whitla for their reactions and comments. Thanks are due also to several readers who feared to be acknowledged in print. Special thanks to my two favorite Harvard students, my children, Anne and Elizabeth Lewis, since their comments were helpfully informed by their inside knowledge of both the author and the College. To my brother Richard Alan Lewis go my particular thanks for pointing out the analogy between grades and dress sizes, and I am grateful to Pamela Keel for directing me to the facts about clothing measurements. My wife Marlyn McGrath Lewis taught me everything I know about the larger mission of Harvard College, and provided endless love and support while I was dean and throughout the writing of this book. I am more grateful to her than words can express.

Whether he was acting out of faith or foolishness, I am glad John Taylor Williams agreed to be my literary agent. I am grateful to Peter Osnos of PublicAffairs for having confidence in this project, and to my editors there, Clive Priddle and especially Lindsay Jones, for making it a reality. Lindsay's editorial skill and support made the last stages of the writing the easiest while improving the manuscript the most.

Any errors that remain are entirely my own. So are all the poor judgments and bad attitudes; none of those who were kind enough to read the manuscript in draft should be assumed to share my views. While I was dean, I enjoyed warm relationships with many wise colleagues with whom I occasionally disagreed—chief among them Jeremy Knowles and Neil Rudenstine, who knew that universities are stronger when ideas are freely exchanged and respectfully debated. Those at Harvard unable to tolerate such disagreements were, happily, very few.

What Universities Have Forgotten

America's great research universities are the envy of the world. For decades they have been wellsprings of invention and creativity in service to society. Society in turn sees the undergraduate colleges within the great research universities as the pinnacle of educational opportunity for aspiring young people. The wedding of research and teaching in universities puts the greatest experts in contact with the most promising students. In top-tier universities, the distinction of the faculty and the achievements of the students are greater each year than they were the year before. Countless families dream that their sons and daughters might attend Harvard, Princeton, Yale, or Stanford. They see admission to such schools as recognition of their children's achievements and enrollment as a guarantee of a bright future.

Older alumni talk about how much universities have changed—how many more women and minority students there are, how much more casual students' social and sexual lives have become, how many more laboratories and research centers there are than in their days, and perhaps how much academic standards have slipped. Yet the basic framework of undergraduate existence has hardly changed at all.

Those of us who have given our lives to these great universities take pride in thinking that they are at core the same as they ever were, only better because the students and the faculty are both better. We value stability, and even as we promote ourselves as constantly looking to the future, we shy away from radical changes. Distance learning may be a great idea, but the ivy walls of our dormitories and classrooms are part of what it means to be an Ivy League college. College athletics may be out of control in some places, but a college that did not have a football team would be as alien as one that served only croissants for breakfast.

The college within the great, old research university is an American icon, and even at their most progressive, American icons want to remain recognizable to American citizens.

Yet the alumni observers are not wrong either. Deep changes have occurred in these old colleges, changes far more profound than the new skin colors and buildings that the alumni notice at their reunions. Old institutional structures survive, but many have lost their meaning. The curriculum is richer than ever, but it is no longer wrapped around any identifiable ideals. Professors still give grades to students, but the grades are now credentials for graduate schools rather than instructional feedback from professor to student. The disciplinary system has evolved into an adversarial minicourt rather than an instrument of moral instruction, an opportunity to help the young grow up and become responsible adults. And intercollegiate athletes, with their heavy training regimens and long competitive seasons, seem to defy an intellectual undergraduate ideal. They are seen instead as specialists taking unseemly joy in physical competition and motivated by materialistic incentives for their college education.

In short, universities have forgotten their larger educational role for college students. They succeed, better than ever, as creators and repositories of knowledge. But they have forgotten that the fundamental job of undergraduate education is to turn eighteen- and nineteen-year-olds into twenty-one- and twenty-two-year-olds, to help them grow up, to learn who they are, to search for a larger purpose for their lives, and to leave college as better human beings. So totally has the goal of scholarly excellence overshadowed universities' educational role that they have forgotten that the two need not be in conflict. Lip service to education remains, in the form of teaching prizes and student public service programs. Some professors embody the ideal of the great scholar of visible moral integrity. Peruse the speeches of the leadership of any university and you will see plenty of talk about the world's problems, about the pursuit of knowledge, about hard work and success. Rarely will you hear more than bromides about personal strength, integrity, kindness, cooperation, compassion, and how to leave the world a better place than you found it. The greater the university, the more intent it is on competitive success in the marketplace of faculty, students, and research money. And the less likely it is to talk seriously to students about their development into people of good character who will know that they owe something to society for the privileged education they have received.

While I served as dean of Harvard College, I tried to address some of these problems, as they manifested themselves at Harvard. Possibly I became part of these problems instead, or of new ones. In 2003 I surrendered my position in the administration and focused again on full-time teaching and research. This book is the fruit of my effort to understand what I grappled with in the dean's office. Viewing the problems across perspectives of space and time, I hope to shed light on where they came from, why they seem so intractable, and what is needed to resolve them.

I have been a Harvard professor for more than thirty years, having started in 1974. Over the decades I have heard many academic discussions about teaching, about the curriculum, about grading, about athletics, and about responding to student misdeeds. I have almost never heard discussions among professors about making students better people. Professors are warned to look for signs of emotional distress in students and to steer them to mental health services. But what most students need more than psychiatric referrals is help shaping the lives that they themselves, and not their parents, will lead. Presidents, deans, and professors rarely tell students simple truths, for example that the strategizing and diligence that got them into the college of their choice may not, if followed thoughtlessly, lead to an adult life they will find worth living.

Events at Harvard, where I have spent my academic career, are the texts I analyze, the source of anecdotes and data on which I base this analysis of higher education. Much of what happens at Harvard happens elsewhere; a similar book could have been written about any of our great old universities. Yet in some ways Harvard is unique; it is the oldest university in America, and so it has set many standards, for good or ill, and even among icons it holds, in the public imagination, a distinctive preeminence. The illustrations I draw from Harvard may be typical or may be extreme, but they are all true, all telling, all indicators of broader trends.

In this book I explain how Harvard and our other great universities lost sight of the essential purpose of undergraduate education. Education is not the teaching of dates and formulas and laws and names and places. Education, in fact, is not mere classroom teaching at all. Pedagogy is often excellent at research universities, and often not. But whether they experienced good or bad classroom teaching, college graduates who pick up their notebooks and transcripts at their twenty-fifth reunion realize that almost none of the facts and figures stuck to their ribs. They are more likely to remember a brilliant instructor than what that instructor taught. Nonetheless, alumni report that they learned a lot in college. In the words of Jorge Domínguez, a liberal education is what remains after you have forgotten the facts that were first learned while becoming educated.* By that standard, what education will today's college graduates take with them?

Ages eighteen to twenty-two are a developmentally appropriate time for young people to leave their parents and become immersed in the life of the mind. They are ripe to draw energy and inspiration from their independence and from an assault of new information and challenging ideas. College, at its best, is where students start to understand themselves and to find ideals and objectives for their lives. They are of an age where the burden of responsibility shifts—students arrive out of a state of dependency on their parents, and depart to take responsibility for themselves and for society. Students much younger than seventeen are not ready for the independence that college provides, and students well into their twenties may be too old to make best use of the opportunity for dramatic personal change. And yet universities seem oblivious to the opportunity they have to shape lives—even though the age of their undergraduates has evolved, over time, by a rational and intentional process, to span exactly these critical years of personal development.

Colleges provide well the practical things that support students' personal growth. They furnish the necessities of daily life within a comfortable community of peers and professors. At the top universities, financial aid is sufficiently generous that few students need to earn large amounts of money to attend. With the amenities for a real education in place, why do colleges within the great research universities now fail in their larger mission?

The how and the why of this failure, and its consequences, are the subjects of this book. Universities have lost the sense that their educational mission is to transform teenagers, whose lives have been structured by their families and their high schools, into adults with the learning and wisdom to take responsibility for their own lives and for civil society. The loss of mission need not be permanent, but the great universities will have to want to restore idealism to undergraduate education in order to realize their potential.

---

*Citations of facts and original sources appear at the end of the book, along with related commentary. A page number and a phrase identify the passage.

Hollow Excellence

Shape without form, shade without colour,
Paralysed force, gesture without motion
—T. S. Eliot (A.B. 1909), *The Hollow Men*

U niversities are complicated places. They serve constituencies that have conflicting agendas. They occupy an exalted place in the eyes of society at large. It is not surprising that they face complex problems and that it is difficult to find wise and principled responses. Watching universities struggle to resolve problems reveals much about what does and doesn't make them tick.

The hard questions facing universities are hard for good reasons. Colleges' failures can result from lapses of institutional will or from faculty laziness. Sometimes money stands in the way of solving a problem. But many hard problems have a long history. They have not been solved because they involve conflicting values, and because there is no natural point of equilibrium between the contrary forces. Universities lack confidence that they know what they are doing. They have lost their sense of how to fit their problems into an encompassing educational mission.

This book reflects on struggles Harvard College faced during the years I served as dean. The problems are how and what we teach, how and why we assign grades to students, how we do or do not help students develop a sense of responsibility for themselves, and how money affects students generally and college athletes in particular. These struggles are interesting in part because each has a cyclical history, a sure sign that the university cannot sustain a truce in a long war of conflicting values. Universities have had wiser voices on these matters at some moments than others, and today we are distressingly short of good sense.

1

All universities, great and small, share these problems. But few universities can boast that their postures today are born of principle and confidence. The hollowness of current responses exposes a loss of wisdom—a loss that is not inevitable but that will take principled leadership to recover.

Teaching. Teaching in its broadest sense embraces all the lessons colleges convey to students during the formative years they spend as undergraduates. Classroom pedagogy is one aspect of teaching, but so are the purposes and structure of the curriculum and the perennial issues of advising and student-faculty contact. Every quarter century or so, colleges reconsider their curricula in response to developments in culture and society. Curricular reviews, then, should provide opportunities for reflection on society as well as on academia. The roles given to science, engineering, and the humanities are indicators of how the university perceives its role in shaping the worldview of undergraduates.

Harvard's most recent curriculum review began in 2002, a year after the appointment as president of Lawrence H. Summers, an economist and former U.S. Treasury Secretary. Summers's tumultuous presidency turned out to be the shortest since Cornelius Conway Felton died in office in 1862. On a Friday night in January 2006, the dean of the Faculty resigned, reportedly at Summers's insistence. Summers himself resigned a few weeks later in the heat of Faculty complaints about his judgment, management, and integrity. Meanwhile, several review committees advanced curricular recommendations for possible Faculty action in the spring. Some professors grumbled about the review's lack of inspiration, already reported in a harsh critique in the *New York Times*. Others were ready to approve the changes, content that the proposed curriculum would demand little of either professors or students. Yet others thought it unwise to make any curricular changes in a climate of Faculty rancor and administrative chaos.

From the beginning, science and globalization drove the review. These would be the engines of human progress in the coming decades, and Harvard College needed to make these themes central to undergraduate education. The new curriculum would marginalize the humanities. At the same time, the academic disciplines themselves provided the raw materials from which an undergraduate curriculum should be composed, as though students going to college en route to careers in business, law, or medicine were doing something slightly out of place at Harvard. This superimposition of economic motivations on ivory-tower themes has exposed a university without a larger sense of educational purpose or a connection to its principal constituents. We have forgotten that we teach the humanities to help students understand what it means to be human. We have forgotten that students from families with little money may not share the assumptions that well-to-do families have about the purpose of education. And we have forgotten that universities could not teach students about our interconnectedness in a global society were it not for the freedoms that American society provides to citizens.

In early 2006 Harvard's academic self-study was meandering toward an uncertain result. Reports were issued in bureaucratic prose reminiscent of Washington at its worst, touting such objectives for a Harvard education as "to further facilitate flexibility for intellectual exploration and opportunities for cross-disciplinary study." The bottom line was that nothing in Harvard's curriculum was held to be more important for Harvard students to learn than anything else. Like a mother of quarreling children, Harvard looked at its thirty-two academic departments and their countless subspecialties and declared that they were all loved equally. The president, having failed to stamp his plan on the Faculty's thinking, withdrew from the process entirely. The professors who carried out the review proposed instead a curriculum with no meaningful expectations at all, a formula they hoped would please their students and avoid academic turf wars among themselves. Whether the Faculty resists or endorses the proposed low-stress curriculum will test Harvard's claim to leadership in American higher education. Academic leaders have in the past regarded new curricula at Harvard as important models for other colleges and newsworthy indicators of intellectual trends. Early signs are that the flaccid curriculum toward which Harvard was moving in early 2006 will be ignored.

Private universities occupy a privileged position in American society. They are the beneficiaries of a social compact. In exchange for the benefits that universities provide to society, they receive tax exemptions as well as specific liberties in support of their academic mission. Thus the public has an interest in questioning whether universities are holding up their end of the deal on which their privileges rest, whether they are providing the education America's brightest and most ambitious citizens should receive.

Less noisy than curricular debates, but equally consequential for those being educated, are serious discussions of the relationship between colleges and their students. Why, for example, is it so hard for colleges to satisfy families' reasonable expectation that students at expensive colleges will have help negotiating their way to their degrees and to adulthood? Problems of student-faculty contact, instruction, and advising have deep roots, dating to the days in the nineteenth century when Harvard and other universities emerged from colonial colleges that had far more limited ambitions. Many pious statements have been expressed about professors who are both great teachers and great scholars, and some of the pieties are true. But research universities have never convincingly decided what relationship faculty should have with undergraduates. We are still living with the aftershocks of an earthquake that happened more than a hundred years ago, when colleges became universities.

Indeed, the aftershocks are growing stronger, not weaker. Professors are hired as scholars and teachers, not as mentors of values and ideals to the young and confused. Instead of expecting professors to help students, universities hire counselors and advisors, and even take pride in absolving faculty of responsibility by touting peer advising systems that use students to do the job professors should do. Meanwhile, our official rhetoric continues to claim that the professors are the true source of guidance for students. For institutions that take pride in telling the truth, that hypocrisy is embarrassing.

Grading. Few subjects are as great a delight to critics of prominent universities as grading practices. People almost always attribute inflated grades to some modern corruption of higher education, perhaps the chaos at universities that accompanied the Vietnam War era. But evaluation is as old as teaching, and complaints about soft grading are of nearly the same antiquity. The cycles of complaint and reaction are so regular, and they started so early, that "grade inflation" must have deeper causes. In fact, faculty members cannot decide how to grade because they do not agree on the purpose of grading—is it meant as an objective measurement, a credential for the benefit of graduate schools and prospective employers, or is it meant to motivate students to learn and to reward them if they do? With no consensus on the purpose of grading, there is likely to be little consensus on the standards to be used. Unless universities affirm that grading has mainly an educational purpose, faculty will continue to bristle at university policies adopted under pressure of public embarrassment.

Personal responsibility. The relationship of the student to the college is increasingly that of a consumer to a vendor of expensive goods and services. The high purchase price is justified in the mind of the consumer on the basis of even higher future return. Yet colleges can and once did have a very different view of their role with students, a role in helping them set standards of personal behavior for themselves, of helping them learn to live up to an honorable ideal of personal integrity. That role of moral education has withered, conflicting with the imperative to give students and their families what they want for the money they are paying. Under pressure to make students happy so that the all-important survey rankings will stay high, colleges feed students candy rather than tougher stuff that will strengthen their ethical bones. As a result, we hold students as fledglings rather than push them out of the nest. Simply put, colleges no longer do a good job of helping students grow up.

In one area colleges cannot make students happy because they are each other's adversaries: The disciplinary system, created as an instrument of instruction, has come under severe pressure in the highly public case of date rape. Should universities try to be ahead of society in setting standards for the prevention and adjudication of peer rapes, as they have been in so many areas of social progress? The choices are not easy, especially when society itself is unsettled on some of the important tensions, such as the balance between the presumption of innocence of an accused male and the presumption of truthfulness of a female complainant.

The apparatus of the old disciplinary system, meant mainly to handle adolescent indiscretions, has responded clumsily to these serious criminal charges. The placating responses made by Harvard—the creation of new definitions for rape and new judicial processes for responding to allegations of rape—dramatically illustrate the extent to which a great university has forgotten that its first job should be to turn students into adults. Colleges have designed an artificial and infantilizing sexual world for students to live in. As a result, expectations about personal actions and their consequences in college are wildly out of line with those in the world students will face beyond college. In the area of student sex, colleges act as though the way to turn students into responsible adults is to treat them like children.

Money and students. There has never been a time when money did not matter to universities, but the raising, charging, and spending of money affects higher education to an unprecedented degree today. At most universities, severe financial pressures have reduced offerings to students. But at the Ivy League universities and other highly competitive schools, students receive more and better amenities and services and a curriculum that is bigger, if not necessarily better. The competition to enroll the best students drives these colleges to build better dormitories and gyms and to offer more generous financial aid programs, at the same time as they charge higher and higher tuition to those able to pay the "sticker price." To keep their students and families happy, colleges shape their programs around student demands and desires. It would be easy to think that the higher-education marketplace is working in favor of these fortunate students, even as it is working against students at second-tier colleges and state universities.

In fact, the free market is not working to students' advantage, because not all students need the same things. Universities are acting not on what students need but on what they myopically claim to want. The great universities have used their financial resources to open their doors to qualified students of limited means, but have thought little about how they fit into the consumer culture that governs the relationship of students to the university. Students who have little money are especially concerned about jobs and careers, for example, but Harvard portrays employability as antagonistic to the true purposes of a liberal education. At the same time, the empty curriculum is so removed from the real world that many students learn how capitalist economies create jobs from the solicitations of companies eager to hire them. Something is wrong with our educational system when so many graduating Harvard seniors see consulting and investment banking as their best options for productive lives.

Intercollegiate athletics are an important special case in the struggle over students and money in higher education. College sports are a major cultural phenomenon in America and a force shaping the undergraduate experience at virtually all colleges. For many Americans, athletic skill is the one form of excellence developed in universities that they can recognize and admire. But a great deal has been written in recent years—as in not so recent years—about the distortion of academic values caused by overemphasis on athletic competition. Universities, especially the leading state universities, spend vast sums on athletic programs in which only a handful of students participate. Few universities break even financially on their athletic programs; certainly none of the Ivy League schools do.

Nevertheless, the harsh critiques of college athletics have caused remarkably little to change. Americans, for reasons rooted deep in our past, want colleges to take athletic competition seriously. But the scale at which money now changes hands raises in sharp form old questions about intercollegiate athletes: Are they really amateurs? Does the NCAA definition of amateurism correspond to a noble amateur ideal of indifference to money and competitive success? And why does money pollute students but not colleges? These questions are particularly germane in the Ivy League, which does not offer athletic scholarships and whose athletes are disproportionately from low-income groups. *really?*

The entire philosophical basis of the amateurism standard in intercollegiate athletics is questionable. Institutional policies and practices have not caught up with the changed realities of the socioeconomically diverse student body. Amateurism was born as a vehicle for separating the social classes in Victorian England. When the concept was imported to America, the social-class rationale was no longer stated explicitly but was enforced implicitly by the ban on compensation. Today, with colleges enrolling more low-income students and with high-income parents pouring large sums of money into the coaching and training of their children, the amateur-professional division no longer draws the correct distinction. It benefits universities but not their students. It discourages, more than it supports, students' pursuit of excellence in the one domain where excellence can be unambiguously determined. At the same time as the standards of dignity and mutual respect associated with amateurism need reinforcement, the financial constraints on students need to be relaxed, albeit very carefully and selectively.

Universities have only a weak and superficial grasp of the scope of their educational mission for undergraduates. They are often puzzled about what they should teach, and are uncertain, even unprincipled, in their responses to educational problems. Two main forces combine to produce these troubling circumstances—competition and consumerism.

Competition

Competition has become intense—among students, among faculty, and among universities themselves. Competition is in itself neither good nor bad, but it has both good and bad consequences. Unquestionably, the rewards of being part of a top-tier university have caused competition for both student and faculty slots that has made both groups better in certain important ways. Yet while the competition has drawn better faculty and students to the top universities, it has driven the two groups apart.

The professors, vying for positions and promotions at the great research universities, are ever more narrowly trained, more specialized, and more advanced in their specialties. Tenure is given mostly for research, in part for teaching, and not at all for interest or skill in helping students become adults. Few of today's professors enter academia as a mission, a noble calling. Of those who do, few survive to tenure at top universities. The pressure to publish a great deal in a short time makes academic writing duller, less adventurous, and more technical, since junior faculty members opt to write what they know to be acceptable to the journals and academic presses. In the sciences and some of the social sciences, the dependence of research on government financial support distorts the directions in which truth is sought. As patentable inventions hold the promise to enrich the university, professors view their relations with industry as being as important as their relations with students.

Anyone analyzing the hiring and promotion standards of a research university will wonder not why the professors care so little about students, but why so many do care, in spite of the lack of incentives and rewards. Sometimes in the sciences, but especially in the humanities, the scholars who make the greatest contributions are those whose depth of knowledge is matched by their breadth of understanding, those able to draw on interesting things that were learned even though they seemed irrelevant. Such breadth is exactly what makes professors inspiring and wise mentors to the young. Sadly, it is given scant value in the process by which young faculty members are hired and promoted.

Raising the standards for tenure has narrowed the selection criteria for faculty, bringing in men and women more accomplished in their particular research programs but less concerned with the welfare of students at large. There are many notable exceptions. At Harvard, the Masters of the residential Houses have chosen to give their time and energy to their communities. Senior professors who knit together a residential fellowship of faculty, graduate assistants, and undergraduates, they compromise their careers as scholars and sacrifice their personal privacy and that of their families to live cheek by jowl with hundreds of students. No one would choose that existence without a deep desire to help young people mature. But the narrowing of the faculty, the trend away from polymaths and toward specialists, and the lessening of concern for students' hearts and souls in favor of almost exclusive interest in their minds are natural consequences of the way professors are now chosen.

Universities aspire to increase the ethnic and gender diversity of the faculty, though that goal will be hard to attain. Rarely do they even suggest that professors should be responsible for students as whole human beings during their crucially formative years, or that professors should be chosen, trained, or evaluated with that objective in mind. Many pressures affect the process that creates the Harvard faculty: There are imperatives to hire the people who will make the next great scientific discoveries, the people who can carry forward some tradition of learning that will disappear from the earth if it does not exist at Harvard, the people who will make an impact in the world of arts and letters, the people who will have influence in Washington and in Beijing, the people who will help the Harvard faculty more closely resemble the Harvard student body, the people who will be acceptable in a classroom setting. And the process of faculty hiring takes place in an intensely competitive environment—every other research university has the same goals. Yet there is no competitive pressure for faculty who will help students to become better people.

Professors have become more specialized in their interests, which are ever more distant from what ordinary citizens understand or care about. Academic presses now publish books selling fewer than 300 copies. "The demands of productivity," a humanities editor says, "are leading to the production of much more nonsense." At the same time, students have become more representative of America and even of the world. Students whose ethnicity, gender, social class, economic circumstances, or geographical origin would have made them unlikely to attend Harvard or Princeton or Yale a generation ago now comprise a majority of the student body.

The faculty and the students share their success in academic competition but are wildly different in their goals in life. Few students arrive at college wanting to be professional academics; most professors have never wanted to be anything else. Many families regard top-tier universities as gateways to a secure future; many professors feel themselves isolated from, and even contemptuous of, the larger and less academically inclined society. Many professors see a liberal education as fostering as much respect for their particular academic virtuosity as for the next professor's; many parents see a liberal education as the entrée to a bright future in the world of finance, medicine, or law. And few students, parents, *or* professors see a liberal education as what it once was: a period in which young people can be freed from the presumptions and prejudices with which they were raised, freed by the power of ideas to pursue their own path in life.

As the pool of college-bound students has enlarged over the past half century, the student bodies at the top-tier universities have grown very little in size. There are many excellent universities, and the preeminence of the top tier in the public imagination is an irrational—if understandable—national obsession. The top few schools are perceived as the big prizes, and everyone knows which schools they are. Ambitious families watch *U.S. News and World Report* closely every August, eager for their children to attend one of the colleges near the top of the page.

The larger applicant pool and the generally stable size of Harvard's student body have combined to cause the one thing everyone knows about Harvard admissions: It is next to impossible to get in. Parents, teachers, and alumni are understandably bewildered and angry when a high school student with impeccable objective qualifications, the best student seen in years, is turned down for admission. Even if academic talent were the only admissions criterion, objective tests are far too insensitive to distinguish among the students in the Harvard applicant pool. The top quarter of the class scored at least 1580 (sum of verbal and math) on the SAT I, and even students in the bottom tenth percentile posted scores of around 1320. Valedictorians are a dime a dozen at Harvard—the admissions office could fill the whole class with them if it wanted to. As it is, about 90 percent of Harvard students graduated in the top 5 percent of their high school class.

Because so many applicants present high grades and test scores, Harvard makes admissions decisions with the aid of nonnumeric information. What might catch the imagination of the admissions committee when considering one student but not another can be hard to divine. As often as not, admissions officers look for a capacity to make the absolute most of the available opportunities. A student who has achieved the maximum with limited opportunities is more promising than a student who has achieved more in absolute terms but less relative to what was possible. Some see in this philosophy a flawed sort of "comparable worth" theory of admissions. Is fine poetry by a child of parents who do not read books more worthy than an excellent science project by a child of two biology professors?

It is understandably difficult for parents and applicants to recognize that admission is not a game with prizes granted to the students with the longest résumés. Achievements of the past may provide evidence of promise for the future, but the objective of the admissions process is to invest in the future, not to reward the past. The laborious recruitment and selection process, with all its contradictions and disappointments and balancing of imponderables, is an attempt to create a community of individuals who, after living and studying together for four years, will go on to change the world for the better in all kinds of different ways. The large mission is to affect all of society—including the academic world, though future academics have never been the principal product of Harvard College.

That subjectivity is hard for disappointed candidates and their parents to understand, and it can also puzzle the professors. A good student, one who shows promise even to go on to postgraduate work in science or the humanities, may lose out to a less stellar student who is extraordinarily excellent at some nonacademic pursuit. How can this be right, when Harvard is, first and foremost, an academic institution? Harvard seeks more than its share of academic stars, but relatively few students each year gain admission solely on the basis of academic qualifications. The larger objective of the selection process is not to pick people who have the best high school transcripts but to pick people who will make a difference in the world. Those who are simply "good students" finish the academic race far behind Harvard's dazzling top students. Deprived of the only thing that distinguished them in high school, "good students" can wind up sadly adrift at Harvard. Students need something in which they can achieve excellence and take pride. A healthy college does not consist entirely of high school valedictorians, many of whom would be miserable in the bottom half of their college class. Raising the academic level of Harvard College by admitting more valedictorians and letting them compete against one another for academic honors might, for better or worse, produce more professors and fewer doctors, engineers, businesspeople, and lawyers; it would surely produce more suicide victims.

The student body has undergone radical change over the past forty years. Fewer than 40 percent of those who graduated with me in 1968 attended Harvard on financial aid; more than 70 percent of Harvard students do today. Most of my classmates were white, and most were men. Today, few generalizations about the student body would withstand scrutiny. Name any identifiable group, and the odds of gaining admission today are below 50 percent. Yet universities relentlessly compete for the top students in the applicant pool. There are only so many prizewinning mathematicians, top quarterbacks, and published poets among high school seniors, and every university wants to enroll the best of the best.

The bottom line is that most Harvard students are talented, but the reasons aren't always obvious in the professor-student context. Students have told me they were reluctant to consider attending Harvard, having a snooty or brainy stereotype in their minds, until they met other accepted students who were also making their decisions. Students are relieved to discover that their fellow students "seem normal." Of course, they aren't really "normal"; it isn't normal to be as smart as Harvard students tend to be, and it isn't normal to have a cross-section of American ethnic and religious groups sleeping in double bunks. But what is normal to these students is that the cleverness and compelling individual stories and ebullient ambition are broadly shared, even though geography and ethnicity and gender are varied. A typical Harvard entering class includes half the members of *USA Today*'s All-USA High School Academic First Team, and more than a third of all the National Merit Scholars in the country. A certain level of distinction is normal at Harvard, and it is both enjoyed and ignored.

The result of Harvard's reaching out in so many directions is unprecedented, intense pressure for admission. Harvard and other colleges get blamed for the stress of the admissions process, but the colleges are only allocating a scarce resource sought by more and more people. Families, mistakenly believing that there is a magic formula for admission, program their children to accumulate credentials and try to keep every aspect of their children's lives spotless.

This competition, like all competitions, has its merits—students come to college with remarkable skills and achievements. But since they have seen their secondary education as aimed at winning the admission game rather than at laying a foundation for later life, they arrive ill equipped for the freedom that college provides. Some respond by substituting for the admissions game a competition to get admitted to a top graduate school or to get a job offer from a top company. Others have a sufficiently firm psychological foundation to make good use of their freedom. But too many students, perhaps after a year or two spent using college as a treadmill to nowhere, wake up in crisis, not knowing why they have worked so hard—or realizing, perhaps, that they do not want the future for which their parents pushed them so hard and sacrificed so much.

It is the fortunate student, in such an existential dilemma, who can find guidance from a professor. More likely, if help is to be found anywhere, it is in the sympathetic ear of the staff—the hired advisors, the psychological counselors, the athletic coaches, the financial aid officers, perhaps the graduate student teaching assistants or even fellow undergraduates designated as official advisors. Faculty members often think that anyone admitted to such a prestigious university ought to be grateful to be studying what the professors are offering, and they grumble about why admissions slots have been wasted on such unmotivated students. A vicious cycle results: The university administration responds to student dissatisfaction with the faculty by hiring more student support staff, rather than by endangering the university's competitive position in the market for professors by expecting better of them.

Competition is neither good nor bad, any more than other economic realities have intrinsic moral direction. But the competition for success in the marketplace of the great research universities has insidious negative consequences for the way they operate and for what students should expect from them.

Consumerism and the American dream

At the same time as universities compete for the top students, the price universities charge for attendance has soared. A single year's bill at most private universities, not just the top-tier ones, is now about the same as the median U.S. household income. The top universities provide generous need-based financial aid, which enables the less economically advantaged students to attend without placing backbreaking burdens on their families. Low-income parents have, nonetheless, made sacrifices to prepare their children for college, which they rightly recognize as the way to economic security they have not enjoyed.

When the high-income group paying top dollar and the low-income group seeking social and economic advancement arrive at a university that has no particular educational mission in mind, the high expectations and demands from the students and their families meet shallow, pacifying responses from the university. Some families want value for money, and some want a clear shot at the future. Some complain about the full range of material deliverables, from double bunks and food service to the lack of institutionally structured social life. Others combat the senseless academic requirements hammered out by faculty, years earlier, in some interdepartmental compromise no professor or dean can remember or explain. At Harvard, at least, students are bewildered by how the university proudly denies preprofessional curricular options to students who in great numbers will enter the professions after they graduate. The universities, eager to maintain their attractiveness in the marketplace, respond by matching concessions to complaints rather than offering educational vision. They improve students' physical amenities; they create beer halls on campus; and whatever the curricular complaint, they respond by relaxing requirements so that students can do what they want to do. What the universities will not do, however, is to place unsustainable demands on the professors, who are themselves free agents in a competitive market. And the universities wonder why students are still unhappy.

Students are unhappy because too many faculty members are not interested in them, except as potential academics, and the curriculum is designed more around the interests of the faculty than around the desires of the students or their families. Both the university and those attending it miss the larger point: The way to make the university experience more satisfying is to recognize and support its larger educational purpose.

In a competitive environment, in which the university wants the best students from the entire world's population and the best faculty from all the world's Ph.D.'s, public image has become much more important than when universities relied on self-reproducing pools of students and professors. Offices of communications and public relations play significant roles in every major university. Deans and professors are discouraged from talking to the press, lest they say something "off-message" from an official university position. As an unhappy consequence, media scrutiny regularly draws attention away from the real issues, and public embarrassment drives decisions that should be made with more principled deliberation.

When the press of bad news drives policies, universities patch things that look bad rather than understand and repair things that truly are broken. By spending time on grading policies or on the number of football players in the freshman class, as all the Ivy League colleges have done in recent years, these great universities have addressed symbols in which the media or other targeted groups have interest. But they have missed the opportunity to improve undergraduate education in far more significant ways. General pronouncements about commitment to worthy ideals, such as close student-faculty contact and stiff grading standards, sound dignified and make good copy. University leaders like sweeping generalities because they entail none of the internal risks of going after negligent professors or departments—though they also yield none of the potential rewards of focused efforts.

A particularly troubling pathology occurs when even the governing boards do not know what is going on. Universities were never truly ivory towers, and they should not be; they are privileged with independence and public support because they serve society. Thus public scrutiny is appropriate and important. But one irony of the current climate at Harvard is that as the school has adjusted to relentless scrutiny from external media, the institution that historically provided "public" scrutiny, the alumni-elected Board of Overseers, has become carefully managed and quite docile. Its members learn of important changes at Harvard by reading about them in the papers. Remarkably, this shift has continued even as the regulation of corporate governance in other businesses has intensified as a result of the misdeeds of notoriously inattentive boards of directors.

Universities increasingly communicate, even to their own families, via press releases rather than through thoughtful letters and reports. Reasoning becomes degraded as news communiqués avoid complex subjects. Summaries and sound bites give the media an exaggerated sense of the importance of institutional pronouncements while hiding problematic sides of the stories. Thus the universities repeatedly fail to explain illuminating tensions such as the costs of initiatives, the balance between announced goals and opposing imperatives, and what isn't being done so other things can be done.

Such changes in the style of management and communication are not unique to Harvard, or even to universities, but they have occurred quickly and visibly at Harvard. Consider, for example, the fate of the annual reports of the president. These reports were first published in 1825 at the insistence of the Board of Overseers, so that its members would know the president's views of the state of the university. Though the reports comprise a selective version of history and always had a role as propaganda, for nearly two centuries they provided a record of facts and trends and a jumping-off point for discussion and debate by faculty and alumni, as well as fodder for later analyses. A decade ago, publication of the reports stopped. There is only one official view of Harvard now—the one the press office feeds to the news media.

When appearances and immediate gratification drive decisions, it is hard to keep everyone reading from the same script. Universities are full of independent-minded individuals—students, faculty, and well-intentioned administrators. Lacking a larger guiding vision and under pressure to fix immediate problems quickly, different parties make discordant decisions. Irreverent students are quick to pick up on the clashing messages and to become cynical about the university's lack of mission.

An illustrative case study is the upheaval at Harvard about grade inflation in 2001 and 2002. At the height of the public furor, a dean cautioned the faculty that grading was so soft that students were not motivated to do their best work. Two years later, in the middle of a curricular review process that sought student approbation, and despite the increase in grades in the interim, the topic had vanished from the discourse, except when grades were called a "burden" on students. Is it any wonder that no one inside the university takes the issue seriously?

Or consider this display of cloudy vision from the academic year 2004–2005. In the fall a committee on student alcohol abuse called for freshman educational programs and observed that the problem of dangerous drinking could not be solved without also addressing "the broader fabric of student life and the social and cultural issues associated with alcohol use on campus." By spring, pressured to improve campus "social life," Harvard was preparing to convert a campus eatery into a pub—in spite of the fact that the only students living nearby were freshmen.

Look good and make people happy. The two do not always go hand in hand.

Undergraduates, universities like to say, are their core and primary customers. At Harvard we often hear that the College is still the center of the university, even though undergraduates no longer pay the bulk of the bills. Yet undergraduates are often the first people to be blamed for universities' failures. Advising is bad? Well, students won't seek it. Not enough enrollments in the language spoken on Pluto? Well, students today are so careerist they aren't interested in the beauty of Plutonian literature. If they don't show up for lectures, it must be because they are indifferent to learning or too interested in sports, not because the professor has given them little reason to attend. If many students take the easiest possible courses to fulfill distribution requirements, the students are heathens or slackers, even if their faculty advisors cannot give a rationale for the rules.

The tendency of university leaders and faculty to shift the blame for the failures of colleges onto the backs of the victims has tragicomic variations. If the undergraduates can't be blamed for something, maybe it's the fault of the graduate students; they are scapegoated, for example, for the poor quality of freshman advising at Harvard. Academic leaders restrict honors degrees to the top half of the class without telling students their class rank, and yet simultaneously blame students who graduate at the twentieth percentile for not making an effort to rise to the thirtieth. Universities affect horror when students attend college in the hope of becoming financially successful, but they offer students neither a coherent view of the point of a college education nor any guidance on how they might discover for themselves some larger purpose in life.

Especially at universities that have extraordinarily selective admissions processes, blaming the student body can be a proxy for frustration by faculty and university leaders about what America has to offer in the way of raw material for the educational mill. As long as universities strive to enroll students representative of American and even world society, and the faculty are selected primarily on the basis of narrow scholarly distinction, the tension will persist between what bright, ambitious, talented, but otherwise ordinary students want and what university faculty think they should want. Indeed, the tension is likely to get worse as socioeconomic and geographic barriers to higher education continue to crumble even as socioeconomic inequalities in the United States continue to widen. It will require courage to confront this tension directly, but sooner or later the stress will cause a rupture if it is not first relieved through candid discussion.

The hollowness of undergraduate education derives from great successes. Universities have become preeminent research institutions but also genuine meritocracies, admitting students on grounds of talent, ambition, and promise rather than family background or ability to pay. These students are not soulless, but their university is. As unfortunate as the side effects have been for undergraduate education, they are not inevitable. The stakeholders can force change. The public has a stake because of the contributions these institutions make in educating many of the most talented young people for a variety of significant roles in society. The alumni, trustees, and professors who recognize what has happened can apply enough pressure to steer the ship to a new heading. Changing direction requires candor about the forces that have caused the errant course. It also requires leadership that views the university idealistically, as something more than a business and something better than a slave to the logic of economic competition.

Repairing universities does not require entirely new thinking. Few of the illnesses besetting college education today are new. Concern about academic competition, grading policies, and students with more brawn than brains is particularly raw today, but none of these phenomena surfaced in universities for the first time in the late twentieth century. Presidents, professors, deans, and students have thought about these issues before and have had things to say—sometimes wiser words than those we hear today, if at other times even more absurd. We look to the history of these issues to avoid the vanity of exceptionalism—the notion that the great universities of the twenty-first century are uniquely subject to these controversies because they have become so extraordinarily advanced. We look to the past because only by seeing where problems came from can we design long-term solutions.

Of one thing we should be certain: The loss of purpose in America's great colleges is not inconsequential. Harvard, Yale, Princeton—these places are not mere curiosities. They, and the standard they set for other universities, drive all of American higher education, on which so much of our future depends.

It was not always thus. In the middle of the nineteenth century, Harvard, the oldest of the universities, thought it was more important to America than it was. It was a college of old fogies in a nation of bubbling populism. The curriculum was fossilized, the teaching indifferent, the student body hereditary. Meanwhile, westward expansion, the industrial revolution, and waves of immigration were energizing the country. Only the jolt provided by a series of farsighted presidents saved Harvard from insignificance and propelled it toward its position of influence on higher education and on American society. Rivalry with other great universities improved one and all, and they became home to Nobel prizewinners and future leaders of commerce, industry, and government, for which these institutions are now justly famous.

The standing of universities a century and a half ago has since been turned on its head. America's great universities are the world's best; they are wells from which imagination, invention, and creativity are drawn to the benefit of American society. The country's future leaders learn the lessons, both good and bad, that they teach. Students' discoveries and innovations will be the source of national prosperity in the coming century. Those students' personal ethics will be the standards of government and of corporate America. Yet universities rarely speak as proponents of high ideals for future American leaders. With their focus extending beyond national borders, universities have become modest in their hopes for the United States. Reluctant to engage in political and moral controversies, they do not encourage their students to seek meaning in their studies and purpose in their lives. The future of America depends on superior education at our premier universities, not only through their curricula but also by the lessons they teach about the roles of individuals and of society. It is time to ask whether these institutions are doing the job the nation wants them to do.

CHAPTER 1

Choice and Direction

How the Curriculum Became Aimless

[L]et us give ample time, teachers, and oversight to the undergraduates, but let what we do for them be informed by the true University spirit; that is, let us treat them just as novices preparing to enter the higher scholarly life in some one of the multitudinous departments of modern research.

—Josiah Royce, 1891

The only way that I can see of improving . . . instruction is through increased stress on offering what should be taught rather than what the teachers wish to teach.

—LeBaron Russell Briggs, 1909

When an energetic student named Bill Gates showed up in my applied mathematics class during my second year teaching, I had no trouble figuring out that he was bright. In my first lecture of the term, I posed a simple problem neither I nor anyone else knew how to solve, just to show the class how problems that look easy can be hard. Gates came to my office a few days later with a solution, which he later published in a math journal along with the other professor who was teaching the course with me.

No, I figured out quickly that Gates was very smart, but smart students were nothing new to me. When I had been a Harvard undergraduate, between 1964 and 1968, I had been in classes with lots of smart undergraduates. To teach people like that was the reason I had accepted Harvard's job offer.

I had missed the takeover of University Hall in spring 1969, the police bust, the tear gas, and the angry confrontations between and

among students and professors. After graduating, I spent two years
fulfilling my service obligation during the Vietnam War. By 1974,
when I was finishing my Ph.D., Harvard College was calmer than it
had been when I left it six years earlier. The military draft and the as-
sassinations of Martin Luther King Jr. and of Robert F. Kennedy had
cast long shadows over my senior spring, but the sun had set on that
era. College students of 1974 did not see the university as the enemy.
Teaching them was an exciting prospect for me, but if I hadn't been
able to teach at a place like Harvard, I would have gone into the computer industry.

I learned a lot from Gates about talent, education, and excellence. I
certainly learned humility. A Bill Gates doesn't turn up in every Harvard class, but every class has some students who are smarter and more
inspired than most of the professors. I learned to be skeptical about
claims of the "value added" by universities. A Princeton professor I
know quipped that the fact that my most successful student was a
dropout confirmed his theory that Harvard's value added is negative—
the more Harvard education you have, the less far you go in life. I
learned that Harvard students' brilliance and drive can sometimes stay
with them for their whole lives and that changing the world is not an
irrational ambition for those sitting in front of me in class. I learned
that it was a privilege to be a Harvard professor, and that has stayed
with me every day of my teaching career. That is probably why, when
the young Bill Gates dozed off in the back of my classroom, I did not
yell at him too loudly. I may have sensed that he was working late at
night on something more important than my problem sets, though I
only later realized he had been writing the computer program that became Microsoft's first product. In any case, I couldn't blame him for
being sleepy; I was an inexperienced and boring lecturer. And the least
that should be expected of Harvard professors is to provide an education worthy of the students who are receiving it.

The college curriculum—the academic program students follow to
earn their degrees—is more than a rule book of requirements and regulations. It is an expression of what a college believes education means.
As such, a decision to change the curriculum can precipitate a war of
ideas about the purpose of college.

In early October 2002, Harvard began what President Lawrence Summers called "the most comprehensive review of Harvard's curriculum in a century." Dean of the Faculty of Arts and Sciences William C. Kirby promised from the outset to ask the most fundamental question: "What will it mean to be an educated woman or man in the first quarter of the 21st century?"

The review progressed in fits and starts over the next three years, sometimes rushing to meet arbitrary deadlines and sometimes backing up and starting over. The indecision about what would come out of the review might have been predicted from Dean Kirby's first words, which implied that the new curriculum would not be revolutionary, whatever Harvard might think it meant to be an educated person. Majors, or something like them, would continue to exist. A series of self-answering questions signaled the moves of a standard academic game, in which those with most of the power pretend to consult others in order to solicit faculty support. Kirby asked if there would be "a shared foundation" to a Harvard undergraduate education, then quickly added that there should be. He also asked, "How can we give our students the freedom to shape their own education through elective choices?"— when elective courses *are* the way students determine their own course of study, unfettered by specific curricular requirements. The twenty-first-century Harvard curricular review was off to a disingenuous start.

Core, specialization, electives—these were old categories, into which Harvard had divided graduation requirements since the 1940s. The difference in this launch of a new curriculum was the lack of a sense of where it was headed, or even why the voyage had been undertaken. Kirby never said what shared foundation he had in mind, but he touted as an educational value the freedom of students to study what they wanted.

Seven months later, a faculty committee produced a hurried report that left the basic questions unanswered. The report promised fewer requirements and more choices for students, pledging to "maximize the flexibility that students have." It identified internationalization and the scientific revolution as areas of greater emphasis, hewing perfectly to the script of President Summers's inaugural address in fall 2001.* Most of

---

*The high principles of more science and more internationalism took a curious turn on their way into practice. A faculty committee appointed by the dean modified the curriculum to allow students to have fewer Core requirements if they studied abroad than if their whole education was in Cambridge. The required science courses are the ones students most often choose to avoid.

the other recommendations were structural and pedagogical, for example, calendar reform and limits on the number of courses in a major. The report used the standard academic device for sweeping issues under the rug when a committee decides they are not important—a formal recommendation that they be studied further. Critics of the report quickly complained of its incoherence. Its principal author even acknowledged that the new curriculum had no particular direction but promised that a "guiding philosophy will emerge" during the subsequent year. A student critic was less hopeful, describing the report as "60 pages of stunningly bland and half-baked recommendations that straddle the line between unspecific and impossible."

A year later a draft report on the new general education requirement was floated. One member of the committee responsible for the report described its substance in this way: "In the end the committee thought the best thing was to put a row of empty bottles up there and see how the faculty wanted to fill them." Student reporters described the Faculty as "frustrated by an endeavor that has faltered for lack of time, guidance, and a unifying principle."

How could the Faculty of a great university talk for two years about the most basic questions of undergraduate education and come up with a curriculum consisting of empty bottles?

Certainly there were operational problems with the review. The president was inexperienced, overly ambitious, and impatient. While many professors were involved in review committees, some were surprised to find their names attached to recommendations they had never voted on and reports they had never seen. The review was heralded as "holistic," taking on the curriculum as a whole rather than adjusting just one part of it, but in truth it was disorganized and fragmentary. A member of my department confided that the review violated two fundamental engineering principles: Understand what problem you are trying to solve before you design a solution, and don't change so many things at once that you won't know what cause has what effect.

A look at the college curricula of other great universities suggests a deeper problem. Universities are having a hard time making the case that the education they offer is about anything in particular. "Breadth" and "choice" have become goals in themselves—not always consistent goals, since students generally have to be forced to take broad programs. When colleges talk about how broadly students will be educated or how much they will enjoy their freedom of choice, they conveniently avoid saying much about what students will learn. And breadth and freedom in academia are like lower taxes in politics—it is hard to be against them, even if they come at the cost of important sacrifices.

Every time curricula are redesigned, it is more difficult to prioritize any field of knowledge over any other. Typically students are required to distribute their course selections across odd categories such as "Quantitative Reasoning" and "Social Analysis" in Harvard's current curriculum. The more those categories result from academic border skirmishes rather than an overarching vision, the more likely they are to be ugly compromises, forged out of what Harvard students accurately called "a tangled web of earnest, academic motivations." The professors doing the design may be content with defending their own turf. But the students, who during their journey through the college curriculum have to visit the homelands of many professors, wonder at the end of the trip what it was about.

How did this happen? Understanding the "tangled web" requires going back to the beginning. Harvard had the first curriculum in America, and it was long on purpose and short on choice.

From the beginning, Harvard had a grand mission. The charter of 1650 says that the original donors made their gifts "for the advancement of all good literature, arts, and sciences . . . and for all accommodations of buildings, and all other necessary provisions that may conduce to the education of the English and Indian youth of this Country in knowledge and godliness." So all the intentions were there at the beginning: to create knowledge, to educate youth, and to teach what young people should know and how they should live. There was even a commitment to diversity.

For anyone reading the charter from the perspective of the twenty-first century, it is tempting to be nostalgic about Harvard's sticking to its essential purposes "through change and through storm," as our anthem, "Fair Harvard," would have it. Perhaps the words have shifted their meanings somewhat over time as society has become more enlightened, just as has happened to that other founding document written in Philadelphia a century and a half later. So "godliness" might now mean "morality" or even "humanity," just as "men" is now read to include both blacks and women in the U.S. Constitution. With the benefit of such generalizations, Harvard has continued, we might like to think, to pursue the advancement of the arts and sciences and to transmit knowledge and values to young people.*

Unfortunately, that liberal ideal does not line up very well with the way Harvard actually operated for most of its history. Harvard produced little knowledge during its first two hundred years. Its purpose was not the creation of knowledge, or even the study of "literature, arts, and sciences" in anything like the sense in which we would understand those terms today. A more accurate rationale was recorded only four years after the founding, and has, since 1890, been engraved on the gate at the main entrance to Harvard Yard. Once the bare necessities of life had been assured, the Puritan author wrote, "one of the next things we longed for and looked after was to advance learning and perpetuate it to posterity; dreading to leave an illiterate ministry to the churches, when our present ministers shall lie in the dust."

Harvard's primary jobs were to train a literate clergy and to preserve the knowledge that had been brought over from England by the Puritan settlers, more than a hundred of whom had graduated from Oxford or Cambridge. The two purposes were intertwined, because for a young man inclined to scholarship, very few professional choices were available outside the church. Students not destined to join the clergy—about half the class, even in the College's earliest days—got the same education as the prospective ministers: Logic, Rhetoric, Greek, Hebrew, Ethics, Metaphysics, and a bit of Mathematics and Science (Latin was taken for granted). That was the curriculum. In Latin a *curriculum* is a racecourse, and if you weren't going to be a minister, the point of running through the Harvard curriculum was simply to get to the end of it. Some Harvard graduates became teachers, but the others would not have much use for their Greek and Hebrew and Metaphysics in later life.

In the seventeenth century, the faculty consisted of the president and two or three "tutors"—recent graduates of the College waiting for

---

*Indeed, in writing the mission statement for Harvard College, which appears in the student handbook, I chose to take advantage of the charter of 1650 in exactly this way. I wrote the mission statement in 1996 as a byproduct of National Collegiate Athletic Association (NCAA) certification of Harvard's intercollegiate athletic program. It turned out that for 360 years Harvard College had never had a mission statement, and though it was hard to see that we had missed having one, I had to write one because the NCAA said we couldn't be a real college without it.

a ministry to open up to them. The president may have done some lecturing, perhaps simply reading from a book—there were not enough books for the students to do the reading on their own. That is what a "lecture" originally was—*lectus*, in Latin, is something read. But most teaching was done by the tutors. A tutor stuck with a class as long as it and he both remained at Harvard.

Here was student-faculty contact with a vengeance. A tutor was with his students throughout the day, including morning and evening prayers, and even slept in the same room with them. His job was as much to sustain discipline and keep order as to teach; there was no fraternization between the ranks. The system worked because the College was tiny. No graduating class had more than twenty-five students until 1721, and not until 1860 did Harvard graduate a class of one hundred.

Aside from lectures, students learned by studying individually, by recitations (repeating what they had been taught), or by disputations (rhetorical debates, in Latin, faithful to a rigid logic passed down from medieval times). Since a tutor's job was merely to pass along what he had been taught, there was no need for advanced learning and no specialization; the same tutor taught all subjects to his students. Students were younger than college students are today; they might enter Harvard at fifteen and leave three or four years later. So of necessity, Harvard was more like a school than an institution of higher learning, indeed more like a reform school than the relaxed American high school of today. The quality of instruction was poor, and as decades passed, teachers who had been trained in England died and were replaced by men educated at Harvard itself. They were supposed to be conveying to the next generation what they had received from the generation before, but the lessons became more distorted with each retelling.

In the 1720s, Thomas Hollis endowed professorships of divinity and of mathematics at Harvard, and disciplinary specialization began. Isaac Greenwood, one of the twenty-five students who graduated in 1721, studied science in London and returned to Cambridge to become the first Hollis Professor of Mathematicks and Natural Philosophy in 1728. With Greenwood, both the style and the substance of a Harvard education began to change. Greenwood gave collegewide lectures on the latest developments in astronomy and other sciences. His classes did not rely on readings from textbooks, since there were none for the material he was teaching. Greenwood presented new discoveries, and his students took notes.

Things did not end well for Greenwood. The first person appointed as a professor in arts and sciences, he was also the first dismissed. The Harvard Corporation, Harvard's principal governing board, found him "guilty of various acts of gross intemperance, by excessive drinking," and cut him loose in 1737. Greenwood was but the first of a long line of creative rakes in the academy, as libertine in their habits as liberal in their thinking.

Greenwood's successor as Hollis Professor, John Winthrop, was the first teacher at Harvard to exercise academic freedom and to run afoul of religious orthodoxy for doing so. He demonstrated that earthquakes have natural causes, and for this and other scientific explanations over his long tenure from 1738 to 1779, he attracted the opprobrium of the clergy, the admiration of Harvard students, and the curiosity of the laity.

Through the 1700s, the curriculum gradually became more specialized and somewhat more up-to-date. In 1769, instruction was reorganized. Thereafter the same tutor taught the same subject to all classes rather than teach all subjects to the same class. Aristotle was finally retired as the textbook on logic. The ancient abstractions that had been the subjects of formal debates were replaced by discussions relevant to the affairs of the day: In 1758 one John Adams, later the second president of the United States, engaged the question "Is Civil Government absolutely necessary for Men?" Yet in other ways, Harvard and the other colleges that had appeared in New England since Harvard's founding were becoming less important. The percentage of the American population attending college was shrinking, not growing, and some of the most learned and influential citizens, Benjamin Franklin for example, did not attend college at all.

At the same time, religion was evolving in New England. In the first years of the nineteenth century, the stern Calvinist orthodoxy lost its control of Harvard, and Unitarians came to power. Harvard remained a devout institution but with a more favorable view of human prospects. Enlightenment and scientific rationalism became discussable, but there were no American models for incorporating them into an educational framework. College remained basically a place where gentlemen were drilled in the same lessons their fathers had received. For more important changes, American universities would have to look to Europe.

At the beginning of the nineteenth century, Harvard was behind the times, a provincial institution stuck in methods and subjects developed for its original mission of service to Puritan New England. But the nation was becoming less isolated. Americans in public life were taking their children with them to Europe to become worldly; John Adams took John Quincy Adams to France in 1778, and Thomas Jefferson's daughter Patsy accompanied him to England in 1784. But Harvard remained inbred for decades longer. The 1812 Harvard catalog listed thirteen professors, three tutors, the president, and four members of the corporation—all twenty-one of them Harvard graduates. In 1815 only six instructors had studied in Europe since the school's founding 179 years earlier. The dreary drill of the same old subjects continued. The great Massachusetts senator and abolitionist Charles Sumner reflected on his years at Harvard, 1826–1830, and proclaimed, "I am not aware that *any one single* thing is well taught to the Undergraduates of Harvard College." Nor was the work particularly demanding. A retired president of the university recalled that in the early 1820s "A youth who was regular in his habits, and who made some sort of an answer, however wide of the mark, at half of his recitations, commonly obtained his degree."

Yet by Sumner's time, Harvard had begun to change, as four young men went abroad to study in Germany and returned to teach at the college. The nineteenth-century German universities were the best in the world, unimpeded by the rigid curriculum of required studies still in place at Harvard. One of the four Harvard scholars in Germany, George Ticknor, wrote to Thomas Jefferson, "If truth is to be attained by freedom of inquiry, the German professors and literati are certainly in the high road." The free and open style of learning in Germany was nothing like the dull drill that continued to dominate at Harvard.

The great writer and philosopher Ralph Waldo Emerson graduated from Harvard in 1821. Emerson was inspired by one of the four German-educated teachers, Edward Everett, who arrived at Harvard as Eliot Professor of Greek Literature on his way to becoming president of Harvard and governor of Massachusetts. As Emerson recalled:

There was an influence on the young people from the genius of Everett which was almost comparable to that of Pericles in Athens. . . . He had a great talent for collecting facts, and for bringing those he had to bear with ingenious felicity on the topic of the moment. . . . He had a good deal of special learning, and all his learning was available for purposes of the hour. It was all new learning, that wonderfully took and stimulated the young men. . . . All his auditors felt the extreme beauty and dignity of the manner, and even the coarsest were contented to go punctually to listen, for the manner, when they had found out that the subject matter was not for them.

The brilliant lecture, profound in its rhetoric, awesome in its "special learning," and captivating even to students who did not fully understand it, had been born. Harvard College was too small a confine for Everett, and he began giving popular lectures in Boston and beyond. To this day, eloquent professors continue to double as public intellectuals.

Harvard was not ready for such teaching. Ticknor assembled an extraordinary set of lectures on Spanish literature, a scholarly triumph unprecedented in the New World and a better treatment of the subject than had been achieved in Europe. But his lectures and those of his colleagues were laid over the rigid old curriculum with its pedagogical fabric of mandatory recitations. The students could not exercise much choice, and so the professors could not exercise much imagination. As a result, scholarship could not take root at Harvard as it had in the German universities. Ticknor complained to the Harvard Board of Overseers, "We are neither an University—which we call ourselves— nor a respectable high school,—which we ought to be." Even Harvard's greatest teachers were not sure what their job was. The old mindless repetition was insufferable, but there was no educational framework into which the new learning fit.

Electives for students and departments for faculty

Ticknor's complaints might have gone nowhere but for student revolts against the stultifying mode of teaching. There had been serious disturbances in 1807 and 1819, but the worst was a student rebellion in 1823 that resulted in expulsion of more than half the graduating class shortly before Commencement. The governing boards—the Corporation and the Board of Overseers—recognized that the oppressive control of undergraduate studies and life had to be relaxed. In 1825 students were given some choice of subjects: They could take French, Italian, German, or Spanish in place of part of the required Latin and Greek. This marked the beginning not only of elective studies but also of introductory classes in subjects students thought useful. The fixed curriculum of wisdom received from the ancients was at an end.

In the same round of reforms, the Board of Overseers divided the faculty into "separate departments . . . arranged as to embrace . . . studies of an analogous and connected nature." Groups of faculty specialists were empowered to control the curriculum in their areas of expertise. This significant departure from past practice provided an opportunity for educational creativity that had been impossible as long as the subjects to be studied were determined by the governing boards. The decentralization of academic authority made administrative sense too—surely the scientists and not the classicists should be deciding what science to teach and who should teach it.

Yet the creation of departments was a fateful step for the way universities think about scholarship. The 1825 vote of the Overseers marked the moment when depth and specialized learning began to ascend in university culture over breadth and the interconnection of knowledge. Today many academics feel that the walls erected in 1825 have grown too high and too strong, and the rage now is for interdisciplinary and cross-disciplinary studies such as "cultural studies" and "mind, brain, behavior." Harvard's current curricular reports are laced with language endorsing interdisciplinary studies for undergraduates. The reports propose nothing about what should be learned but are firm in endorsing the interdisciplinary learning style. The form of Harvard pedagogy should match the style of contemporary scholarship, but no one can say what knowledge Harvard graduates should take away with them.

Also in response to the 1823 riots, the academic calendar was modified to create a proper summer vacation, on the theory that students were most likely to be restless and rebellious in hot weather. To this day, almost all student disruptions occur in the period between spring break and exams, and in March deans start praying for a cold, wet April.

The last Harvard professor on the Corporation left it in 1823, and there would not be another for a century and a half. This marked the end of the old idea that the "Fellows of Harvard College," as the Harvard Corporation is still officially known, were faculty colleagues with a voice in their own ultimate governance. Today, not a single member of the Harvard Corporation, except the president, even lives in Massachusetts. The professors resent the Corporation's secrecy and isolation from the affairs of the university in much the way that in 1823 they objected to the Corporation's decision "to degrade them to the rank of ministerial officers, and to subject them to the discretionary government of [the president]." In early 2005, only weeks before the Faculty cast an unprecedented vote of lack of confidence in Summers's leadership, a Fellow said he was unaware of Faculty discontent with the president. The small, isolated governing board had made the same mistake that led to the riots in 1823. It did not know what was going on at Harvard. A year later, after two Fellows opened up communication with professors, the Corporation took the grievances seriously. By that time the crisis was too severe; only the president's departure could bring calm.

Elective opportunities expanded greatly in the 1830s, only to be limited again in a conservative counterreaction. The end result was that Harvard became less oppressive to its students but no more stimulating. The recitation system survived and, by enforcing a protocol of interrogation and response, guaranteed that teachers and students would have little substantive interaction. One alumnus explained, "the expression 'Not prepared,' on the one side, and 'that is sufficient,' on the other, uttered in varying keys calculated to produce repulsion, were too often the Alpha and Omega of acquaintance" between instructor and student. Henry Adams, who was a Harvard student in the 1850s, described the feeling of the place as accommodating, low-pressured, and pointless, in that

> no one took Harvard College seriously. All went there because their friends went there, and the College was their ideal of social self-respect. Harvard College, as far as it educated at all, was a mild and liberal school, which sent young men into the world with all they needed to make respectable citizens, and something of what they wanted to make useful ones. . . . In effect, the school created a type but not a will. Four years of Harvard College, if successful, resulted in an autobiographical blank, a mind on which only a water-mark had been stamped. . . . Harvard College . . . taught little, and that little ill, but left the mind open, free from bias, ignorant of facts, but docile. The graduate had few strong prejudices. He knew little, but his mind remained supple, ready to receive knowledge.

Things have changed at Harvard, but elements of this description are hauntingly familiar today. The international prestige of the name and the ambitions of parents provide nonacademic rationales for students' college selections. If Harvard graduates leave with prejudices, or even ideals, they probably did not pick them up from what they studied. They may be ready for anything, but not because curricular demands gave them skills and expertise. More likely they are smart, motivated, self-confident, and Harvard-watermarked, like the fine sheet of blank paper of Adams's metaphor.

In the mid-1800s, self-satisfied Harvard had serious competition from other New England colleges, and its reputation was declining. An Overseer told an alumni audience in 1844 that "Harvard has, of late, been constantly losing ground in the esteem and patronage of the community at large, and is fast becoming simply a high school for a portion of the youth of Boston and its vicinity." It took a radical break with the past to give direction to the university, at the cost of direction to the education it offered. President Eliot's twin ideals of academic excellence for the faculty and freedom of choice for the students had consequences with which universities are still coming to grips.

Charles William Eliot became president of Harvard in 1869, an important moment for Harvard and for America. Barely one in two thousand New Englanders attended college at all, and the percentage had decreased over the previous decades. At the same time, America was coming alive: The transcontinental railroad was completed that year, and industry was growing at a dizzying rate. Yet the social club that was Harvard risked becoming irrelevant to the nation, if it could survive at all.

Only thirty-five years old when he was appointed and a chemist by training, Eliot remained president for forty years, during which he utterly transformed the university. He made his priorities clear from the start. In the opening words of his inaugural address, he declared that Harvard's domain would be all of human knowledge.

> The endless controversies whether language, philosophy, mathematics, or science supplies the best mental training, whether general education should be chiefly literary or chiefly scientific, have no practical lesson for us today. This University recognizes no real antagonism between literature and science, and consents to no such narrow alternatives as mathematics or classics, science or metaphysics. We would have them all, and at their best.

At their best. From the perspective of the twenty-first-century academy, the phrase sounds trite. But the notion that the university would
be about excellence, about having the best students studying with the
best faculty in a temple of the most advanced learning, was an innovation. Harvard's vocabulary shifted drastically under Eliot. In the years
from 1825 up to Eliot's presidency in 1869, the words "excellence" and
"excellent" appear in the annual reports of the president and deans
only fourteen times; during Eliot's forty years they appear 411 times.

Eliot's inauguration was a rare moment in history. One man gave a
speech that promised to change everything, and then he did. People
who heard the speech recognized that a revolution was at hand. "We
are going to have new times here at Harvard," wrote one alumnus right
after the speech. "No more old fogyism."

When Lawrence Summers became president in 2001, some thought
his impact might rival Eliot's. Yet he will be remembered for his failures. Eliot advocated change and made it happen; Summers used the
bully pulpit for forgettable sound bites backed up by little action. Education became neither more scientific nor more international—in
fact it did not improve at all. He voiced opinions but advanced no
reasoned intellectual agenda. Eliot transformed Harvard by relentless
cycles of thought, persuasion, and execution; he grew a parochial
college into a great university. Summers complained of Harvard's
parochialism, but through arrogance and poor planning, he squan-
dered Eliot's legacy.

Eliot's call for excellence came with the equally revolutionary determination to make all subjects available to all students. Students' freedom to choose their studies had diminished in the years leading up to
Eliot's installation, and what choice remained was tied to the student's
class year. For example, a student could not read an author slotted for
senior-year Latin except by taking Latin all the way through, no matter
how much Latin he knew coming into the College. In his second year,
Eliot created the concept of a "course" with a name and number, open
to students of several class years. A couple of years later he added the
innovation of informing students which professor would be teaching
each course before students had to decide which courses to take. Little
by little, the required curriculum disappeared. By 1884 there were only
a few required courses, and in another decade most of those had been
eliminated. At the same time, the number of students, the variety of
courses offered, and the number of faculty offering them grew enor-

mously. The university of which Eliot became president in 1869 had 570 undergraduates and 45 professors; the university from which he retired in 1909 had 2,277 undergraduates and 194 professors.

Eliot's plan was to open Harvard to new students, faculty, and subjects. But he knew that teaching needed drastic revision if the plan was to be successful. And like the new industrialists who were revolutionizing transportation, communications, and manufacturing, he envisioned that mass production and increased quality might go hand in hand.

> The actual problem to be solved is not what to teach, but how to teach. The revolutions accomplished in other fields of labor have a lesson for teachers. . . . When millions are to be fed where formerly there were but scores, the single fish-line must be replaced by seines and trawls, the human shoulders by steam-elevators, and the wooden-axled ox-cart on a corduroy road by the smooth-running freight train. . . . With good methods, we may confidently hope to give young men of twenty to twenty-five an accurate general knowledge of all the main subjects of human interest, besides a minute and thorough knowledge of the one subject each may select as his principal occupation in life.

So the duality between general education and concentration, usually encapsulated in President Lowell's dictum about Harvard graduates knowing "a little of everything and something well," was in Eliot's mind four decades earlier.

But everything had to grow at once: more professors to teach new subjects, more students to fill their classes. In 1877, eight years into Eliot's presidency, the *Harvard Lampoon* published a caricature of him with the manifesto "Higher Standard, 60% for a Degree, Harder Exams, More Professors, More Rooms, More Money." Twenty-first-century Harvard is experiencing another bigger-is-better growth cycle. It announced that it would enlarge the faculty to improve the student-faculty ratio and to expand into new scientific fields, and then in almost the next breath announced it would build up to eight new undergraduate Houses so it could have more students.

Eliot thought Harvard should expand for both practical and idealistic reasons. The faculty had to grow because its members were becoming more specialized and the university was endeavoring to teach everything. The student body had to grow because the advancement of

Figure 1.1 Eliot as seen by students in 1877, eight years into his presidency.

democratic civilization demanded it. As Eliot saw it, "unless a general acquaintance with many branches of knowledge . . . be attainable by great numbers of men, there can be no such thing as an intelligent public opinion; and in the modern world the intelligence of public opinion is the one indispensable condition of social progress."

Within a decade, Eliot reported that "the recitation, considered as an opportunity of examining a student to see whether he has learned the lesson of the day, and to give him a mark of merit or demerit, has well-nigh disappeared from the University." Instead of rote regurgitation of facts, the recitation had "become for the teacher an opportunity to give conversational instruction by asking questions . . . with a view to correct misapprehensions and to bring out the main points of the subject . . . for the student . . . an opportunity to ask questions, to receive . . . the explanations and opinions of the instructor." These interactive classes were analogous at the undergraduate level to seminars that were becoming prevalent in graduate education. Once Harvard had raised expectations for mature discourse in classes, it also needed to raise the age at which students matriculated. In 1872 Eliot reported that over the previous two decades Harvard had lost the "school-boy spirit" that had been natural when boys arrived at the age of fifteen; the average age of admission had risen above eighteen and has remained there ever since.

The impact of the more informal and reciprocal form of teaching was dramatic. Henry Adams, whose own student experience had been so indifferent, found that students reacted in an entirely different way to the history course he taught in the 1870s. "Since no textbooks existed, the professor refused to profess, knowing no more than his students, and the students read what they pleased and compared their results. As pedagogy, nothing could be more triumphant. The boys worked like rabbits, and dug holes all over the field of archaic society; no difficulty stopped them." Faculty members who had been around longer could barely believe what they had been missing. As one professor said in 1886, "Formerly, the only business of a teacher was to hear recitations, and make marks for merit. Now, he has the opportunity of teaching. This is one of the greatest educational discoveries of modern times,—that the business of a teacher is to teach."

Unfortunately, personalized teaching was expensive, and, as Adams noted, "The whole problem of education is one of its cost in money." During Eliot's years, there was a fourfold increase in the size of the student body and a slightly greater increase in the number of professors, but the number of teachers and researchers who were not professors grew from 15 to 416. In 1895, Eliot proudly stated that "The unusually larger proportion of teachers to students (about 1 to 12) makes personal care for individuals the rule and not the exception. The whole method of the College is intended to minister to individual needs, through the elective system, and the adoption of individual modes of instruction."

At the time of Eliot's inauguration, he noted the synthetic opportunities lectures provide "for inspiration, guidance, and the comprehensive methodizing which only one who has a view of the whole field can rightly contrive." But he also noted their potential weaknesses, warning that "lectures alone are too often a useless expenditure of force. The lecturer pumps laboriously into sieves. The water may be wholesome, but it runs through. A mind must work to grow." A decade later, according to Eliot, Harvard lecture courses had been modified to contain "a large admixture of the Socratic method. The lecturer does not read or speak continuously himself, but frequently interrupts his exposition to address a question to an individual or to the class, or to invite the class to ask questions and suggest difficulties."

Whatever the pedagogical advantages and deficiencies of lectures, they had and continue to have enormous practical and economic merits. They are suited for a mass market and are easily repeated. The exceptional brilliant teacher can engage many eager students at once. Indolent or unprepared students like lectures as well, since they can satisfy their obligations with little effort and minimal risk of embarrassment.

As the university grew rapidly under Eliot, it needed a way to address the deficiencies of the lecture system without incurring the heavy personnel costs of faculty seminars. Sections were the solution—small groups of students from a large course, meeting with an apprentice teacher. Eliot had opened the graduate school of arts and sciences in 1872. It provided the scholarly training needed by the next generation of teachers but previously available only in Europe, and, after 1876, at Johns Hopkins. Just as important, it provided a corps of subprofessorial teachers on which Harvard and other research universities have relied ever since for undergraduate teaching. The pathologies of small-group instruction by untrained assistants were recognized in Eliot's day as now. In 1877 a student described his section mates in terms easily recognizable by today's undergraduates.

> First, and perhaps the most despicable of all, is the man who takes notes. . . . [H]e is always taking them; during every lull in the recitation you may hear the steady scratching of his pencil. When the instructor said, "Mr. De Browne, will you please close the door?" I looked at the scribbler, and lo! he was jotting that down, too! . . .
>
> Then there is the man who asks questions. Why does he do it? It is not for information surely, for he asks questions when he already knows their answers. . . . But I don't so much object to him, because he uses up the time. . . .
>
> Such are the eccentrics of the section. Its hero I have still in store. . . . When he is called upon, we fresher Freshmen know that the clever answer will be, "I have no books, sir,—am quite unpre-

pared,—really know nothing whatever about the subject." This, then, must be the "Harvard indifference" about which I have heard so much. I am trying for it now, and I hope to be expert when I go home at Christmas.

Indeed, these types are so familiar that in 2004 a *Crimson* columnist, oblivious to the earlier account, enumerated them in slightly varied form. "The People in My Section" included the Antagonist, the Expert, the Flatterer, the Offended, and so on. But now, as in 1877, the problem lies not with the students but with the instructional system. To combat the impersonality of large lectures, inexperienced graduate students teach small groups of undergraduates. All parties know that teaching is a sideline to thesis research for most of these teaching fellows, and the undergraduates react with inattention, cynicism, or cunning.

A few years before the end of Eliot's presidency, the largest course in the College had 520 students, almost as many as had been in the entire College when he began. The lecturers needed more assistants to staff more sections. The dean of the Faculty acknowledged that these courses were becoming less effective as vehicles for education: "If the large lecture courses are to have more than an uncertain stimulating value some reorganization must come." Eliot began to recognize the strain on the system. Large courses "might be made still more efficient than they are," he said, "by the expenditure of more money upon them in the employment of more assistants, at higher pay, for a larger number of hours per week."

But three years later, the Overseers demanded that he spend less money, not more. Throwing the industrial metaphor of Eliot's inaugural address back at him, the governing board demanded "increased educational efficiency." Dean of the Faculty LeBaron Russell Briggs suggested that the only way to achieve economies might be by "requiring professors to do the work now done by assistants," and for the first time labor conditions for faculty emerged as a recruiting issue. "Many of the best professors would not come or would not stay if required to do the work now performed by assistants," Briggs worriedly observed.

The unexpected consequences of Eliot's four-decade program of liberalization were becoming apparent. It was costly to let the professors think of themselves mostly as scholars—costly and detrimental to undergraduate education. The only solution might be to limit professors' freedom to choose what they taught—a freedom they would not willingly relinquish. "The only way that I can see of improving, with our present force, our already rich and varied instruction," wrote Dean Briggs, "is through increased stress on offering what should be taught rather than what the teachers wish to teach."

During America's vast post–Civil War expansion, higher education became increasingly important to social advancement. Lincoln was elected president of the United States without a college education, but that never happened again. Charles Darwin and James Maxwell created new sciences that changed human consciousness of our place in the universe. The steam engine produced industries that transformed everyday life. Education had to change as well.

For the first time, education became consumer-oriented. As early as 1850, the Massachusetts legislature pushed Harvard toward instruction in useful learning, arguing that under the elective system "that which was desired would be purchased, and that which was not, would be neglected." Thirty years later, Eliot boasted that the free market he had created within Harvard was working to students' advantage, as "in all departments the instructors have felt prompted anew to make their exercises interesting, profitable, and indeed indispensable, to their students." In 1890 Harvard opened advanced studies to undergraduates, bringing into college classrooms the scholars who had been hired to pursue research and to teach graduate students.

But the new teaching role given to academic specialists had an unintended consequence: It pushed undergraduate education into the background. Eliot had abolished the deadly recitation, and student-faculty relations had warmed. But just as the students had been freed to study what they wished, the faculty had been freed to teach what they wished. By the 1890s, undergraduates had great flexibility in what to study, but less than ever of what was taught was meant for them.

In 1891 philosophy professor Josiah Royce reflected excitedly on the growth of graduate studies at Harvard, rejoicing that the changes taking place would free graduate education in the arts and sciences from its old dependence on undergraduate instruction and "make it all the sooner what in time it is sure to become—the most important department in the University." In Royce's optimistic view, every one of the specialized areas of study leading to the Ph.D. contributed something of practical importance to society.

> The modern University study of Political Science is educating the public for that serious time of grave social dangers which seems to be not far off. Academic work in Natural Science is constantly opening new fields to the industrial arts, and giving new insights into the business of life. Academic study of Philosophy is preparing the way for a needed spiritual guidance in the religious crisis which is rapidly becoming so serious.

Was there anything holding the university together, now that its job was no longer to provide a common background to undergraduates? The university was now about academic scholarship itself, Royce explained, rather than about educating students.

> The traditional college had as its chosen office the training of individual minds. The modern University has as its highest business, to which all else is subordinate, the organization and the advance of Learning.

That sounds like what we would today call a research institute—a place where distinguished scholars gather for extended periods of time to think great thoughts, unfettered by the obligations of classroom teaching. The common complaint that graduate students get all the attention started with such visions of universities as places mainly of scholarship. The undergraduate was significant in such an ideal university only as a guest in a house belonging to others.

> In the true University the undergraduate ought to feel himself a novice in an order of learned servants of the ideal—a novice who, if in turn he be found willing and worthy, may be admitted, after his first degree, to the toils and privileges of this order as a graduate or, still later, as a teacher; but who, on the other hand, if, as will most frequently happen, he is not for this calling, will be sent back to the world, enriched by his undergraduate years of intercourse with his fellows, and with elder men, and progressive scholars. The ideal academic life then is *not* organized expressly for him.

Professors were becoming professionals in a way they had never been before. They were preparing the next generation of scholars—graduate students, or undergraduates who identified themselves as graduate students in the making. They were also preparing an educated citizenry. But increasingly, the teaching talent that had been used exclusively to the benefit of the citizens was diverted to serve the interests of the scholars. A commentator observed in 1901:

> There is nothing remarkable or out of place in the fact that advanced or specializing courses, in whatever subject, are given by the best men. But the tendency has recently been to transfer to these courses lecturers who have hitherto been connected with the large undergraduate courses. . . . The loss to the undergraduates, indeed, is plainly the gain of the Graduate School. But it may seriously be questioned whether such gain to graduate students—many of whom, after graduation, mingle little in the world of affairs—quite compensates for the loss to the undergraduates.

As teaching became increasingly specialized, the Ph.D. became a license needed to get a teaching job, though it was difficult to identify a connection between the training certified by the one and the qualities needed for the other. In 1903 Harvard philosopher and psychologist William James exploded in frustration when one of his best students could not be hired for a teaching position because he had not endured the ritual of writing a Ph.D. thesis:

> Will anyone pretend for a moment that the doctor's degree is a guarantee that its possessor will be successful as a teacher? Notoriously his moral, social, and personal characteristics may utterly disqualify him for success in the classroom; and of these characteristics his doctor's [Ph.D.] examination is unable to take any account whatever.

More than a hundred years later, many undergraduates do perceive themselves to be subordinate, unworthy novices, to use Royce's words. Meanwhile, the graduate students who become professors acquire contempt for "the world of affairs" from which they will be cut off. Research universities are still struggling to resolve the tension between the old ideal that undergraduate students should benefit from a broad program of learning and the reality that those doing the teaching are costly research scholars, unprepared for educating a body of under-graduates with much more diverse futures. Down to this day, the "moral, social, and personal characteristics" of faculty remain qualities not merely untested by the system that trains them but entirely un-mentioned in the process that selects them.

Offering students the freedom to choose their studies, as Brown University does most famously but almost all universities do to a signif-icant degree, is popular with students but leaves little at the center of college education as a whole. Offering professors the freedom to teach what they want is consistent with their primary status as research schol-ars, but encourages faculty indifference to the personal circumstances of students. By intentional curricular design or by the unseen hand of student choice, students don't spread out evenly but aggregate to cre-ate huge courses, with all the problems they bring.

These tensions between the instructional wishes and needs of un-dergraduates and the professional skills of the faculty created fault lines that are still with us. Will the curriculum respond to the desires of the students, the preferences of the faculty, or the educational needs of society? Will the students be the ones the professors most want to teach or the ones whose education will most benefit society? Will the university be run for the benefit of students, faculty, or society? Re-search universities have not answered these questions, first raised when both students and faculty were left to their own devices.

CHAPTER 2

Meritocracy and Citizenship

What Should Graduates Share?

Youth is the time when the character is being molded and easily takes any impress one may wish to stamp on it. Shall we then simply allow our children to listen to any stories that anyone happens to make up and so receive into their minds ideas often the very opposite to those we shall think they ought to have when they are grown up?

—Plato, *Republic*

[O]ur ancestors did not forget the interests of learning. . . . Enlightened themselves, they benevolently wished that the rays of science might fall on their descendants. And the wish was excited by a rational conviction, that as long as learning should be cultivated, freedom and virtue would not lack advocates.

—Letter from John Clarke to his son at Harvard, 1796

We are faced with a diversity of education which, if it has many virtues, nevertheless works against the good of society by helping to destroy the common ground of training and outlook on which any society depends.

—*General Education in a Free Society,* 1945

When Harvard opened its doors, a college education was a privilege of membership in cultured society. Over time it became a gateway by which the brightest and most ambitious of the masses could rise in social and economic status. In the early twenty-first century, a college degree is the minimum qualification for most jobs above the level of manual labor. Almost 90 percent of respondents to one survey thought that a college education is as important today as a high school education used to be, and almost three-quarters of today's high school students plan to pursue a bachelor's degree.

Not everyone needs to go to college at a research university. There are many superb colleges in the United States, and a great portion of the college-bound population does not want a four-year, residential institution in which few of the students are above age twenty-two. But the colleges in the top-tier universities are in a special position. They are loaded with intellectual talent among the faculty, overwhelmed with applicants eager to attend, and well endowed. They therefore have the best opportunity to define for themselves what it means to be educated, rather than simply to respond to market forces at every turn.

The entering students are a cross section of society, with little more than youth, ambition, and intelligence in common. They are headed to destinations all across the landscape of places, careers, and lifestyles. Defining the common ground for this diverse student body is a charged and troubling task. If the uniting principle is anything more than excellence at whatever the student chooses to study—"the highest development of his own peculiar faculty," as Eliot put it in his inaugural address—the attempt to define the core of a college education becomes an institutional identity search. But professors are reluctant to imply that one specialty is more important than another. Instead, their conversation may focus on what hours and sizes the courses should be rather than on what their content should include.

Yet there are some things that the diverse student body has in common, and the curriculum should recognize it. College students tend to be young. Youth implies being open to change, to discovering one's loves and talents, and to aspiring to a newly imagined future. It also implies an unfinished process of personal development. Colleges take in children for whom parents are responsible and graduate adults who should be responsible for themselves and, especially at the great universities, responsible for society. The ages of eighteen to twenty-two are an ideal time for students to understand the values that tie them to other living people and to those who have gone before.

Most students arriving at the top colleges have been heavily conditioned to the importance of gaining admission—so completely conditioned that, having gotten in, their internal compass gives them little guidance about what to do next. They are the most promising students in the country, but the great universities give them little sense that they owe something more than tuition money for the privilege of their education. Many resemble the politician so compellingly portrayed by Robert Redford in *The Candidate*—willing to do anything in order to win, but bewildered by the freedom gained by winning. Redford's character, at least, in the last moment of the movie acknowledges his bewilderment. Some college students never become so self-aware. For those that do, few institutional signals call on them to repay to society the debt they have incurred.

For colleges within research universities, the goal of graduate education confuses the debate about the purpose of undergraduate education. Graduate students are not so young when they start, and they are in school so long that they are certainly not young when they finish. Maturational distractions that are expected of undergraduates are treated with little sympathy when they afflict graduate students. It is less important for graduate students to come to grips with their place in the great chain of being than to find their place in the academic ladder, or rat race. And although all new graduate students have promise, their opportunities have already started to narrow when they matriculate for their Ph.D.'s. They risk not being taken seriously as promising academics if they give voice to thoughts of going into business or law. Professors can help them get where they are supposed to be going, but will rarely help them figure out if they want to go there.

College is not graduate school. Professors in research universities are in a good position to mentor graduate students because they have been there themselves. Undergraduates need something that professors may be utterly unprepared to give. And professors will often prefer graduate students who, like themselves, are devoted single-mindedly to learning, who are focused on knowing as much as possible about a limited domain, and who are skilled at hiding any personal agonies.

The tensions between these three bodies—undergraduates, graduate students, and professors—began long ago. When the dread of leaving a continent illiterate no longer justified the rote relearning of the classical curriculum, something else had to bind the college together.

Making a forest from the trees

Abbott Lawrence Lowell was a persistent critic of Eliot on the Harvard faculty. Lowell watched with disapproval as Eliot dismantled the last fragments of the common curriculum, developing the graduate school while letting undergraduates have free rein to select their courses. In the last years of Eliot's presidency, Lowell chaired a review of under-graduate education. His faculty committee discovered that the major-ity of Harvard students were not working very hard under the elective system or taking many courses above the introductory level.

When Lowell succeeded Eliot as president in 1909, he immediately pointed out the destructive force of intellectual diversification, however much it had been necessary. Things had been simpler when there were only a few students, who all studied the same subjects together, lived to-gether, and aimed at one or two of the same professional careers.

> The college of the old type possessed a solidarity which enabled it to fulfill that purpose well enough in its time, although on a narrower scale and a slower plane than we aspire to at the present day. . . . In the course of time these simple methods were outgrown. President Eliot pointed out with unanswerable force that the field of human knowledge had long been too vast for any man to compass; and that new subjects must be admitted to the scheme of instruction, which became thereby so large that no student could follow it all.

And a price had been paid for that: "The new methods brought a di-vergence in the courses of study pursued by individual students, an in-tellectual isolation, which broke down the old solidarity."

Lowell offered a curricular remedy that has since become a stan-dard: "The best type of liberal education in our complex modern world aims at producing men who know a little of everything and something well." A Ph.D. program, miniaturized of course, was a good model for the "something well" part of the curriculum, but the practi-calities of the "little of everything" part were problematic. Lowell had a clearer idea than Eliot of how educational breadth might be achieved, but making it happen was something else. The obvious idea would be to have students take

> a number of general courses in wholly unrelated fields. But instruc-tion that imparts a little knowledge of everything is more difficult to provide well than any other. To furnish it there ought to be in every considerable field a general course, designed to give to men who do not intend to pursue the subject further a comprehension of its un-

derlying principles or methods of thought; and this is by no means the same thing as an introductory course.

And who would teach such courses? In Lowell's answer there are hints of disappointment about his predecessor's faculty-hiring practices, reservations still felt today by deans of undergraduate education in research universities.

> A serious obstacle lies in the fact that many professors, who have reaped fame, prefer to teach advanced courses, and recoil from elementary instruction. . . . Effective instruction in fundamental principles requires men of mature minds who can see the forest over the tops of the trees. It demands unusual clearness of thought, force of statement and enthusiasm of expression. These qualities have no necessary connection with creative imagination.

In December of Lowell's first term as president, the Faculty agreed to require students of the Class of 1914 and beyond to develop both concentration and breadth in their studies. Breadth was mandated by dividing courses into four broad areas and requiring students to take courses in each area according to certain further restrictions. The areas were (1) Language, Literature, Fine Arts, Music; (2) Natural Sciences; (3) History, Political and Social Sciences; and (4) Philosophy and Mathematics. This scheme was what would now be called a "distribution requirement." It is, in fact, a distribution requirement identical to the one proposed in 2005 for Harvard undergraduates, except the 2005 proposal has only three areas instead of the four areas of 1910. In 2005 the fourth group from 1910 is split, with philosophy joining the first group and mathematics the second. The 1910 version is actually better than the 2005 version, as it reserves a special place for fields distinguished by the training they provide in analytical reasoning.

Harvard's 1910 distribution requirement was not the nation's first; between 1901 and 1908, Yale, Cornell, and Wesleyan had all reacted to excesses of their own elective systems by adopting requirements across divisions. But a system of concentration plus distribution at Harvard was an ingenious, or perhaps cynical, adaptation for undergraduate use of structures supporting graduate education. The departments in which a student might concentrate, and the departments that were slotted into the four curricular divisions, were the departments that had been created for Ph.D. studies. Lowell's dream of general courses that were not introductory did not materialize during his presidency. Nor did he ever resolve the problem that the "clearness of thought, force of statement and enthusiasm of expression" so valuable in college teachers were qualities largely unrelated to scholarly excellence.

Distribution requirements are the easy way out of the imperative for general education, easy for both students and faculty. Professors can teach from their home bases and yet take credit for contributing to the breadth of undergraduate education. Students treat curricular requirements as the rules of a game they are challenged to win, seeking out the easiest course in each division. Distribution requirements tend to have more teeth in the sciences than in the humanities. Science-oriented students may regard humanities requirements with annoyance or derision, but nonscientists often regard science requirements with real fear. Veterans of curricular wars realize that a distribution system imposes a science requirement without singling out science as a special case.

❧

Columbia University was the first to take general education to the next level and to define a true core of texts that all graduates would have read. This development occurred in 1919 for what sociologist Daniel Bell called "a curious mixture of parochial, sociopolitical, and philosophical motives."

At Columbia, the institution of a mandatory course in Contemporary Civilization followed the abolition of the Latin requirement for admission a decade earlier. The liberalization of the entrance requirements opened the doors to ambitious immigrant children sharing few cultural assumptions with the well-educated students who had been Columbia's principal customers. This knocked the supports—an assumed knowledge of the literature of Rome—from underneath a large curricular apparatus. The end result of the reactions and counterreactions at Columbia was a college, as Bell described it, "dedicated firmly to the tradition of the liberal arts rather than to professionalism; that . . . sought for social diversity in its student body; and that . . . was committed to no doctrinal philosophy of education other than exposing the student to major intellectual ideas and expanding his imagination."

Columbia added a uniform humanities requirement in 1937, and a form of common core exists there to this day, after several cycles of reform. Chicago's core curriculum was more intellectually doctrinaire from the beginning, and passions surrounding it remain so strong that the president was forced to resign in 1999 for daring to argue that it needed fundamental change. More modest changes implemented in the core courses three years later precipitated a brief but intense conservative reaction. Yet even at Chicago the curriculum never had quite the rigidity with which mythology credits it. A true "great books" curriculum, as proposed but not adopted for Chicago, was taken up by St. John's College in Annapolis, Maryland, and remains there to this day. (St. John's now has a campus in Santa Fe as well.) The school offers no electives for the students, and there is no discretion for the faculty teaching them. All students read the same books in a planned four-year curriculum.

The system of large lecture courses at Harvard and the requirement that students take some courses (no matter which ones) outside their area of concentration led to huge enrollments in easy courses, fondly known as "bow-wows." Lowell's successor, James Bryant Conant, like Eliot a chemistry professor, unsentimentally raised the level of both faculty and students. In Conant's view, improving the students and the faculty were "two aspects of one problem." The problem required new solutions, because America itself had changed. The days of expansion were over, and America was, in Conant's eyes, entering a period of social stasis. The proportion of the population attending colleges had "increased many times," and had now reached one in two hundred. Harvard's job for the future would be to pick the best of what America offered.

> With the population apparently nearing a stationary point, the next hundred years' history of higher education in this country must of necessity be radically different from that of the last. The frontiers have vanished, the migrations of the nineteenth century can hardly occur again; the tremendous changes caused by the sudden industrialization of the country are unlikely to find their parallel in the years ahead. As compared with the past, we appear to be entering a

static period in our social history. Many powerful factors tend to force even the most ambitious youths into a groove predetermined by geographical and economic considerations. This being the case, the problem we now face as a nation is not one of expanding to any great degree our facilities for handling college and university students. It is rather that of improving the selective machinery in our school system which should sort out those who can profit most by four years of college and a subsequent professional training.

As Conant saw it, half a percent of the population in college was enough. The challenge would be to select that half percent. In the words of historians Morton and Phyllis Keller, Conant "sought to build a university given over as never before to *meritocracy,* * that is, attracting students and faculty whose distinction lay not in their social origins but in their intellect and character."

Creating a meritocracy of the faculty required the institution of a more objective and orderly system of appointing professors, especially to permanent positions. Professors would be "up or out" after eight years without tenure. Conant also established the systematic use of outside experts to review tenure cases. This procedure would combat academic cronyism and the practice of professors anointing their own successors, often from among their Ph.D. students. Executed at their best, these reforms guaranteed that Harvard professors would be distinguished scholars. In practice, it often resulted in the appointment of narrow specialists, the best in the world at something that was not very important in the first place. The reliance on outside expertise could also make reputation more important than reality, and not test at all a candidate's commitment to teaching or to the welfare of the university.

❧

World War II resulted in as thoughtful and idealistic a curricular study as had ever occurred and as may ever occur again, at Harvard or anywhere else. *General Education in a Free Society,* published in 1945, was a printed volume of 267 pages that came to be known as the "Red Book"

---

*The term *meritocracy* was coined as a pejorative in a 1958 satirical novel by British sociologist Michael Young, *The Rise of the Meritocracy.* The book warned that society might not be well-served by order based on merit rather than heredity, but the term is now generally used in a positive sense.

because of its binding. Its official author was a committee of Harvard professors, but most of the writing was that of a single man, professor of Greek literature John Finley, only forty-one when the report appeared. Finley's pen evoked the same nobility about Harvard's mission as he ascribed to the Athenian state in the books he was writing at the same time.

The report's scope went beyond the education that Harvard students or even college students generally should receive. It described what the entire educational system of America needed to do to prevent another catastrophe like the one that had nearly destroyed the civilized world. General education was not, the report said, education in knowledge in general, whatever that might mean. General education had a specific objective. It looked to the student's "life as a responsible human being and citizen" and to certain "traits of mind and ways of looking at man and the world." General education had a point of view. "A successful democracy (successful, that is, not merely as a system of government but, as democracy must be, in part as a spiritual ideal) demands that these traits and outlooks be shared so far as possible among all the people." No set of facts could comprise a general education; what citizens needed were the shared values of a diverse people.

> The heart of the problem of a general education is the continuance of the liberal and humane tradition. Neither the mere acquisition of information nor the development of special skills and talents can give the broad basis of understanding which is essential if our civilization is to be preserved. . . . Unless the educational process includes *at each level of maturity* some continuing contact with those fields in which value judgments are of prime importance, it must fall far short of the ideal.

In spite of its attention to secondary schools as well as to higher education, the report's influence was mainly on colleges, and indeed its importance beyond Harvard was more in legitimizing the idea of a special set of general education courses than in standardizing what those courses would be. The Red Book established that courses designed to train specialists in a discipline might not enlighten others not oriented toward that specialty. Newton's laws might be important even for a philosophy major planning on law school, but the philosophy major would not learn physics well in the class meant for physics majors. The physics majors likely came to physics courses with a view of the world as a rational and predictable system whose rules can be discovered empirically. That very perspective was the most important thing for the philosophy major to learn from a general education course. The curriculum proposed for Harvard in 2005 abandoned not only the notion of a foundation that educated citizens should share but even the special mission of teaching an important subject to an intellectually diverse student body.

The Red Book recommended that Harvard require that six of the sixteen courses needed for graduation be specially designed General Education courses. There would be three broad areas of learning—humanities, natural sciences, and social sciences—and students would be expected to study some of each. There would be a single course in the humanities (Great Texts of Literature) and a single course in the social sciences (Western Thought and Institutions), both courses taken by all students. "These two courses, as well as the projected introductory course in the physical sciences, would form a comparatively coherent and unified background for an understanding of some of the principal elements in the heritage of Western civilization." Additional courses would be crosscutting but not quite so sweeping in their scope.

By the time the Faculty had accepted the General Education program, the idea of any single course being required for all undergraduates had given way to some choice among specially designed alternatives. Western Thought and Institutions was indeed offered under the rubric "Soc Sci 2" and became a classic, an inspiring experience for thousands of Harvard students. But students could take History of Far Eastern Civilization instead—and many who did so had their lives changed by learning something not at all part of their own intellectual heritage. Courses like the affectionately named "Rice Paddies" maintained the thematic unity of the General Education program even as they relaxed the Western orthodoxy of which the Red Book had been born. Broadening the curriculum strengthened it at first, but over the next two decades, more idiosyncratic courses began to appear in the curriculum.

As early as 1962 a *Crimson* editorial complained, "General Education has become increasingly specialized." Thirty years after the publication of the Red Book, the forces of specialization and choice had won a complete victory over the postwar ideal of a common experience for a diverse student body united by citizenship in a democracy. When social unrest swept over the Harvard campus in the late 1960s, the curriculum was dismissed as "a hopeless anachronism," "chauvinistic and dated." The lack of logical unity in the remains of the curriculum fed student cynicism about the educational values of the university. As one professor described it in 1970, "For students these days a liberally educated man is not construed in terms of the introspective gentleman, but rather in terms of the socially perceptive activist."

The General Education curriculum was conceived in dedication to shared values. It was not revolutionary, as critics at Columbia and Chicago were quick to point out; the Red Book gave too little credit to the general education curricula in those colleges. But a curriculum unified by the importance of democratic values was more galvanizing when conceived in 1945 than it had been in 1937 or even in 1919.

The narrow escape from totalitarianism in 1945 yielded rare intellectual unity. Students supported the curriculum's educational purpose, even as, over time, some came to dislike its regulatory strictures. A report by the Student Council written as the curriculum was being formulated stated that "it is in a period of confusion and catastrophe rather than in times of glittering prosperity or preoccupation with material problems that students must think deeply about permanent values, and about the future of civilization itself." Given the difficulty that universities now have in developing inspired curricular missions, perhaps a national crisis would be necessary to achieve consensus on the purpose of a college education.

General Education was an effort to find "some over-all logic, some strong, not easily broken frame . . . strong enough to give goal and direction" to the entire educational system. "This logic must further embody certain intangibles of the American spirit, in particular, perhaps, the ideal of cooperation on the level of action irrespective of agreement on ultimates—which is to say, belief in the worth and meaning of the human spirit, however one may understand it." In General Education, thinking about values was meant to cut across the curriculum and to be part even of the science curriculum. Although "[i]n the natural sciences facts are studied in abstraction from values . . . this separation, while pragmatically valid, leads to disaster if treated as final. Values are rooted in facts; and human ideals are somehow a part of nature."

During the 1950s and 1960s, the General Education curriculum was modified, generalized, relaxed, and opened up to departmental substitutions. As a result, it eventually lost much of its intellectual integrity. It may have fallen apart because prosperity swept over America, and a generation of students arrived in Cambridge unconscious of threats to civilization that had inspired their predecessors. But it disintegrated also in part because it was almost impossible to teach. With few choices, courses were huge. Few professors could knit such broad learning into an intellectually integrated whole and then deliver it with panache in large lectures. As one writer said, it

> required a staff of instructors with an inhuman degree of cooperativeness and availability, as well as a willingness to venture out of established territories of special knowledge into the uncharted and the general. Nothing in the Harvard Report of 1945 was going to keep language from being taught by linguists, science by scientists, and history by historians: They were all, by virtue of *their* educations and predispositions, poorly equipped to make their classrooms an experience in humanistic learning.

Indeed, some of the greatest teachers in the General Education program were not among the university's most prolific scholars. John Finley himself, the principal author of the Red Book, devoted most of his energy to teaching and to serving as Master of Eliot House, roles for which he became legendary.

Despite the difficulties in sustaining its sense of common purpose through decades of implementation details, the General Education curriculum was a testament to the quality of mass education that can be achieved when a few professors are inspired by ideals that students too are moved to embrace. Better than any curriculum I have known at Harvard or elsewhere, it responded to the universals about students—youth and promise—without defaulting to an "anything goes" elective system. The Red Book defined general education as "that part of a student's whole education which looks first of all to his life as a responsible human being and citizen." It was a moment when everyone could agree that responsibility and citizenship were key issues on which colleges should engage their students.

But the times changed, the teachers of the great General Education courses passed on, and the next generation of faculty did not share their postwar ideals. As the logic of the curriculum disintegrated, it became a dumping ground where departments could pasture faculty not trusted to teach concentrators. The Vietnam War, racial strife in America, and the concomitant violent upheavals at Harvard were merely deathblows to a curriculum already breathing its last.

General education after the Red Book

In 1974, in response to the disintegration of the General Education program, dean of the Faculty Henry Rosovsky initiated another review of undergraduate education. In explaining the need for the review, he cited the "vast changes [that] have occurred in advanced research in the past few decades," "the feeling that an older community of beliefs and values has been displaced without a satisfactory substitute," the need "to use our resources effectively," and "a sense that the undergraduate population has not received its fair share of the recent intellectual additions to our resources."

It took more than four years for the new curriculum to be designed and brought to a vote, and another three years for new courses to be generated and the full requirements to be put into effect. The so-called Core Curriculum (something of a misnomer since there were so many ways to satisfy the requirements) had ten course areas. Each student had to satisfy a specified set of eight Core areas, omitting two that were "close" to the student's field of concentration. An eleventh area was later added and the number of required courses was subsequently dropped to seven. Harvard's course catalog explains that

> the Core seeks to introduce students to the major *approaches to knowledge* in areas that the faculty considers indispensable to undergraduate education. It aims to show what kinds of knowledge and what forms of inquiry exist in these areas, how different means of analysis are acquired, how they are used, and what their value is. The courses within each area or subdivision of the program are equivalent in the sense that, while their subject matter may vary, their emphasis on a particular way of thinking is the same.

Like General Education, the Core created many inspiring courses, and brought distinguished senior members of the faculty, some of them master teachers, into the lecture hall with a broad cross section of the student body. Some courses with very encompassing and ambitions aims drew huge audiences. Michael Sandel's class Justice is as much a Harvard classic as Sam Beer's Soc Sci 2. And the Core did something perhaps even more ambitious: It instituted a system of quality control. Some faculty members resented the Core standing committee for interfering with their freedom to teach what they wished, but the committee's vetting of individual courses eliminated many of the bad courses and poor teachers that had crept into the dying General Education curriculum.

As excellent as Core Curriculum courses could be, the Core structure was a frustration from the beginning for both students and faculty. Unlike the General Education courses of the Red Book curriculum, many Core courses were quite specialized and narrowly focused. Yet only under restricted circumstances could a student substitute a departmental course for a Core course. Students eager to understand the world in which they were living were puzzled, for example, that the Core course Gendered Communities: Women, Islam, and Nationalism in the Middle East and North Africa satisfied a requirement but the History Department course The World in the Twentieth Century did not.

The Core's lack of any unifying framework of ideas or of facts provoked student cynicism from the beginning. A separate Core area, called Moral Reasoning, in theory honored the realm of "values." But moral understanding was simultaneously isolated from the other areas of the Core. Not only was there no "over-all logic" to the curriculum, but there also was no sense that values emerged from facts, even scientific facts.

The Core structure was, in reality, a way of instituting a breadth requirement and stimulating the creation of courses for nonspecialists while dodging the culture wars of the 1970s. The notion that "approaches to knowledge" provided a useful organizing principle for a broadly based education was not even original; the Red Book had explicitly said in 1945 that the division into Natural Sciences, Social Sciences, and Humanities should be understood in terms of their different "methods of knowledge." In fact, this theme was reminiscent of a much earlier time in Harvard history, when the curriculum was meant to teach students how to think rather than to impart useful knowledge— an approach ridiculed by an 1882 *Crimson* editorial as "the old-fashioned country-college system of prescribing studies merely for mental discipline." By putting the emphasis on ways of thinking rather than on substance, the Core Curriculum embraced the entire Harvard faculty, all of whom, presumably, knew how to think, however obscure their special interests. Yet the overarching rationale that the Core taught "approaches to knowledge," however serviceable, was never credible. No Harvard review ever attempted to determine if science students learned to think differently by taking a Social Analysis course, for example. The College's disciplinary committee saw little evidence that taking Moral Reasoning courses made students less likely to cheat or steal. Even the Core's founding documents made no claim that the Foreign Cultures requirement advanced a distinct approach to knowledge, It aimed merely to provide students a taste of certain knowledge.

The Core, nonetheless, has to be counted a success, however cynically students and faculty viewed it. It forced, and in some cases inspired, the faculty to teach courses overseen by a vigilant bureaucracy of their own colleagues. Because deans and presidents played a Tom Sawyer role, persuading professors that teaching in the Core was a high honor, many good and few poor courses came to life. But as a curriculum, the Core made no sense, especially to students. In its later life, it lost the support of the deans and was opened to anyone wanting to teach in it. When any professor could teach a Core course, it was no longer an honor to do so. Once the Harvard administration turned against it, it collapsed because the deans concentrated their rhetoric on its previously unspoken weaknesses. It was, in truth, not only not a Core. It was not even a curriculum.

❧

The review Dean William Kirby launched in 2002 was more ambitious than that of the 1940s or 1970s. The charge was refined to include advising and "direct educational contact between faculty and students" as important objectives, echoing another message of the president's inaugural address. It also added "'scientific literacy'" (quotation marks in the original) to the substantive matters to be ensured by the new curriculum, a rather more modest expectation than the grand ambition stated in the president's inaugural address: "Part of our task will be to assure that all who graduate from this place are equipped to comprehend, to master, to work with, the scientific developments that are transforming the world in which we will all work and live."

Kirby and Benedict Gross, dean of Harvard College, advanced the need for a more global or international curriculum by referring to Harvard's past: "As the 'Red Book' of the 1940s sought to outline how Harvard students should be educated as 'citizens of a free society,' we should aim to prepare students to live as citizens of a global society."

What could the deans have meant by contrasting the "free" society of the 1940s with the "global" society of the new millennium? Harvard, we were told, sees its students as "citizens of a global society" who will "live and work in all corners of our planet." Perhaps the deans meant that in the new curriculum, economic and political contingencies should take the place of Enlightenment ideals as the most important lessons for Harvard to teach its students. But the "freedom" in the "free society" for which the Red Book prepared students was not a chance, post–World War II creation at Harvard—it is a very old ideal. The "liberal" in "liberal education" means "free."* Human freedom, and the capacity of education to free the mind and ennoble the soul, have long been bedrock values of a Harvard education. Globalization is a critically important phenomenon of our time, and students certainly need to understand it. But the political and economic reality of globalization has not *replaced* the need for democratic idealism.

The reports that emerged from Kirby's review proposed a new instructional genus: elective courses that will "attract large numbers of students and provide common intellectual experiences for many students." The description of these courses was provocative—they were called "Harvard College Courses" at first and more recently "synoptic" and "integrative" and "portal courses." But progress in substance has not matched the progress in nomenclature. As of late 2005, none of these courses had been offered or even planned, and just as Dean Kirby kicked off the review by advocating a "shared foundation" without suggesting what it might be, the reports that emerged from the review presented no particular knowledge that should be universally or even broadly shared. They rejected the Core's "approaches to knowledge" organization of the curriculum but suggested no alternative. This vagueness was not lost on President Summers. As he began to realize that the review would not come out as he had hoped, he urged that the curriculum should be about *something*.

Free, to paraphrase information libertarian Richard Stallman, as in *freedom*—not as in free beer.

Are we going to teach literature by teaching courses about the great works of literature, or are we going to teach works of literature by teaching about one particular period in one particular country? Increasingly, we need to have the courage to define what greatness is, what's most important to know and to teach students.

The question was among Summers's few comments about the humanities and excited some interest because of that. But literature was probably meant only as an example. In his inaugural address, he had, along the same lines, observed that few at Harvard would admit to being ignorant of Shakespeare, but too many find it acceptable not to know the difference between a genome and a chromosome. The deeper question Summers raised is, What is most important to know, and to teach students? Will Harvard students of the future have any common knowledge, any shared educational experience, any particular point of view from which they will all have seen the products of civilization? Will there be a meritocracy of ideas as well as of professors and students?

The "empty bottles" resulting from the review in spring 2005 gave little hope for an affirmative answer. And a report on General Education, finally released in fall 2005 after many delays, confirmed that President Summers, having offered no vision of "greatness" himself, had failed to inspire the Harvard Faculty to come up with any of its own. If Summers and Kirby hoped to leave a mark on the meaning of a Harvard degree as profound as those of Conant's General Education program and Rosovsky's Core, they failed in their ambition. They discovered that a great curriculum does not crystallize out of scribbling by bureaucrats or squabbling among professors if the leaders cannot breathe into it direction and purpose.

The proposed general education requirement is three courses in each of the old General Education areas of Natural Science, Humanities, and Social Science—under new and trendier names. The courses, moreover, could be departmental courses, not specifically designed for the purpose of general education. The empty bottles could be filled with anything, as long as the right departments were offering it. The grand synoptic courses might be there, if any professors could be coaxed out of their departments to teach them in the absence of a structure to ensure that students would take them. But there is absolutely nothing that Harvard can expect students will know after they take three science or three humanities courses freely chosen from across the entire course catalog. The proposed general education requirement gives up entirely on the idea of shared knowledge, shared values, even shared aspirations. In the absence of any pronouncement that anything is more important than anything else for Harvard students to know, Harvard is declaring loudly that one can be an educated person in the twenty-first century without knowing anything about genomes, chromosomes, *or* Shakespeare.*

The proposed curriculum preserves the freshman writing and foreign-language requirements. Otherwise, the only common knowledge it strongly advocates for students is whatever can be gathered from a "significant international experience," the residue of the dramatic early call to prepare students for life in a global society. In the name of expanding "opportunities—not requirements—for students," the Moral Reasoning, Quantitative Reasoning, and Foreign Cultures requirements are all slated to be dropped. And sixty years after *General Education in a Free Society,* America has all but disappeared from a Harvard education. Not only does the new general education report fail to promote any shared values or ideals; it also dismisses the idea that the old General Education program was really about that anyway. The Red Book was just an attempt to create a "benign national ideology . . . at the start of the Cold war," according to the new report, by offering "courses specifically designed to meet contemporary exigencies."

The Enlightenment ideal of human liberty and the philosophy embodied in American democracy barely exist in the current Harvard curriculum. The new curriculum promises to be even less supportive of what the post–World War II Red Book committee thought a college curriculum might provide for society. Harvard's Core Curriculum does not even give students the option of understanding their own country.

The 2004–2005 Core Curriculum included the following options for students wanting to fulfill their Historical Studies requirement by taking a course in the history of American institutions: Offerings include

---

*The dean and some faculty members argued that students would use their curricular freedom for intellectual adventure, but the opposite also seems likely. Students trying to achieve honors, which Harvard values highly, would tend to choose courses in subjects they already know, in the hope of competing successfully for high grades.

Medicine and Society in America, The World in 1776, Pursuits of Happiness: Ordinary Lives in Revolutionary America, Slavery and Slave Trade in Africa and the Americas, World War and Society in the 20th Century: World War II, The Warren Court and the Pursuit of Justice, 1953–1969, and America and Vietnam, 1945–1975. There were seventeen courses about the history of other parts of the world. As a profile of what Harvard thinks students might be encouraged to learn about America, the list is very strange. Of course, it is not really a profile of what Harvard "thinks" about anything—it is just the natural result of professors choosing to teach subjects close to their expertise. Many of the teachers are superb, and the courses fascinating. But there are no courses on the lessons of the American Revolution or the Civil War, on the thinking of the founding fathers or the development of the Constitution. A student who wanted to learn any of these subjects through the Core would be without options.

A similar critique could be made of other parts of the Harvard catalog, both the Core courses and the departmental courses in History and Government. In a largely elective curriculum, students infer importance and value from the choices the university offers. Interestingly, students flock to courses on American institutions when they are offered. The course on the Warren Court is always oversubscribed, as is a course on the American presidency offered in the Government Department (and therefore not satisfying any Core requirement).

But instead of promoting learning about America, Harvard's twenty-first-century review insists that students learn more about the rest of the world. The focus raises a puzzling question. Will America be, in Harvard's eyes, merely another country, one among many? There seems to be nothing in particular Harvard wants its graduates to understand about the United States, other than what comes in proportion to its wealth and military influence within the global society. Perhaps Harvard no longer thinks of itself as an American college at all but is looking to become a global college, in the same way that during the last century it became a national rather than regional college.

At one level, basic American values are taken for granted by our students and faculty. No one I know at Harvard would be opposed to free speech or equal opportunity. Indeed, these terms are brandished regularly by students and faculty for a great variety of causes in which the university becomes embroiled, from "Justice for Janitors" to faculty resistance to the USA Patriot Act.

On the other hand, there are deep divisions within the faculty and the student body about how such principles apply in practice—just as deep as the divisions in America and, sometimes, within its Supreme Court. Though Harvard is often caricatured as a liberal campus, the student body is politically more balanced than the faculty, in part because it is so much more geographically and socioeconomically representative of the United States. Thus Harvard students share the country's divisions about such issues as the appropriate use of the nation's military power, the balance of power between the executive and legislative branches of government, the morality and legality of abortion rights, the role of religion in civic life, the relation of church to the state and to the university, affirmative action, and gay marriage. Harvard students should be able to reason and argue about these bitterly contested issues more insightfully than the average American, because we admit and graduate them with the expectation that they will be leaders. But Harvard's curriculum expresses no expectation that they will approach such debates with wisdom.

Little within the Harvard curriculum helps students think, reason, and argue about how our shared heritage applies to the controversies of today. Instead, debate and discussion about public controversies take place in the extracurricular realm. But with the exception of the vigorous and politically neutral Institute of Politics, the structures within which the discussions happen tend to be birds-of-a-feather groups: Republicans talking to one another about affirmative action, or pro-choice students talking to one another about abortion. It takes a courageous student to start a genuine dialogue about a controversial subject, and great effort is needed to pull into the discussion students who have not already made up their minds. Professors have little interest in creating the discomfort that results from dialogue about fundamental but divisive issues. Ensuring that the intellectual and emotional environment is "comfortable" for students is an almost unquestioned priority in American higher education, even at Harvard—in spite of the fact that real learning about values can take place only when one's own values are challenged.

In spring 2002, the faculty committee that chooses student commencement speakers selected the U.S.-born Muslim son of a Bangladeshi-

American father and an Irish-American mother. Had the parents been reversed and the student's name been Christie, the speech might not have attracted much attention. But his name was Yasin, the speech was announced with the title "American Jihad," and a firestorm erupted among students and alumni and in the world media. The title was, as it turned out, the most jarring thing about the speech, which was an eloquent but uncontroversial example of commencement-time talk about personal struggle, faith, and growth. But by long tradition, only the titles of commencement addresses are released in advance, and there was widespread speculation about the speech itself, and even what the speaker might say if he chose to depart from the text the committee had approved. To crown the irony, the title wasn't even the one Yasin had presented to the selection committee. It had been suggested as a punchier alternative by a member of the committee, who happens to be Jewish.

In the end, a healthy dialogue resulted, mainly among Jewish and Muslim students, and the title was restored to "Of Faith and Citizenship: My American Jihad," Yasin's original proposal. There was no protest to speak of, and rain kept the crowd small anyway. Still, College officials and students who had known Yasin as a temperate and constructive force on campus were saddened by the personal attacks on him and by the failure of the university to use this incident to teach something important about diversity at Harvard, an international outlook, and freedom in America. President Summers, who in the aftermath of the September 2001 attacks had called on everyone at Harvard to "treat all other members of our community, from all backgrounds, with civility, decency, and respect" and to "affirm . . . the ideals and values that lie at the heart of our university and our nation," remained silent until Yasin received a death threat, and then issued this statement:

> Concerns have been raised about the planned commencement speech of Zayed Yasin, who was chosen as one of this June's student Commencement speakers by a duly appointed faculty committee. We live in times when, understandably, many people at Harvard and beyond are deeply apprehensive about events in the Middle East and possible reverberations in American life. Yet, especially in a university setting, it is important for people to keep open minds, listen carefully to one another and react to the totality of what each

speaker has to say. I am pleased that there have been a number of constructive conversations that have addressed potential divisions in our community associated with his speech. Finally, I am told that Mr. Yasin recently received a threatening e-mail from an unidentified source. Direct personal threats are reprehensible and all of us who believe in the values of this university should condemn them in the strongest terms.

Some observers were surprised that the strongest defense a Harvard president would offer for a Harvard student—a student well-known on campus, with an unblemished record, and duly chosen by the university to speak at Commencement—was that no one should threaten to kill him. A statement from Howard Georgi, the Master of Yasin's House, was more personally supportive, saying that Yasin "is thoughtful, reasonable, and works to encourage civil discussion and dialogue." But it took a student journalist to make the larger point. Calling President Summers's statement "lukewarm," the student wrote,

> I have met the enemy, and it is not Zayed Yasin. . . . I am glad that I went to a University that would choose such a speaker during such difficult times. I am glad that we would not let the events of Sept. 11 pervert the meaning of one of the world's great religions without letting someone, one of our own, speak in its defense. I am glad that in a time of great sorrow, ours remains one of the great institutions of the world, standing in defense of the freedom of speech and debate that is fundamental to an academic community. . . . This brand of intellectual discourse and constant questioning is both so Harvard and so American. We cannot allow it to be taken away from us—that, truly, would be the triumph of evil.

The following fall, President Summers rose in morning chapel to complain that in universities "[s]erious and thoughtful people are advocating and taking actions that are anti-Semitic in their effect if not their intent." A few weeks later he said, "We are ultimately stronger as a university if we together maintain our robust commitment to free expression" while reaffirming his "concerns about speech that may be viewed as lending comfort to anti-Semitism." Many found puzzling his suite of pronouncements from June to November. In his temperate defense of Yasin's benign speech with its controversial title and his attack on actions that are *viewed* as lending comfort to anti-Semitism or are anti-Semitic *in effect*, the president seemed to suggest that Harvard embrace a new sort of "robust commitment to free expression"—one in which the important element is not what the speaker actually says or means but what the listener hears.

At its core, the Zayed Yasin incident was not even a free speech issue. Yasin did not have a right to stand in front of tens of thousands on Commencement day and say whatever he wanted. He had volunteered to give a particular speech, and Harvard honored him by asking him to do it. President Summers's tepid support shows the weakness with which Harvard, when under public relations pressure, holds to principles even more commonplace than the right to free speech: that those we honor should be treated with dignity, that people should be judged by their words and not their appearance, and that Americans can share values without sharing race or religion.

Globalization is "in" at Harvard. President Summers and Dean Kirby repeatedly warned that Harvard is too "Americanist" and must not produce provincial graduates with meager awareness of the rest of the world. According to Summers, "Our intellectual universe needs to be expanded beyond American preoccupations." At a fundraiser in 2002, he cited a member of Congress who, when asked if he would be traveling abroad during the congressional recess, responded, "No, I've been there." In his annual letter, which elsewhere urged a curriculum that "maximizes choice and flexibility," Dean Kirby suggested nonetheless that an international experience might become a graduation "expectation," whatever that might mean. "Should we not expect that every student have a significant international experience—be it foreign study, an internship, public service, or research abroad—before graduation?" The president made the point with more peremptory phrasing, saying he was "disturbed" that Harvard "lagged behind" most other schools in the fraction of undergraduates who studied abroad:* "You know something? The best place

---

*It is an odd irony to think that Harvard should be engaged in a competition with other universities to send away more students who have so eagerly sought to attend—especially since a number of colleges with robust study-abroad programs adopted them in part because of housing shortages, limited academic opportunities, or locations in sleepy towns that do not hold the interest of their students for four consecutive years.

to learn how to speak Japanese is in Japan." Citing the example of Afghanistan's unexpected emergence as a country that mattered to the lives of Americans, Summers stressed that Harvard has the job of "preparing people for a broad international understanding."

Most of the Harvard students who would be the beneficiaries of this emphasis on international education are citizens of the world's major democratic nation. Their own country is rarely mentioned in anything written recently about Harvard's plans for undergraduate education. Harvard recognizes no responsibility to see that its students who are American citizens understand the underpinnings of their democracy, or that its students who are foreign citizens comprehend the values enshrined in American institutions. The closest Harvard officials have come in recent writings about the curriculum to acknowledging that Harvard is located in a particular nation is a statement in Dean Kirby's cover letter to the 2004 report: "As a leading American institution, Harvard College has a responsibility to educate its students—who will live and work in all corners of the globe—as citizens not only of their home country, but also of the world, with the capacity not only to understand others, but also to see themselves, and this country, as others see them."

The report does not attempt to flesh out the thought that Harvard has at least some responsibility to educate students as citizens of the United States. The Report on General Education that appeared after another year and a half of deliberation failed to mention Western civilization at all, except in the historical introduction and in one sentence disavowing any "assumptions about the centrality of the West and its values": "The Committee did not want to give, even inadvertently, the impression that it was trying to turn the clock back to an era in which a consensus about what all students should know was more easily reached." The current curricular reports do not even suggest that international students at Harvard might return to their homelands with informed respect for the principles of American democracy.

Knowledge of American institutions and the enlightened heritage from which they emerged certainly cannot be taken for granted. It is precisely because there is so little agreement even among well-educated Americans about how our democratic principles should apply in practice that we owe it to our students to help them become the citizens on whom the future of the nation will depend.

The claims that Harvard as it stands is excessively Americanist, and that its intellectual agenda is too narrowly focused on "American preoccupations," lack factual foundation. For example, of the eighty-three professors teaching in the History Department in the year 2003–04, twenty are identified as U.S. historians; the rest cover the range from Latin America to Vietnam. Even throwing in all of Western Europe as the source of the intellectual tradition from which the United States emerged, more than half the department is concerned with other parts of the world. The prevailing intellectual atmosphere at Harvard is not globally myopic.

While it was once the university administration that limited study-abroad opportunities in order to assure quality control, it is now the student body that needs persuasion to leave Cambridge while they are undergraduates. Students recognize that the education they are receiving at Harvard is better than that available at most foreign universities. Students are also reluctant to sacrifice opportunities to engage in extracurricular activities at the very high level Harvard offers. By contrast, students are eager to spend time abroad when their college education is behind them. Competition is fierce for the limited number of postgraduate fellowships to study or travel abroad. In the 2002–2003 school year, there were 153 applications for four scholarships to study under one postgraduate program in England. Harvard students seem to view experience abroad rather the way President Eliot did: "that foolish beginning but excellent sequel to education."

Snappy lines about Japan and Afghanistan are a poor substitute for thoughtful analysis of how best to give students a "broad international understanding." The best way to achieve international understanding is not to have everyone go abroad before graduating. As the Roman poet Horace wrote two thousand years ago, *caelum non animum mutant qui trans mare currunt*—that is, those who go running across the sea change their climate but not their mind.

Learning about the world pulls students in two directions. Many students by the time they graduate are eager to experience life for a time in a foreign culture, but many are reluctant to sacrifice one or two of their quota of eight terms at Harvard to do it. Students for whom Harvard represents a pinnacle of educational opportunity almost beyond the imagination of their underprivileged families may be disconcerted by Dean Kirby's amiably meant quip that "If you're going to come to Harvard College, it would be very good to have a passport." Of course, study abroad makes sense for students of international history, literature, government, or other fields for which the best centers of learning may be located elsewhere. But there is no better place in the world to study mathematics or biochemistry as an undergraduate than at Harvard. For students in such fields, the attraction of going abroad is experiential, not academic. And Harvard's rationale for its new emphasis on study abroad is also largely based on the premise that it will be a good experience for students. As Dean Kirby explained, study abroad has been emphasized

> [b]ecause the world our students will live and work in goes beyond Massachusetts Bay and beyond the United States of America. Ours is a world of interacting, changing but still *different* societies and cultures. Wherever our students are from, the world they will face will be one mostly made up of foreigners—of people with different pasts and different presents, who speak, write and think in different languages, at least some of which have to be learned in order to understand the people who speak them.

Harvard, which justifies its high prices on the basis of the quality of its faculty, libraries, and research facilities and has consistently opposed academic credit for experiential learning in areas such as community service, now proposes that the experience of living abroad be an almost essential expectation for an undergraduate degree. The Curricular Review Report stated explicitly that a "significant international experience," not an academic course of study abroad, is what every Harvard student should have. The report even denigrated the idea of a Harvard student fulfilling the international-experience expectation by studying at the likes of Oxford and Cambridge, noting that "a purposeful mission in a non-Anglophone culture or third-world society would instill a higher level of global competency than would a similar experience in England or Australia."

There is something unseemly and anti-intellectual about such experiential prescriptions for higher education, when the "experiences" will be so varied in locale, comfort, and purpose that they will have nothing in common. They will cost money,* Harvard's or families', and under the proposed curriculum they will replace academic coursework in Foreign Cultures, which will no longer be required. Of course, some international experiences teach things that cannot be learned any other way. The question is not whether travel or study abroad can be instructive but whether it is the best use of a scarce and precious resource: time at a college in a great research university. The best way to learn about poverty may be to live in poverty, but no one suggests that Sociology majors should spend a year of their college education in the slums. Given the cultural polarization of the United States, it would be more valuable to have every student from a blue county live in a red county for a summer, and vice versa, than to force them all to go abroad before graduating. I have found parents and students alike skeptical that those with the privilege of attending one of the world's finest universities should learn "global competency" by substituting experiences abroad or courses at inferior universities for the opportunity to study, think, and debate with others at Harvard.

The great universities, the universities that educate a disproportionate share of the nation's future industrial, political, and judicial leaders, struggle to explain the overall point of the education they offer. Anything resembling moral principles or suggestions of ultimate values has been isolated within the curriculum, if not removed from it entirely. And as universities focus on lands beyond American borders, the democratic freedoms that have protected and nurtured these institutions are barely acknowledged in what they teach. If the country is depending on Harvard to produce another Supreme Court nominee thirty years hence, Harvard is not getting the freshmen of the Class of 2009 off to a good start.

The great universities are respected and certainly prized in America, but the public regards with increasing skepticism the values they represent—and their failure sometimes to represent any values at all. As

---

*For the academic year 2005–2006, Harvard quoted $44,350 as the cost of attendance, including tuition, room, board, books, and incidentals, but not medical insurance. If a "significant international experience" is "expected" of all students in the future, then the cost of that experience will have to be added to the total. (Cost estimate from How to Finance a College Education: A Guide for Families, Harvard Financial Aid Office, 2005–2006.)

their cost soars toward $50,000 per year, and their intellectual content becomes more estranged from anything comprehensible to ordinary citizens, they will be regarded as sources of economic security for their graduates but not of intellectual or personal inspiration. As a result, the critical judgments of educational quality and the downward pressure on costs that have been applied so vigorously to K-12 education may find their way to the university marketplace as well.

Private universities have long been free from meddling by American society. But that freedom is part of a social contract. Universities are given freedom—and tax exemptions—because they serve American society. In a time of war, a war that seems much more real in most of America than it does in the 02138 zip code, will America continue to believe that its universities are holding up their end of the deal?

On the first anniversary of the attacks of September 11, 2001, I was asked by the *Harvard Crimson* to write anything I deemed appropriate to the occasion. The question I raised at the end of my piece still troubles me. "Since Sept. 11, there has been an unprecedented recollection of this country's founding principles of freedom and equality," I wrote. "How will the Harvard Faculty balance the reality that the U.S. is one nation among many in an ever smaller and more interconnected world, with a recognition that the particular 'free society' in which Harvard exists is founded on ideals which Americans continue to be proud to defend and preserve?" The answer offered in the proposed curriculum ignores the fact that Harvard, that old place founded "to advance learning and perpetuate it to posterity," is an American university. At Harvard today, all knowledge is equally valued as long as a Harvard professor is teaching it, and that does not bode well for posterity.

CHAPTER 3

Contact, Competition, Cooperation

The Downside of the Pursuit of Excellence

The object of the undergraduate department is not to produce hermits, each imprisoned in the cell of his own intellectual pursuits, but men fitted to take their places in the community and live in contact with their fellow man.

—A. Lawrence Lowell, 1909

The era had not yet come when professors asked, "But if I use my time in talking to students, when am I to get my work done?"

—Rollo Walter Brown (A.M. 1905), 1948

After teaching my courses the same way for thirty years, in the thirty-first I decided to try something new. Instead of requiring students to do their problem sets and projects by themselves, without divulging their work to other students, I tried the opposite. Every student had a partner in the course, and the two members of a team submitted homework jointly. Both students in a pair got the same grade on the work. Team members could work together in any way they wished, as long as teams did not share their solutions with other teams.

My students were nonscientists satisfying a general education requirement in quantitative reasoning. I wanted them to understand some of the principles of electrical engineering and also something about the way engineers work. I wanted them to experience, in a modest and relatively low-stakes way, what professional engineering teams do all the time. I hoped most students would learn that in human interactions, the whole is better than the sum of its parts.

I also wanted them to understand that life sometimes is unfair. An engineering team gets paid if its client likes the results it delivers. Either everyone on the team reaps the benefit, or everyone takes the blame. The client doesn't care if one individual on the team did her job but another did not do his; the client cares only what the whole team delivers. I knew that most college students with the exception of athletes were unlikely to have had much experience with such sublimation of the individual for the benefit of a group.

Little in the Harvard curriculum provides that kind of experience. Students majoring in the humanities and social sciences take seminars, but those classes often have an environment of competitive sharing, with rewards going to the students who have the best ideas to share and are the quickest to share them. I decided to give traditional examinations in my course, so that in the final reckoning, slackers would not profit excessively and those stuck with delinquent partners would not be excessively disadvantaged.

The experience was a sobering one. Some students did fine—especially students who were just happy to pass their quantitative requirement, and students who became so intrigued by the material that they lost sight of the strategic and tactical issues of evaluation. Some students mistrusted the system because it was unfamiliar, but they gradually relaxed. But others were simply angry about it.

Several students voiced similar complaints, and I will label the canonical complainer Alice and her partner Bob. "It isn't fair that I got only a 70 on this problem set," said Alice. "Look at it—the part I did is all right and the part he did is only half right. Why should I be punished for the fact that he didn't do a good job on his part?" I reminded Alice that there was no "her part" and "his part"—both were responsible for the whole thing. Maybe splitting it down the middle and stapling the two halves together had not produced the best result. Maybe Alice should try a different approach next time; perhaps she and Bob should first try to do all the problems by themselves and then sit down to compare and merge their results. Alice returned after the next assignment complaining that this approach didn't work either. Bob would not get started on time, and she wound up having to do most of the work. I pointed out that she had made a disappointing discovery about Bob, but she was not powerless. She had established that she could not achieve *both* of two desirable ends: an excellent homework solution and an equitable division of labor. But she could still achieve either the one or the other, and it was within her power to decide which. She protested that there was enough pressure on her already to do well in college without being expected to struggle with those kinds of decisions.

Another student phrased his complaint more directly. Working with a partner, he said, "is more of a challenge than working alone." Couldn't he just do the work by himself? No, he couldn't, I responded. It might be a challenge, but unless you become a professor, you are likely to have to work in a group, with the entire group taking responsibility for the result.

These students, if they knew anything about cooperation and communication with peers, kept it locked away in a part of their brains they did not use while doing academic work. They had been conditioned to a particular way of pursuing excellence—making sure *others* did not profit from *their* excellence.

Students are social animals—more than professors tend to be. In most academic fields, professors prosper by individual brilliance. The writings and discoveries that gain them the greatest fame are those for which they can claim to be the sole creator. In this way professors are different from most students and from the adults in the professions and careers to which most students are destined. One of the effects of the unrelenting competition among faculty is an idealization of "the life of the mind" that belittles skills on which almost all nonacademic work relies. And one of the effects of the unrelenting competition to enroll the best students and to keep them happy is to give them what they demand, in residential and social life, whether or not those things are, in the long run, in their best educational interests.

The educational role of residential life

When A. Lawrence Lowell succeeded Charles William Eliot as Harvard's president in 1909, the first words out of his mouth emphasized the student as a member of society and refocused the university on undergraduates who were not destined for academic careers. "Among his other wise sayings, Aristotle remarked that man is by nature a social animal; and it is in order to develop his powers as a social being that American colleges exist."

Harvard had not been created for intellectual "hermits" on their way to becoming professors, "each imprisoned in the cell of his own intellectual pursuits." But as the size of Harvard had increased under Eliot's long presidency, Lowell argued, so had students' isolation and anonymity. As a result, Lowell continued, "college life has shown a marked tendency to disintegrate, both intellectually and socially."

Lowell recognized that the subordination of undergraduate education to the pursuit of scholarship had a social cost for undergraduates. In a large college, Lowell observed,

> The personal contact of teacher and student becomes more difficult. Large communities tend to cliques based upon similarity of origin and upon wealth. . . . Great masses of unorganized young men . . . are prone to superficial currents of thought and interest, to the detriment of the personal intellectual progress that ought to dominate mature men seeking higher education. This drift . . . is the cause of the exaggerated importance of the secondary interests as compared with the primary object of education; of what Woodrow Wilson, when President of Princeton, called the overshadowing of the main tent by the side-shows.

Lowell's solution to the problem was the creation of the "Houses," residences where a few hundred students of different backgrounds would form living communities with each other and with faculty and tutors. His intention was intensely democratic. A. C. Hanford, dean of the College under Lowell, explained the same principles for the freshman dormitories:

> The man of limited means and the rich, the high school and private school graduates, the son of the banker, and the son of the farmer were to be thrown together. Freshmen coming from different schools and of varying origins were to be given an opportunity for making new contacts, social distinctions were to be broken down, and a democratic class spirit developed.

Lowell was at once a nostalgic throwback—the small college he remembered was gone forever—and an inspired visionary. His ideal of a college community would mix students of different backgrounds and of different interests. But like many a Yankee aristocrat who had come of age in the nineteenth century, Lowell carried social prejudices that are repugnant today. He was not at all progressive on the education of women, and he persecuted homosexual students. He excluded the few blacks at Harvard from the House system, supposedly in their own best interests. Lowell also limited the number of Jews at Harvard.

Though Lowell's vision of social unity was short-sighted, his idea of an integrated residential community was correct in principle. Several decades passed before the Houses really represented cross sections of the College, not just because of Lowell's quotas and prohibitions. Less wealthy students from the Boston area continued to live at home, and wealthier students took fancy apartments rather than move into the Houses. Even so, the Harvard of Lowell's era was a congenial place for most students. In practice, the student community was more open-minded than the president. Stanley Marcus, the scion of the Nieman-Marcus department stores, came from Dallas to attend Harvard in the 1920s. His description of being a Jew at Harvard contrasted with Lowell's efforts to limit the number of Jews admitted in the first place. "Harvard turned out to be everything I had dreamed it would be," he wrote in his autobiography. "During my years at Harvard I encountered only one instance of obvious religious discrimination," losing an election for a club presidency—what he called one of the "minor obstacles a Jewish student had to learn to handle." Certainly other Jews at Harvard who arrived in the 1930s and 1940s felt the prejudices more sharply than Marcus did, but over the years all forms of discrimination faded and Harvard realized an unencumbered version of Lowell's vision. Today students of both sexes are assigned to the Houses at random, except that they can ask to be accompanied by a few friends. Virtually all students now live in the Houses at Harvard, though no one is required to do so.

Unlike the Oxford and Cambridge Colleges to which they bear a family resemblance, Harvard's Houses were never meant to be the venues for academic instruction. Yet their entire purpose was educational in a broader and deeper sense.

The House Plan is a great experiment, in some respects the greatest tried since the College was founded, but it is the consummation of the changes that have been going on for many years. . . . They are all directed to giving the student more individual attention, and at the same time making him more dependent upon his own efforts; to enlarging self-education under guidance, with more guidance. This involves a serious and mature attitude of mind on the part of the undergraduate. It signifies the tone of a university as contrasted with that of the schoolboy. The problem of the college is a moral one, deepening the desire to develop one's own mind, body and character; and this is much promoted by living in surroundings and an atmosphere congenial to that object. . . . The Houses are a social device for a moral purpose.

By adopting only selectively the liberalizations of the late twentieth century, the Houses weathered the revolutions that swept over colleges, including the move to coeducation and the struggle over ethnic-identity politics. One can argue about whether Harvard students are any more "serious and mature" than students elsewhere, but they are socially integrated to a degree that is rare in American colleges. Other colleges have tried to achieve a similar result, but only Yale, whose housing system was established a few years after Harvard's, has fully succeeded.

The experiment is very difficult to repeat. A true community cannot be large, and the economically efficient scale for dining and other services is closer to a thousand than to a few hundred. Where voluntary segregation has arisen, it is almost impossible to eliminate. But the most powerful forces working against integrated housing are not the economic ones. Depriving students of freedom of choice is a hard sell, in housing as in course selection. Students are young adults, the argument goes, and should be allowed to make their own choices and their own mistakes. If they choose to live with only black students, or only athletes, or only other people who need to save money, or only people from New England prep schools, who is the college to tell them they should not? Indeed, it is argued, birds-of-a-feather aggregates are educational assets, since a critical mass can promote a minority interest or culture.

This train of logic and pressure produced "theme dorms" such as the Italian Language and Culture House at Stanford and MIT's "Chocolate City." But the opportunity to learn from those sharing interests or roots limits the opportunity to learn from those who are different. The fundamental tension is expressed in a defense of Chocolate City: "People group together by whom they get along with. If we say that any two people can live next door to each other, then we are evading the obvious. Yes, any two people can live next to each other, but not any two will be neighbors." One student scolded me in similar language for insisting that projects be done in teams. "I have enough pressure on me trying to do well without having to worry about working with some random person in whom I have no interest."

Theme houses, housing assignment policies that comply with students' natural inclination to self-segregate in the interest of "comfort" or promotion of a particular culture, are a concession to inmates wanting to run the asylum. Like the elective curriculum, housing policies put students' freedom of choice in conflict with the educational imperative, to insist on education ahead of free choice. In fact, although no individual student would ask to have his or her freedom of choice curtailed, most students recognize the educational value of integrated housing. I never met a dean with responsibility for theme dorms who would not have preferred to see them abolished, but they are politically difficult to eliminate once they are entrenched. Ongoing developments in the housing systems at Princeton and Dartmouth show that those who have the privilege of designing housing policies anew rarely choose to risk self-segregation. It takes some courage, and a great deal of money, for colleges to insist on the educational value of putting students together with "random people in whom they have no interest." But if Americans don't learn in college the value of tearing down those walls, the walls will not come down in the world into which those students graduate.

Integration may not survive under the pressure to quell unrest and to give students what they demand. Reversing a long-standing policy that spaces would not be allocated to groups of students based on race or gender, Harvard announced in fall 2005 its intention to create a women's center. Harvard was only doing what most other colleges did long ago, but President Summers was said to have declared only a year earlier, "A women's center is one of the last things I want to see on campus." That, however, preceded his notorious comments about the cognitive abilities of women, which changed the Harvard climate dramatically. Harvard reacted by accommodating almost any request presented on behalf of women, including that for a women's center. Students themselves, steeped in Harvard's integrationist tradition, were quick to speak up in opposition. In the staff editorial a few days after the announcement, the *Crimson* editors wrote, "The integration of Harvard and Radcliffe—bringing together space that was once gender-segregated—was a victory for equal rights. That women's groups would now be calling for gender-specific space is a matter of heavy irony." As often happens now when Harvard comes down on one side of a delicate balance, it provided no explanation of the driving principles, since there were none. The responsible dean, almost certainly acting on orders from above, said only that "our women students want a women's center, and therefore I want one." An instructive moment was sadly lost, a moment when students might have learned how to think about integration and segregation, about why a women's center but not a women's dormitory or a black students' center is consistent with Harvard's educational vision.

Student-faculty contact in a college of lectures

It is a challenge, though not an insurmountable challenge, to create student communities that cross lines of socioeconomic background, race, and avocation. Creating communities that cross the student-faculty divide is more difficult. Students say they crave contact with professors, and most professors say they enjoy contact with students. But none of the research universities can really claim to have solved the student-faculty contact problem.

Lecture courses are a standard bogeyman in discussions of student-faculty contact, but because they are a practical necessity, universities view them as sources sometimes of shame, sometimes of pride. Dean Kirby referred to lectures as "distance learning" and he urged "limiting severely the opportunities for students and faculty to avoid intense engagement with one another." Yet Harvard also takes pride in the size of some of its courses, acknowledging that size is sometimes correlated with quality. During summer 2004 the University's home page prominently featured a photograph of a full lecture hall and the caption "Harvard students enjoy learning from world-renowned lecturers, such as Michael Sandel, whose 'Justice' course regularly attracts between 700 and 900 undergraduates."* And the integrative courses that are heralded as innovations of the new general education curriculum are promised to "attract large numbers of students."

---

*Sandel's Justice (Moral Reasoning 22) is one of Harvard's best courses, but such bragging about its size is unseemly. One reason it is so large is that Harvard requires most students to take a Moral Reasoning course but never offers more than a few courses in this rubric.

Universities not only generate knowledge and pass it along to young people but also integrate knowledge. Lecture courses at their best can do all these things. They are educationally different from, not intrinsically inferior to, small-group instruction.

A "course"—a series of classes extending over three or four months—is a good unit of teaching in part because the instructor can start from first principles and at the end talk about the state of the art. Courses structure knowledge as well as teach it. Lecture courses are successful if the lectures are illuminating individually and tell a larger story when taken together.

The lecture has a bad reputation as an instructional vehicle because it is used in ways to which it is not well suited. Lectures are a terrible medium for communicating long sequences of undifferentiated facts. Yet professors sometimes treat a course like a tube of toothpaste: they squeeze out a little bit of material every day, starting at ten past the hour and stopping exactly on the hour, regardless of how that moment relates to the structure of the subject matter, and they try to ensure that the tube is empty at the end of the term, clenching the tube in both fists during the last week if necessary. At their worst, lectures today are not much better than they were in 1825. According to George Ticknor:

> Professor Jardine of Glasgow . . . says, after an experience of above half a century in different modes of instruction, that "there certainly never was a wilder scheme devised by the perverted ingenuity of man, than that of attempting to improve the minds of youth, and create intellectual habits, by the sole means of reading a lecture, without further intercourse between teacher and pupil.". . . Lectures . . . , on the present system, . . . are a waste of the time both of the hearers and the instructers [*sic*].

At their best, however, lectures are not an endless series of short lessons, as many as will fit in an hour, but more like chapters in a book, each one giving a new dimension to what has come before. At the end of the course, the student can have a sense of integrity and satisfaction with the experience as a whole. A good course is not merely a well-taught course, any more than a good book is simply a well-written book. Good courses have good concepts behind them. A student can come away from a course enlightened, even if the lecturer's delivery is imperfect.

Thus "good teaching" needs a larger interpretation than the term is usually given. Good teaching is more than talking smoothly and keeping the class awake, more than the capacity to give "clear, well-structured lectures" on which Harvard's course evaluation questionnaire asks students to rate professors on a one-to-five scale. In his book *Coming Apart,* Roger Rosenblatt described the great Harvard Celtic scholar John Kelleher in these terms: "He was the wisest and most complete teacher and dedicated scholar I had ever seen. It wasn't his brains or his learning that drew me to him. Or his abilities as a teacher. His near-confounding stammer drove most students away; it was discouraging and, at times, heartbreaking to see him struggle with his tongue, as if it were a snake filling his mouth, merely to get it to lie still and allow him to speak his mind." Kelleher's learning spanned continents and millennia, and his unpretentious personal style and inspiring wisdom transcended his elocutionary incapacity. Like a humble monk, he moved and educated his students through the power of his ideas, not his discourse.

Lecture courses are not only a great medium. When used appropriately, they are an economic necessity, even for Harvard. Harvard's student-faculty ratio is eight to one, quite good, and most classes enroll fewer than twenty students. Many seminars are intentionally limited, and some courses, on subjects such as cuneiform, are important for the survival of knowledge even though they will never be popular. Given the size of the College and the number of courses, the average course size is higher than the median, probably fifty or more. Once a course has more than a hundred students, it doesn't really matter how big it is. A lecturer who can engage an audience of a hundred in a conversation can do it with five hundred; a lecturer who reads his notes to five hundred will read them to a hundred also.

Harvard judges teaching when it hires and promotes faculty. But the evidence for the teaching skill of a fresh Ph.D. is inevitably limited—often to the impression left on a group of faculty colleagues after a heavily rehearsed fifty-minute presentation of the candidate's thesis research. Harvard makes adequate teaching a requirement for promotion, but the process used to assess teaching is far less rigorous than that used to judge scholarship. Promotion committees use the Committee on Undergraduate Education (CUE) Guide as their primary source of information about teaching quality. This guide uses student evaluations of courses gathered for an entirely different purpose—

helping students decide which classes to take. Students are not told that the way they fill out the forms may play a key role in tenure decisions, and the "purpose" stated in the guide itself does not mention its use as evidence in tenure cases.

In any case, student course evaluations principally measure students' assessment of instructors' appearance and demeanor, not any more thoughtful analysis of the quality of the education they are providing. Two Harvard psychologists showed that the numbers students assign lecturers after watching only thirty seconds of video with no sound correlate very highly with student evaluations of the entire course at the end of the term. Students watching the brief videos had no information about what the instructors were saying and ranked instructors on personality traits such as optimism and confidence, not on teaching quality. This experiment conclusively establishes that student course evaluations are simply consumer preference metrics of the shallowest sort.

While senior faculty members judge scholarship by obtaining detailed, confidential evaluation letters from dozens of outside experts, they almost never expend the effort to visit classes of their junior colleagues or study their course materials in order to assess teaching quality directly. The appraisal of teaching in the tenure dossier rarely amounts to more than a pro forma letter listing a few student evaluation scores. Even then, excellent teaching doesn't count much more than the merely satisfactory.

Almost from the moment when scholarship became the dominant factor in professorial appointments, teaching was seen as at best an unrelated skill, and perhaps even in natural opposition. An 1878 survey of American colleges concluded, "It is as original thinkers and authors that the majority of college professors attain a reputation; but the qualities that fit one for pursuing original investigations . . . may unfit him for . . . the teacher's task. It is, therefore, oftentimes true that a great scholar, of national reputation, is only an indifferent teacher." Conversely, great teaching can be viewed in academic circles as a kind of performance art, fine if you can do it but raising doubts about the teacher's seriousness as a scholar.

With the standards for promotion based so much on research productivity, new faculty members are often left to plan their courses on their own, probably imitating the style in which they were taught. Their colleagues may not encourage them to spend much time thinking about becoming better teachers, or dreaming up imaginative new courses, because they do not want to signal, unfairly, that time spent learning to teach will help them to be promoted. Still, Harvard is not without examples of what can happen when the incentive structures and hiring standards for faculty are changed. A quarter mile from Harvard Yard, the Harvard Business School puts pedagogy high on the list of institutional missions. Students who move from the College to the Business School are astonished by the improvement in teaching quality.

Creation of a grand course is an intellectual achievement in itself. If this were recognized in faculty hiring and promotion, students would, in the long run, be well served. The lecture format is here to stay, and universities would be better off embracing a philosophy that teaching a superb course was evidence of great intellect, not an accidental skill, when they decide what great minds to seek out for hiring. Student-faculty contact should come elsewhere, but that does not make lecture courses bad. There are a few faculty members, I suppose, who run for the door as they utter the last words of their lectures, but most people I know hang around to talk to students, accept lunch invitations when they can, and respond to e-mails with some fidelity. An alumna once told me about a lecture course she had taken. The professor had been a wonderful teacher, but she neither wanted nor got a personal relationship with him. What she wanted was a personal relationship with Virgil, and the professor had given her that.

About thirty years ago, Cynthia*—the woman just mentioned—received individual instruction from Professor Conrad during her junior and senior years. Cynthia met with Conrad, who was one of the greatest classical scholars in the world, every Wednesday afternoon for two years. She and Conrad read the great Latin lyric poets, Propertius and Ovid among others, together in Conrad's study in the university library. As Cynthia was doing a joint major between classics and English, they sometimes read English poets too. Sometimes they drank sherry while discussing the works and their language, themes, and significance.

Nothing "happened" between Cynthia and Professor Conrad, except that she was so inspired by his penetrating mind that she went on to earn a Ph.D. in the humanities. But today such an educational experience could not happen, for at least three reasons:

---

*The names of both student and professor have been changed in this account.

1. No male professor can be alone with a young female student for long hours, especially with no one sitting outside the door to hear what is or is not going on. There is too much risk of a complaint of a sexual advance. The case of Cynthia and Professor Conrad would be stunningly dangerous today because much of what they were reading was love poetry. The opportunities for misunderstandings and false charges are not limited to professors and students of opposite sexes.

2. Serving alcohol to underage students is illegal and puts the university at serious risk.

3. It is a very inefficient use of a very expensive resource to have this kind of teaching done by senior faculty. They may want to do it, but there are only so many hours in the day, and many other important tasks can be done only by professors—advising Ph.D. students, chairing search committees for new hires, reviewing junior faculty for tenure, and so on. If tutorial of this sort occurs at all, there are overwhelming incentives to have it done by junior faculty, graduate students, or faculty on annual contracts.

Every university touts the quality of its professors and promises that they will be available to undergraduates. And every university privately recognizes that student complaints about inadequate faculty contact are persistent and intractable. But we expect the most from the greatest universities, and they are the most disappointing. Harvard faculty averaged only 2.92 out of 5 on a 2002 survey question about availability, compared to an average of 3.31 at other top-tier colleges.

Personal relationships between students and faculty have always been rare. In 1825 Ticknor said, "The amount of personal attention received by any student, on an average, from his instructers [*sic*] at college, would be thought insufficient for the instruction of children in the humblest primary or charity school, where only the rudest elements of education are attempted." Andrew Preston Peabody, a junior at the time of Ticknor's grim assessment, said of student-faculty relations that

the relations between the Faculty and the students were regarded . . . as those of mutual hostility. The students certainly considered the Faculty as their natural enemies. There existed between the two parties very little of kindly intercourse, and that little generally secret. . . . It was regarded as a high crime by his class for a student to enter a recitation-room before the ringing of the bell, or to remain to ask a question of the instructor.

There have been endless cycles of promised reform followed, some decades later, by more complaints. In 1845 an Overseer called for students to have "more intimate social relations" with instructors by assigning "to every member of the faculty his quota of students." The relationship was to have a parental element.

> With [students] it should be [the instructor's] duty to make himself acquainted, to study their characters, to watch over the formation of their habits, to give them advice on all subjects of importance, as to recreation, reading, and modes of study, and to act as their special moral guardian, in pointing out sources of danger and of evil, and in shewing to his pupils, both by precept and example, the "more excellent way."

Any hope for such relationships between students and faculty was doomed by the vast growth of Harvard and the transformation of the faculty into scholarly professionals in the twentieth century. In 1950 a faculty report complained that an "increase in the number of students without corresponding increases in the size of the faculty . . . helped cause a broad, new tendency towards mass education." Cynthia was lucky with Professor Conrad. Even in the 1970s his way of teaching was going out of style. There are no signs it will come back any time soon.

Extracurricular life as education

Despite their complaints about student-faculty contact, Harvard students show generally high levels of satisfaction with all aspects of their college careers. Still, they invariably report on surveys that their extracurricular experiences were better than their academic experiences. University leaders have long worried that students spend too much time on frivolous pursuits and not on the academic rigors that are the central purpose of the university. Dean Kirby welcomed freshmen to Harvard with the message "You are here to work, and your business is to learn." The *Crimson* reported that President Summers sneered about running "Camp Harvard," though he recalled only referring to some of the college staff as "camp counselors."

Extracurricular organizations were a natural but unintended consequence of Eliot's sweeping changes: the end of the mandatory curriculum and the great increase in the size of the student body. In 1870 when there were about two hundred freshmen and thirty or forty students per classroom, the instructional unit naturally was also a social unit. Twenty years later, when students could choose their own courses, they had a different set of companions in each. Their class cohort was too large for all students to get to know one another. Memorial Hall, built to provide a dining commons, could no longer accommodate the whole College—there was a waiting list for meal contracts. And morning prayers, in earlier days another common experience, were no longer mandatory.

So it is unsurprising that clubs of every description sprang up during Eliot's presidency. The *Harvard Index* of 1891–1892 lists dozens, everything from the Chess and Whist Club to Delta Phi and the Total Abstinence Union. Because students had more classmates than they could ever get to know, by the end of Eliot's presidency the "tie of class" no longer served to hold the College together. So it remains to the present day. Extracurricular life combats the anonymity of large numbers, the isolating force of the competition for individual excellence, and the incoherence of a largely elective curriculum.

The available data suggest that students' activities outside classes don't hurt their grades but do improve their attitudes. Richard Light studied how extracurricular activities affect students' outlook, and his conclusion rings true to my experience.

> The big finding is that a substantial commitment to one or two activities other than coursework—for as much as twenty hours per week—has little or no relationship to grades. But such commitments *do* have a strong relationship to overall satisfaction with college life. More involvement is strongly correlated with higher satisfaction.

Yet when student achievement falls below some hoped-for goal, the focus is often on the waywardness of the students rather than the poor quality of education offered by the faculty. Extracurricular activities are invariably portrayed as frivolous distractions. Dean Kirby began Harvard's curricular review with a neutral promise to "examine the relationship between undergraduate life (residential and extracurricular) and undergraduate education," but before the review had progressed very far he explained his view of that relationship. "Extracurricular activities may enrich the life of this and other colleges, but college is a serious place for education."

If students are not enjoying their studies, it is the job of the university to fix their academic life, not to curtail their extracurricular life. Frowning on the things students do like is not the way to make them like other things better.

Discussions of this kind among faculty and deans often use or suggest mechanical or hydraulic metaphors. Students need to *balance* their academic and extracurricular activities better than they do, and the university needs to *channel* some of the hours students now put into extracurricular life into more studying. These metaphors suggest that students' lives are seen as zero-sum games, and the university should change the rules so students have to allocate their efforts differently. But students do not find greater satisfaction in extracurricular life simply because they prefer play to work.

Students like extracurricular activities because they require students to work together toward shared goals, and academic life provides few opportunities for exercising that most human impulse. Harvard has also recognized, in the past if not today, that extracurricular activities support and do not detract from its educational mission. In the words of former Harvard president Derek Bok, these activities have a role in "teaching about how to work effectively with others, how to play by rules of leadership or followership."

A vivid confirmation of this analysis occurred during a lunchtime conversation I had with three computer science graduates of the classes of 1994 and 1995 who started a company together and sold it in 1998 for more than $250 million. Over sandwiches I asked them what part of their computer science education had been most important to the success of their software enterprise. After a moment of tight smiles and awkward silence, one of the young graduates spoke up. "The computer science courses I took were really terrific," he said in an attempt to reassure me, "but I didn't learn much that I could not have learned on my own. The most important things I learned were from managing the Quincy House Grill." It made perfect sense—hiring, firing, and inspiring colleagues, working under pressure in close quarters—all were very much the same in the cheeseburger-flipping business he had run at Harvard as in the software business the three had started in a tiny apartment.

Consider the physical activity of undergraduate life, stripped of its content. What students almost always do when involved in extracurriculars but almost never do in their academic lives is work together with other students. Extracurriculars are social activities of a kind largely absent from the academic world in which they live.

By and large, in the academic life students are expected to work on their own. The ideal of the solitary poet or artist or scholar, producing a work of profound brilliance in a lonely garret room, serves as the model of how students should do their coursework. Many young scholars turn away from scholarship precisely because they have decided that there is too much loneliness and not enough interpersonal cooperation in the life they see their faculty advisors living.

Learning would be more engaging in college to the extent that it could be made more collaborative. Employers who recruit Harvard seniors have concluded that among young people who are smart enough to have been admitted to Harvard, significant roles in athletic teams or other student groups can be better predictors of success in the workplace than are high grade-point averages. The head of a corporation told me that his first job after college was with a consulting company that recruited among seniors by phoning all the captains of athletic teams, having found that they had more of the qualities needed for success in the business world than high-GPA students tended to have.

Most of the top professors, having won the academic game in which independence, originality, and creativity are the key values, do not appreciate the importance of getting more out of a team than the individuals could contribute by themselves. This indifference to leadership has contributed to Harvard's disenfranchisement of one of its most powerful leadership training programs: the Reserve Officers Training Corps (ROTC). At Harvard, in spite of official opposition by the Faculty, several dozen students participate every year at MIT. They are motivated, of course, by financial, career, and patriotic considerations as well as by the desire for leadership training.

The official reason for Harvard's disenfranchisement of ROTC is that gays may not serve in the armed forces and Congress has not chosen to lift this ban. Some suspect that antimilitary, even antipatriotic motivations lie just below the surface of Harvard's position. Those opposed to the ban argue an alternative moral imperative, to support the defense of the nation. The balance of principles is among the most troubling issues confronting universities, and the future of ROTC is visibly fought on this high ground. President Summers publicly voiced his support of ROTC, speaking at its commissioning ceremony annually, but he did not call for Harvard to welcome ROTC back to campus—and also did not use his presidential authority to meet the program's financial needs. He responded sympathetically to advocates for ROTC and advocates for gay rights, without explaining for the benefit of the community the balance he chose to strike.

The discrimination issue aside, ROTC is a hard sell at Harvard because professors undervalue the life skills it teaches, just as they look askance at students whose team sports or community service activities mean more to them than their studies. The faculty cannot see across the gulf that the development of the research university created between the permanently committed professional scholars and the student body, with all the social origins and career aspirations undergraduates bring to their education.

CHAPTER 4

The Eternal Enigma: Advising

What to Study, or How to Live?

[T]here are minor details of the [elective] system which are still discussed;—
as, for example, whether this course, or that, be a desirable one; . . . whether
the choice of the individual student be oftenest determined by sound or trivial
considerations; and whether any general advice as to choice of studies could
be profitably given by the Faculty.

—Charles William Eliot, 1877

Faculty members have no special competence to help individual students de-
fine their values, their convictions, their personal commitments. Not all pro-
fessors have resolved these questions to their own satisfaction, and fewer still
can communicate their feelings in ways that will be helpful to others.

—Derek Bok, 1977

A few years ago I asked a student into my office because his grades
in my course in theoretical computer science had taken a nose-
dive. He had started out doing well, but the first weeks of the course
are review for many students, so I assumed he had hit a wall when my
lectures reached the more advanced material. The less forthcoming
the answers about what he didn't understand, the more impatient and
worried I became. After a long back-and-forth that seemed to be
bringing us no closer to the source of the student's confusions, he
blurted out that his girlfriend was pregnant and neither of them had
told anyone.

The conversation shifted abruptly from mathematical abstractions to real people. He didn't know how to talk to his parents. She didn't know how to talk to her parents. He didn't even know how to talk to her, or her to him, it seemed. They didn't know how to think about the pregnancy. And so both were ignoring it—on the surface, but both were living in turmoil.

The advising system is where the divide between students and faculty shows most clearly. Advising students is difficult. They have rich academic opportunities, and they are at a stage of their lives when their talents and ambitions may not be clear even to themselves. Young people are coping with personal dilemmas not easily separable from academic decisions. Many forces conspire to push students to feign confidence in their study and career plans. Parents have high and often specific ambitions for their children. Showing uncertainty to parents may be taken as disloyalty; showing it to peers may be seen as revealing weakness. Students have a tendency to episodic frantic activity—studying, partying, exercising, organizing a road trip for some student group—as a way of avoiding the gnawing question: Am I doing what I really want to do with my college years, and am I heading where I want to go? In college, with its endless distractions, it is easy to find excuses for looking intensely anywhere but inside oneself. My student's pregnancy crisis was an extreme case of something that happens all the time: Students' lives are thrust before their eyes at times and under circumstances that they cannot plan or predict.

Professors tend to be narrowly educated experts who have spent most if not all of their working lives in universities. Having not had broad life experiences themselves, they are poorly equipped to help college students sort out theirs. Most professors can't speak with much competence to academic subjects even ten or fifteen degrees off the headings in which their own academic careers have been steered. Nothing in the way they were educated or hired makes them any wiser about personal matters than a person chosen at random from the phone book. And yet the image of the professor guiding the student, with wisdom and skill, has been the ideal of every college generation for more than a century.

❧

Academic advising did not have to amount to much when students had no choice in what they studied, but once there were electives, students had decisions to make and needed help making them. The answer to President Eliot's question of "whether any general advice as to choice of studies could profitably be given by the Faculty" remains uncertain to this day.

Formal advising started at Harvard in 1888, when a few professors were designated to advise twenty-five freshmen each.

> The relation was intended to be a confidential and friendly one; but as a starting-point every Freshman was required to submit his choice of studies to his adviser at or before the beginning of the year. Most of the instructors who were appointed on this committee found that they themselves had a good deal to learn about the selection of a four years' course of study in Harvard College.

These basics are still with us. The relationship of advisor to student is supposed to be friendly, but if it doesn't have a mandatory bottom line, students won't show up for advice. Students often know more than professors about individual courses and the complexities of the curriculum. But Eliot raised expectations further, asserting that a student "may consult his advisor upon any topic relating to his college life." Just a few years later, Eliot seemed to recognize that faculty advisors were not of much use in helping students pick courses. He instituted a one-day shopping period to help students figure out "the choice of their studies and their fitness for the particular courses which they desired to take."

A decade later, the system had "not produced all the good effects hoped from it."

> In the first place, older men cannot be expected to sympathize thoroughly with the undergraduate temper, or free themselves entirely from the prejudices of their specialties. In the second place, they cannot judge a Freshman's mental tastes and abilities at sight, or even from entrance records. And finally, they cannot, in five minutes, work out for him an ideal course of study for four years, or even one, much less convince him that his own plan, if he has any, is not better.

These words, from a 1901 editorial in an alumni magazine, deserve a close reading by those designing advising systems today. Not one word of the diagnosis is less problematic a century later. Professors who have given their lives to the pursuit of ideas may be uninterested in revisiting the insecurities of adolescence with their students, and they often do not even respect academic pursuits far from their own. Getting to know an undergraduate well enough to give useful advice is a lengthy process, requiring more than a file of test scores. And even if an advisor takes the time to develop a well-considered plan for a student, it will be useless unless the student can be persuaded to follow it. My own freshman advisor was a professor of mechanical engineering, and I thought I wanted to study pure mathematics. That may not sound like much of a leap. But the "prejudices of his own specialty" left him incapable of giving advice about pure mathematics, except insofar as it was instructive for me to witness his prejudices in action.

In 1902 the dean of the Faculty admitted that what Eliot had described as a "detail" a quarter century earlier posed unanticipated subtleties and complications.

> For a Freshman when he faces the elective system the danger of mistakes is grave. His home advisers seldom know the College; his college adviser seldom knows him. Moreover, his college adviser may well hesitate to discriminate among studies which the Faculty declares to be of equal value; or he may believe it his duty to recruit his own specialty; or he may believe it is his duty to keep clear of what anybody could construe as recruiting his own specialty: in the matter wherein a Freshman first needs advice the adviser is neither qualified nor permitted to advise. The burden rests on the Freshman himself; and though it is well for him to take responsibility, for this particular responsibility he may be too immature and short-sighted.

Advising at Harvard has not improved in the intervening hundred years, and the sources of its problems have not changed either. As Harvard prepared to debate its new curriculum in fall 2005, every one of the proposals demanded better advising. But fixing the advising problem was always described as the job of a committee that would report later. Those proposing a more flexible curriculum offered few suggestions about how students could benefit most from their new opportunities. When the advising committee finally issued its report, it recommended that more advisors be recruited and that an advising dean be put in charge of the advising system, but said not a word about the advice that students should receive.

The advising problem can be split into academic advising, moral education, and self-understanding. The division is not very neat, because college students are whole people, and problems in one sector bleed into others, as happened with my student and his pregnant girlfriend.

Academic advising

Shock, or at least feigned shock, greets the idea of having anyone but a professor give academic advice at a great university. The *Boston Globe* reported with disdain that rather than "a top professor who can guide the student's intellectual journey with expertise built over years of teaching," a student's freshman advisor is probably someone "who coaches the women's soccer team, works in the housing office, or serves as President Lawrence H. Summers' events planner." The inadequacy of the advising system is one of the few matters on which deans, professors, and students agree. A professor leading part of Harvard's curricular review acknowledged: "A significant number of freshmen don't have advisers with a lot of academic experience. We do OK with them socially, on what it means to be in college and live in the dorms. But on the curriculum side—what courses and electives to take—we need to do a better job."

Students tend to have broad interests, and if their minds are already made up about what to study, their decisions should be challenged, not accepted at face value. It is part of the job of a good college to help students out of Conant's "groove predetermined by geographical and economic considerations." A few years ago a computer science professor called me to ask what to do with a freshman advisee. The student had been a hotshot computer scientist in high school, but when he turned up in his advisor's office early in freshman orientation week, he wanted advice on majoring in the visual arts. He had needed to wait, he said, until his mother left town before he could tell anyone about his real ambition. This scenario was a success story; usually it takes a year or two, if not longer, for students to tear themselves free from their parents' choices.

The differing perspectives of students and faculty are part of what make advising a challenge, but there is a third piece of the puzzle: the curricular requirements. In Eliot's pure elective curriculum, or in Brown's general-education-free curriculum, there are no mistakes of commission to be made, only opportunities to be lost. But a structured curriculum, be it Harvard's eleven Core areas or Princeton's seven-area distribution requirement, creates problems of two kinds. First, it forces students to pick among the courses that satisfy the requirements, say between a course on Dante and one on Milton. The Dante course isn't better for everyone, and a science professor is unlikely to know whether it would be better for any particular student. Second, a structured curriculum works best if students think it makes sense, and students won't think it makes sense unless the faculty advisors do. When advisors lack confidence that the academic program is good for their students, it is hard to blame students for regarding those requirements as pointless bureaucratic hurdles to be vaulted in the least demanding way possible.

Complex curricular requirements are the result of political compromises and turf wars among faculty. Political compromise can produce a balanced result, but it rarely produces a thing of beauty or elegance, or anything that anyone but its creators will believe in or even understand. To this day I cannot explain the eleven Core categories of the Harvard curriculum, much less provide any rationale for why students need to take one each of Lit&Arts A, B, and C rather than two from A and none from B. Such confusion among advisors, in their one-on-one advising conversations, breeds cynicism in students.

What colleges need is a curriculum, as I once told Dean Kirby, so simple that the faculty can explain it to the students. The general education curriculum proposed in fall 2005 achieves that by lumping all Harvard courses into three broad categories, very much like the Red Book categories, and allowing students to choose any course in an area to satisfy that area requirement. What remains to be seen is whether the faculty will agree to leave those choices in students' hands, given the cost: Nothing at all could be promised about what students would know when they graduate. A science student could graduate having studied no history, for example, by taking economics courses instead. The student's faculty advisor, also a scientist, will probably "hesitate to discriminate among studies which the Faculty declares to be of equal value," as Dean Briggs wrote in 1902, and a Harvard education will have become meaningless.

Moral guidance

Harvard today tiptoes away from moral education, little interested in providing it and embarrassed to admit it does not wish to do so. Its general report on the ongoing curricular review grandly stated that "we remain cognizant of our responsibility to educate morally responsible citizens and leaders." Yet most of the rules of moral behavior that colleges used to teach have gone by the boards. More generally, there is no consensus on what counts as good character, so colleges are reluctant to help students become better people. In 2001, Fred Hargadon, then Princeton's admissions dean, described his college's relationships with students this way: "I don't know if we build character or remind them that they should be developing it." Minor reversals in students' lives, which in another time would have been met with encouragement to strength, courage, and determination, must now be answered with advice about therapy, waiver of rules and deadlines, or other forms of accommodation. I once received a petition to rescind grades that had been given to a student while she was sleepless due to a snoring roommate, even though she had been given extensions to accommodate her insomnia. Once the student had received her grades and found them lower than she hoped, she challenged the appropriateness of the medication she had been given and asked for the opportunity to wipe the record clean and complete the work anew. One reason it is now so hard to flunk out of college is that students are given so many reprieves for finally coming to grips with personal demons, faulty medications, emotional burdens, and cognitive deficits they did not understand the *previous* time they failed a course.

The drive for excellence puts a premium on perfection. The drive for perfection legitimizes excuse-seeking, so that imperfections will be erased or never show in the first place. And seeking to excuse flaws, be they minuscule deductions from graded work or fistfights that others allegedly started, undercuts efforts colleges might make to teach students personal responsibility. It is not a productive set of forces, and it does not nourish good character.

Colleges sometimes attempt to teach ethical thinking and moral issues in the classroom. The Harvard Core Curriculum does exactly that, by including a set of courses in Moral Reasoning, and Princeton's has an area called Ethical Thought and Moral Values. But Harvard's proposed general education curriculum drops the Moral Reasoning requirement, and with it the part of the curriculum devoted mostly to Western moral and political philosophy. It remains to be seen what Harvard will decide, but it would only be following the pack if its curriculum stopped requiring students to think about morals and ethics in the classroom.

But perhaps that is not the only or best way to force students to think about issues of good behavior and good character. Classes in moral reasoning are hard to teach because students are, as always, eager to please and to do well. Today's students tend to believe that moral questions have correct answers—as David Brooks noted in his essay "The Organization Kid," for the first time since before World War I, many young people believe that "the universe is a just and orderly place." Telegraphing to students, if they are bright and sophisticated, that a moral question is about to be raised will propel them into intellectualized gamesmanship. It has never seemed to me that small-group discussion was the best forum for raising difficult moral issues, as the requirement for quick answers encourages rote pieties and snappy argumentation and discourages deep thought. Just as in any other subject area, asking known questions, about the value of diversity for example, is likely to elicit safe and reliable answers. A good treatment of a moral issue can happen only if the "correct" answer is not obvious and students are forced to recognize that they do not really believe everything they are tempted to say. And professors find it difficult to press the younger generation out of their framework of unquestioned truths about acceptable behavior.

The only trick I have found successful is to take students completely by surprise, so that the moral lesson comes to life. In my theory of computation course, for example, I devote five minutes to the tragic story of the founder of the field of computer science, Alan Turing. An Englishman trained in mathematical logic in the 1930s, Turing made groundbreaking discoveries before the first electronic computer had been built, and then played a critical role in the Allied war effort by helping to crack the German Enigma code. Arrested for homosexuality, he endured hormone treatments intended to cure him, lost his security clearance, and committed suicide at age forty-one—a great mind lost to irrational prejudice.

As this brief tale unfolded in my classroom, silence fell, not because the story was so interesting or because the moral is a surprise (few Harvard students would argue for the persecution of homosexuals), but because it was so out of place, so contrary to the rules of the game students and professors play with each other. Students exhaled only when I began a new paragraph by returning to Turing's mathematics. Still, almost every year, a student or two sent me an e-mail afterward, asking for more information. Some were exploring feelings about which they were conflicted, and some were just bewildered that I was, so incongruously and unnecessarily, saying something about good and evil.

Students tend to ask their advisors narrow questions that mask deeper ones. If a question is as simple as it sounds, the student may know the answer already and may merely be filling time, since the advising conversation is mandatory. Should I take the standard Math X course or the more challenging Math X+1? Should I take a history or a physics course? Should I write a senior thesis? Should I go to summer school or try to get an internship at NASA? It is the advisor's job to get the student to think about what he or she is really trying to accomplish. Often the question behind the question is deeply troubling, indeed so hard to face that the student may not realize what the question really is. The real question may be not about math prerequisites but about the balance between risk and challenge for someone who has already gotten into Harvard; not about history and physics but about the student's ambitions versus her parents'; not about senior theses but about a girlfriend who will be in Cambridge over the summer.

Students who come to their advisors with personal problems already have them half solved. But such openness is rare, since students are so reluctant to acknowledge imperfections. Advising conversations that begin on purely academic matters but don't end that way are more important. In the end I gave my student with the pregnant girlfriend a lot of advice, none of it on the academic matters he came to talk to me about. On another occasion I stopped to comfort a woman who was crying after my final exam. I figured that she thought she had flunked, and, not being able to give her any instant reassurance on that score, I thought I might at least engage her in a conversation about summer school or some other way of making up the requirement, should that prove to be necessary. But our conversation turned quickly to more pressing and troubling issues. It turned out she had been sexually assaulted and didn't know what she should do about it.

The most important job of the advisor, even the "academic" advisor, is to help students understand themselves, to face and take responsibility for their decisions, and to support and to free them to make choices that are at odds with the expectations others have for them. Rogerian therapy sometimes works wonders as an advising technique, turning every vague statement back to the student as a more clearly stated question. Advisors can help just by listening empathetically and echoing in a slightly probing form what their advisees tell them.

The expectation that all students be treated equally creates a perverse barrier between students who are in trouble and faculty who might see worrisome signs. Social conventions discourage professors from noticing anything personal about a student, even tears. Faculty members who are uncomfortable having any involvement with students' personal lives are happy to have an excuse not to do so—on the basis that it would "invade the student's privacy" or should be left to professionals. It is safer to treat the student as a brain on a stick, as I once heard Harvard's minister Peter Gomes put it. Worries about students' mental health have caused the college administration to make gestures toward engaging the faculty in students' emotional lives, but the gestures themselves indicate how great the separation has become. A special brochure is sent to the entire Harvard Faculty annually, explaining that "verbalizations of hopelessness" and "tearfulness" may be "identifying warning signs" of distress that should cause the professor to engage the student in conversation and perhaps to urge the student toward professional help.

Giving advice not only requires some intuition about adolescent psychology; it is also a moral responsibility and burden. If professors cannot see beyond the borders of their disciplines when answering a question with larger implications, the student will notice that and will probably not ask another large question.

Yet questions with moral dimensions come up all the time in advising conversations. Consider, for example, the infamous problem of faculty diversity. A hundred years ago, a dean wondered whether it was the responsibility of an advisor to recruit for his field, or to be scrupulously neutral as the student decided what to study. In the past two decades, that question has confronted almost every academic advisor when talking with women and minority students about their ambitions. Professors are intensely aware that the faculty does not look like the student body, and that there will be an institutional and a societal benefit in the long run if more women, black, and Hispanic students become professors. But law firms and businesses feel the same way about their professions, and they may provide a path for a talented student to repay debts and send siblings to college with far greater speed and certainty than would a lengthy Ph.D. program. Is it for us, the faculty, to try to persuade such a student of the nobility of the life of the mind? And if we don't, how many generations will pass through college before the Faculty resembles the student body in gender and ethnicity? The best advice to the individual student may not be socially progressive or advance the university's worthy goals. I always address the student's best interests, but I recognize that others may balance their responsibilities differently.

How did the academy evolve so that professors have to be sent a brochure explaining that a crying student is in distress, and advising them to direct such a student to professionals?

Professors can be expected to be good advisors only if the university pays some attention to the personal character, moral probity, and wisdom of those we appoint as professors. To put it more bluntly: If we really want closer student-faculty contact, if we really expect faculty to guide students' lives and not just their studies, then we owe it to students and their families to appoint professors with whom we would want our own children to have close personal contact.

Professors probably have human weaknesses and evils in the same proportions as the general population. Drinking problems, inappropriate sexual advances toward adolescents, irrational bursts of anger, incapacitating depression—all these exist among professors as they do among other people. What is different is the mischief such problems can create when professors have close contact with students who are eighteen or nineteen years old, nominally adult but not fully mature, and predisposed to think of professors as wise people. Such difficulties present special challenges for the university when considering individuals for positions in which they will affect the lives of hundreds or thousands of students. An especially important part of my role as dean was to filter suggested candidates for House Masterships, delicately trying to determine whether whispers of such indiscretions or weaknesses, on the part of either the professor or a spouse, ought to give pause when considering someone for leadership of a tight-knit and publicly exposed residential community.

The stakes are, if anything, rising. A Massachusetts court recently held that advisors, including faculty who head residences, could be held *personally* responsible for the death of a student by suicide. This chilling decision may make colleges reluctant to allow anyone lacking clinical training to be involved in students' emotional lives at all.

There are serious challenges in reconciling the reality that faculty are not chosen for admirable character with the drive for greater student-faculty contact. In this day and age, no one considers divorce a scandal. But what about three or four divorces: Would that suggest that someone's life might not be quite "together" enough to give wise personal advice to undergraduates? What about psychological cruelty to one's children? These are not crimes, and they happen to people in many other walks of life. But families send their children to college in the expectation that the people who will be advising them are compassionate and moral souls. Universities should not create the impression that advisors are good people unless they are.

Louis Menand has appealed to the importance of professors as role models by recalling the philosophy of John Dewey.

> People learn, Dewey insisted, socially. They learn, as every progressive nursery school director will tell you, by doing. Dewey believed that the classroom was a laboratory in which to experiment with the business of participating in the associated life. American higher education provides almost no formal structure, almost no self-conscious design, for imagining pedagogy in this spirit. But the only way to develop curiosity, sympathy, principle, and independence of mind is to practice being curious, sympathetic, principled, and independent. For those of us who are teachers, it isn't what we teach that instills virtue; it's how we teach. We are the books our students read most closely.

I wish every faculty search committee would read these wise words before it begins to analyze recommendation letters and probe if the candidates' advocates were being honest and impartial. Unfortunately, little of this kind of wisdom finds its way into faculty hiring procedures.

All research universities follow roughly the same formula in describing the qualifications to be a professor. By Harvard policy, professors are hired and promoted on the basis of "teaching, scholarship, and the obligations of academic citizenship," the latter meaning participation in university committees and outside professional societies. Character and personal behavior of a noncriminal nature don't enter the formula at all. In fact, if such a matter were raised in a hiring or promotion meeting, it could properly be ruled out of order and perhaps legally actionable, since it would amount to judging candidates on criteria of which they had never been informed. Hiring committees may, however, consider professional behavior. Stealing your colleague's ideas or overworking your graduate students or putting your class to sleep could be disqualifying sins. But not stealing postage or abusing your children or sleeping with students.

There must be something wrong with this picture, but preferable alternatives are not easy to design. There would be two problems with including some kind of character test as a condition for employment or promotion as a professor.

First, some professors are inspiring teachers and brilliant scholars but despicable human beings. In the past, as long as they kept their private lives separate from their professional lives, it didn't matter. Second, the history of the last century has taught us the dangers of inferring the unsuitability of one's character from one's personal social unacceptability. It would once have been thought quite improper for a woman to be teaching at the university level. Harvard has been particularly retrograde on issues of faculty equality; several women professors had gained tenure at Harvard before any woman was allowed to enter the Faculty Club through the front door. Even the great meritocrat James Bryant Conant said he thought that "a deluge of medium and good men of the Jewish race in scientific positions . . . would do a lot of harm," and the idealistic Lowell was a far worse bigot than that. Gay and lesbian professors of my generation felt it necessary to keep their sexual orientation secret until they had tenure—a step forward, of course, from the permanent secrecy required of previous generations of homosexual faculty and students.

Universities tend to be ahead of the rest of the country in accepting what were once considered social abnormalities, but Harvard's tainted history would raise doubts about any exercise of subjective judgment. It is hard to be confident that discretion applied to such qualities as good character would not be used, by gentle innuendo, to scuttle the candidacies of unpopular people. We do not want our descendants to look back with regret on brilliant minds whose careers we curtailed because they were simply not "one of us."

Officially at least, Harvard goes by the book and ignores everything except teaching, research, and academic citizenship. As a professor, I am not supposed to notice if one of my colleagues has very poor judgment about his personal life or is even what might well be called a bad person. Derek Bok set out the facts quite clearly:

> Universities have largely abandoned the attempt to pick professors on the basis of their moral character. However sincere their concern for ethical standards, therefore, universities must proceed with little control over the adults who have the greatest influence on the lives of students.

This description matches my experience. Time and again in meetings to choose among candidates for faculty appointments or to judge internal candidates for promotion, favorable references to personal qualities have been challenged as excuse-making for academic inferiority, and doubts about personal probity have been countered as indifference to real academic star quality.

Universities could change things if they decided to. It would require consistently committed leadership, not simple formulas, to move toward a faculty of professors who are good models and guides for young people. But visible commitments, such as they are, favor scholarly brilliance over moral probity. Once granted tenure, a professor can be removed only for "grave misconduct or neglect of duty," so it is almost impossible to fire a tenured faculty member for lapses of character. Hiring and promotion decisions, however, should take into account any kind of behavior that calls a candidate's character into question. We should be confident in our ability to recognize bad people when we see them. We do not have to abandon, in the pursuit of academic excellence, the ideal that one should be a person of character to guide young people.

How to achieve that ideal is, however, unexplored. The *Crimson's* 1938 caricature of Harvard's admissions practices is extreme but identifies the tension. "The policy boils down to a sliding scale of personality and brains, with more being demanded of the one as the quality of the other declines. Thus the genius can come to Harvard however repulsive he is, the moron only when his charm is truly dazzling." Good character should be among the considerations in faculty hiring, though not an alternative to brilliance.

If universities can't find a way to consider character when appointing faculty, they should lower the expectations they create about student-faculty contact. We might as well acknowledge, if it is true, that a student might see a top professor in a lecture or even in a seminar but not in any setting where real advising is likely to occur. One distinguished professor with heavy research commitments outside Harvard told the *New York Times*, "I have a Harvard office, but I hardly ever, ever use it." It is as though the basic give-and-take of the elective system has yet to be accepted: that students are free, within reason, to study what they want, and that the professors have a responsibility to help them figure out what to do with that freedom.

Yet universities succeed, rather in spite of themselves, in hiring many professors with an encompassing view of the burden of their educational positions—individuals who lead their lives and pursue their careers in ways that students admire and respect. How? First, as Derek Bok suggested, we can rely on the law of averages: "Fortunately, most faculty members do set high standards of probity, conscientiousness, and service to others." It was an act of exemplary moral courage, for example, for Douglas Melton to risk professional suicide by moving his entire scientific program to an area for which federal funding was prohibited—the use of new embryonic stem cell lines for the cure of diabetes. In an era of increasing religious self-righteousness in America, Diana Eck has devoted herself to documenting America's tradition of religious diversity and promoting worldwide religious pluralism, even in the face of a *fatwa* (Islamic decree) against pluralism in Indonesia where she has spoken. Shortly after becoming Master of one of the Harvard Houses, she adopted the four children of parents killed in ethnic warfare in Eastern Europe, thus very publicly backing her communitarian ideals with a personal commitment.

Harvard is fortunate in having so many humane professors, whose departments probably skirted the regulations against considering personal qualities in appointment decisions. Many of the best seem to have been raised far from the hothouse of university life, and seem to be better human beings for not having deep family roots in academia. Perhaps they have seen more clearly the transformative power of higher education and remember that most of the students with whom they now share the ivory tower have come from the nonacademic world and will return to it.

Officially, these values are as irrelevant as hair color when it comes to hiring practices. Universities do as well as they do in hiring men and women of good character only because during the selection process, the evaluating professors sometimes disregard the warnings to take only research, teaching, and service into account and quietly favor those they think are good people.

A regular part of the ritual of the faculty hiring process is to have the candidate visit and give a research talk, after which a few professors take the speaker out to dinner and continue to probe the fine points and implications of the ideas presented in the colloquium. At these dinners I prefer to find out what the candidates do for fun, where they grew up, and how they spent their summers when they were in high school. I would have loved to hear the answer Diana Eck might have given to the last question—"drilling holes for dynamite, blasting, and mixing cement," as she described it in her book *Encountering God*. It is hard to spend one's entire life, from childhood on, in academic pursuits and still retain the humility and human understanding that make one a good advisor to students who are forming their own identities. The pressures of academic advancement in the best universities are now so intense that those who succeed often see winning academic competitions as a life goal in itself.

Any student who is advised by an expansively wise professor is fortunate, for there are not enough of them to go around. Bok ended his musings on faculty advising by noting that the university could find a way to make up for the shortfall: "[A] university can emphasize character in appointing other adult figures who touch the lives of students in important ways: administrative deans, athletic coaches, faculty heads of student residences, and many more."

Indeed, the job postings for coaches routinely list such duties as "to help [student athletes] develop their full potential as individuals and athletes." That is why the soccer coach makes such a good advisor for any student: Athletic departments, unlike academic departments, consider character, morality, and how to guide the lives of young people when they make hiring decisions.

CHAPTER 5

Why Grades Go Up

A Drama Without a Villain

[I]n the present practice Grades A and B are sometimes given too readily—Grade A for work of no very high merit, and Grade B for work not far above mediocrity.

—*Harvard Faculty Report of 1894*

"Harvard's Quiet Secret: Grade Inflation," announced the Sunday *Boston Globe* in fall 2001. The next day's story was entitled "Harvard's Honors Fall to the Merely Average." The two articles reported that 51 percent of Harvard grades were As and A minuses in the 2000–2001 academic year, and that 91 percent of Harvard students graduated with honors in June 2001.

Nothing I saw during my eight years as dean brought Harvard as much scorn as the grades and honors it awards. "Hilarious," said a Yale dean. "I mean really. Really." "Can't believe it," said a vice provost at Cornell. Critics inside Harvard were more direct. "In a healthy university, it would not be necessary to say what is wrong with grade inflation," said Harvey Mansfield a few months earlier. "But once the evil becomes routine, people can no longer see it for what it is." President Summers said he was "very concerned about both honors inflation and grade inflation," and he worried to the faculty that Harvard had lax standards. He assured students that tougher grading would be to their advantage—the word was out about how soft Harvard grading was, and the school needed "to be sensitive not to put Harvard students at a disadvantage."

After a year of self-study, a sober faculty report was issued the following spring, votes were taken, press releases were prepared by Harvard and consumed by the media, and there was general self-congratulation at Harvard that we had done something about this important problem. The next time there was a report on grades, it was possible to announce that they had gone down a bit.

But they went right back up the following year, to a level higher than ever. And the year after that, they went up again.

Harvard is not alone in being the object of criticism and ridicule for the grades it gives. Many universities have taken the usual steps. They studied the problem, half hoping that people would lose interest by the time the study was complete, and then issued more exhortations, principles, and promises than concrete actions. Brown reported on a major study of its grade-inflation problem in 2002. In 2004 Princeton's dean Nancy Malkiel induced the faculty to adopt "guidelines" on the number of A grades that could be given. Countless websites and books deplore rising grades in colleges, reserving the most cutting attacks for the most prominent research universities.

The way top universities grade is of interest to the outside world because high grades are excellence reduced to concrete form. The mania for excellence finds measurable form in the grades given to individual students and in the range of grades given by an institution. Grades serve as easy proxies for academic standards of any kind, and rising grades are taken as markers of declining standards. Such evidence of declining standards is broadened into an indictment of whatever social force is the critic's hobbyhorse. Society is going to hell in a hand basket, and the great universities are going to get there first.

≈

After the *Boston Globe* series broke, national media quickly joined the attack. The *New York Times* wrote, "Harvard, long a center of excellence in so many forms of study, is becoming known as a pioneer in grade inflation, too." *USA Today* proclaimed, "The fact that 50% of all Harvard students now get A's is a troubling problem." Some columnists were harsher—one congratulated Summers for taking on "the rot of grade inflation in Harvard's classrooms," and another quoted the percentages of A grades at Harvard and argued that "You can't outlaw failure."

Some protested that the rise in grades was the inevitable consequence of improvement in the quality of the student body, but others countered that whether that was true or not, something had to be done about it. Spurred to action, the Faculty of Arts and Sciences undertook a review of grading and honors in fall 2001 and issued a report the following spring. At the last Faculty meeting of the year, the professors voted to toughen up. Harvard grade-point averages would no longer be computed on its unusual fifteen-point scale; henceforth Harvard would use the same four-point scale as most other American colleges. Further, honors degrees would be capped at around 50 percent of the class. With that the Harvard Faculty adjourned for the year; the standards were set to be tightened—three years in the future.

The next day's *Boston Globe*, citing its own reporting on the subject the previous fall, reported that Harvard had "committed itself to awarding more B's to students." The *New York Times* assured readers that the Faculty had voted "to put the excellence back in the A." Soon thereafter, the Harvard Faculty's resolve to take action on grades was reported as far away as Singapore and Australia. Meanwhile, professors moved on—at least some of them relieved that the heat was off and that not much of importance had actually changed.

It was barely noticed that changing the numerical values of As and Bs has nothing to do with how professors assign those grades, or that capping the number of students receiving honors would not discourage professors from giving As and Bs. In fact, the changes Harvard adopted had no effect on grades. The 2001–2002 decline in grades occurred before the changes were voted. Just talking about the seriousness of the problem impacted faculty judgment a bit. The rise that occurred the following year lost all the ground gained during the period of scrutiny, and then some. The president again announced that he was concerned, but the grading issue became a footnote in the context of a broad review of undergraduate education, barely mentioned in the sixty-page report of the review committee.

Rising grades are not the result of some late-twentieth-century decline in society. Despite the claims of critics, grade inflation was not caused by the Vietnam War or by the admission of black students. Current grading patterns are not a warning that after centuries of dispassionate evaluation, universities have succumbed to consumerism, giving students the grades they want rather than the grades they deserve.

In fact, grades have been going up for as long as there have been grades. Figure 5.1 shows the percentage of Harvard students on the Dean's List from the 1920s until the list was eliminated in the early 2000s. The graph is a reasonable proxy for the trajectory of grades over the past eighty years.*

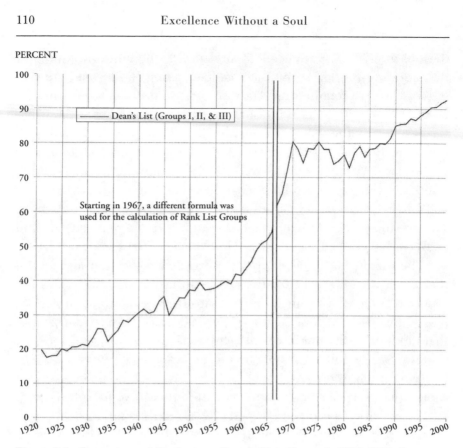

Figure 5.1   Percentage of Students on Dean's List, Harvard, 1920–2000. Source:
Adapted from Harry R. Lewis, The racial theory of grade inflation, *Harvard
Crimson*, April 23, 2001. Data are from public reports of the university.

There was a sharp rise in the 1969–1970 academic year (in that
chaotic spring at Harvard, final exams were optional), but there followed fifteen years of relatively stable grading. The rate at which
grades increased during the three decades starting in 1968 is almost
exactly the same as the rate at which they had been increasing over the
previous three decades. (Hold a straight edge against the jagged lines
on both sides of the 1968–1969 dividing line; the angle is identical.)

The stability of grades over the fifteen-year interval 1970–1985 de-
bunks a favorite theory of conservative critics—that grade inflation was
caused by the admission of black students. Black students did not ap-

---

*There is a gap in the graph between 1966 and 1967 because the mathematical formula
for Dean's List was slightly changed at that point, so the two halves of the graph are,
strictly speaking, incomparable.

pear at Harvard in significant numbers until 1970, the beginning of
the only extended period of stable grading of which records exist.

Over the entire period shown on the chart and even before, professors, deans, presidents, and public commentators issued pronouncements about the significance of rising grades—and the only times they
did not anguish about declining standards were when they celebrated
the improvement in the student body. The history of rising grades at
Harvard suggests that alarmist theories about grade inflation should be
regarded with suspicion.

Grades always go up; only the stories change

One reason that the Harvard Faculty was glad to move on from the
grade-inflation controversy in 2002 was fatigue; we had heard it all so
recently. In June 1996, using the same numerical GPA cutoff for the
summa cum laude (with highest distinction) degree as had been used
the previous year, the Faculty awarded *summa* degrees to 115 seniors,
up by 36 from the year before. "An A means less than it once did," said
former dean of Undergraduate Education Lawrence Buell. Yet there
was little sense that it really mattered. Buell noted that "grade inflation
should not be regarded as a top priority issue in education," and his
successor, David Pilbeam, added, "I haven't spent many hours this year
worrying about it."

Nonetheless, the Faculty cut the number of *summa* degrees it
awarded. In spring 1997, the Faculty voted to limit *summa* degrees to 5
percent of the class, carrying GPA calculations to three places after the
decimal point to draw the dividing line between students with extremely high GPAs. Although it capped *summas,* the Faculty did nothing to limit *magna* (with high distinction) or *cum* (with distinction) degrees, even though the *Boston Globe* had reported that 80 percent of the
class was graduating with honors of some kind. Instead, Harvard
waited until the embarrassments of 2001–2002 to impose similar percentage limits on *magna* and *cum* degrees.

Harvard considered it more important to reduce the number of
summa degrees (from 7 percent of the class to 5 percent) than to reduce the overall number of honors degrees (from around 80 percent
to 50 percent) because the Harvard *summa* is the ultimate mark of distinction in the competitive game professors play: academic excellence.
Whatever will happen to students at the 80th or 50th percentile of the

class, they are unlikely to grow up to be Harvard professors. An understandable, but not very admirable, sense of the superior significance of our academic mission caused the Faculty to place greater significance on withholding the *summa* from a student in the 94th percentile than on denying a degree *cum laude* to a student in the 25th percentile. This kind of urgent debate over such irrelevancies as whether 5 percent or 7 percent of seniors should graduate *summa* must have motivated the quip, "Academic politics is the most vicious and bitter form of politics, because the stakes are so low."

Social critics commonly attribute the rise in grades and honors degrees, at Harvard and elsewhere, to a collapse in values caused by the turmoil of the 1960s. In 1976, the conservative columnist George Will cited with disapproval "an astonishing rise in undergraduates' grades" since the mid-1960s at Harvard, Vassar, Amherst, and the University of Virginia. He commented that "academic life may come to resemble the 'Caucus-race' as explained by the Dodo to Alice in Wonderland: . . . 'Everybody has won, and all must have prizes.'" Will laid the blame on affirmative action (admission, as he saw it, of unqualified minority students who must be passed to keep them in school), consumerism (soft grading by departments in need of enrollments to justify larger budgets), and, most of all, "the egalitarian passion against 'elitism.'" Rather poignantly in retrospect, he suggested that discussions on college campuses about such phenomena "may be the first stirrings of a counterrevolution against the strange egalitarianism that had helped produce 'grade inflation.'"

But Will's polemical explanation doesn't square with the time line of rising grades. In 1966, before the alleged moral collapse of the 1960s could have progressed very far, a Harvard office was already studying the problem of rising grades. The concern was "that practices have grown soft; there has been inflation, and there should be a return to parity."

Perhaps the upward creep started even earlier. The 1950s are generally regarded as the good old days of academia, but grades were rising even then. The difference was that the rise was seen as a cause for celebration, an indication that the students had gotten better, not that standards had gotten worse. "The proportion of the exceptionally bright and interested in each class is now in all probability greater than it has ever been before in Harvard's history," President Nathan Pusey rejoiced in 1954. "Harvard graduates may take pride in the fact that last year forty per cent of all Harvard undergraduates were on the

Dean's List." He also took the sunny view when honors degrees rose past 40 percent of the class: "This increase in Honors is encouraging evidence of a resumption of interest, on the part both of students and Faculty, in a type of scholarly work which was relatively neglected during the war period." In 1951 the dean of the College struggled to understand the pattern of rising grades, which had been observed even then. Perhaps fear of the military draft made students work harder, he thought. "It has even been argued that the Harvard Faculty is growing soft and standards are slipping. But one thing is certain. Harvard students are working hard and are demonstrating an admirable ability to meet with poise and fortitude the pressures."

In fact, rising grades were reported at Harvard in every decade of the twentieth century. Deans, presidents, and commentators have explained the phenomenon using whatever rationale suited their purposes. In 1933 the dean of Harvard College noted with pride that the percentage of students on the Dean's List had risen to unprecedented levels and attributed the rise to the fact that "the undergraduates took their academic work more seriously than usual."

But in the first years of the twentieth century, President Lowell was anything but optimistic about grading. The evidence was everywhere, he thought, that Eliot's elective system had caused students to flock to the easiest courses. The grading practices of some professors were intolerable.

In 1910, E. Thorndike's *Educational Psychology* had given birth to the science of educational statistics. Lowell attacked "snap" courses by pushing faculty toward a grade curve he had calculated (Figure 5.2). He superimposed a professor's grades on what he called the "normal diagram," explaining, "You will see that [the grades in your course] are

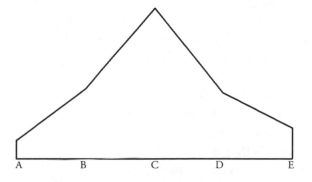

Figure 5.2 President Lowell's "normal" grade curve.

higher than the normal. In my experience this is likely to mean that the course is easier than it ought to be. I know your course is very valuable, but a marking coming closer to the average would, I suppose, make it better still."

Professors resisted, then as now, such oversight of their grading, typically arguing that either their course or their students were special. One compared the grades of every one of the 83 members of his course with the student's grades in the student's other courses, pleading, "Does it not appear that, as students have sometimes said, my grading is too low rather than too high? I have gone over my marks again and again, and have not seen how I could possibly put them lower without being unjust."

Educational leaders bent on raising standards have often used selected statistics and circular reasoning. In 1910 Lowell insisted that he had "tried to maintain something like an equal standard by checking great inequality in the marking of the courses which are largely attended," comparing the marks in large courses, scientifically, to "the typical curve of marks." But the only reprimands went to professors whose grades were too *high*; no one seems to have been told to give *more* As. And when asked how he selected the eight courses for which the grades would make up the "normal diagram," he explained: "Those particular eight elementary courses were taken because they seemed to be sound courses which were well marked. I avoided those which were obviously or notoriously easy." In other words, in calculating the average that supposedly represented the norm, he omitted those courses in which he thought the grading was abnormally lenient—a classic case of circular reasoning.

Students have always flocked to easy courses when they have had distribution requirements to fulfill. Even the 1909 report that created the distribution system expressed concern about the problem of easy courses, pointing out that "in a number of departments there are occasional easy courses which are a serious detriment to the College; and the committee would suggest that each department should strive to stiffen, or eliminate from its list, courses of that character." If Harvard returns to a distribution system of general education as its 2005 report proposes, it should expect students once again to seek out what are now called "guts" in large numbers.

Professors were already complaining about soft grading in 1894, when the Committee on Raising the Standard reported to the Faculty:

"[The Committee] believes . . . that by defining anew the Grades A, B, C, and E, and by sending the definitions to every instructor, the Faculty may do something to keep up the standard of the higher grades. It believes that in the present practice Grades A and B are sometimes given too readily—Grade A for work of no very high merit, and Grade B for work not far above mediocrity." More broadly, the Committee opined, lax grading was compromising the very significance of a Harvard degree. "One of the chief obstacles to raising the standard of the degree is the readiness with which insincere students gain passable grades by sham work. . . . These students maintain themselves in technically good standing with so little work that our degree would be seriously cheapened if its minimum cost were generally known." Only the diction distinguishes this grave message from President Summers's concern that giving Harvard students high grades would disadvantage them.

That is as far back as the history of rising grades at Harvard goes—since that is as far back as grading goes. Letter grades were introduced at Harvard in 1886, so it took only eight years for the first official report that an A was no longer worth what it had been and that the grading system needed reform.

Grades have always been going up, people have always been complaining about it, and nothing much has ever happened that fixed the problem of rising grades for very long. Moreover, grades were never as low as it is imagined that they were in some supposedly good old days. When Harvard's leading critic of grade inflation, Professor Harvey Mansfield, wrote that "everyone knows that C is an average grade," he was referring to a time that never was—not 1890, four years after the introduction of grades at Harvard: That year the average grade, calculated using the conventional four-point scale, was halfway between a B and a C, and the average grade for seniors was a straight B.

Table 5.1   Grade distribution at Harvard, 1950

Grades	A	B	C	D	E	Abs&Inc
%	14.0	38.0	37.9	7.5	2.0	0.6

Nor was C an average grade in Professor Mansfield's freshman year, 1949–1950; that fall, more than half the grades given at Harvard were

As and Bs (Table 5.1). The registrar reported that the average grade of the College was around B– during Mansfield's sophomore year.

Table 5.2 Grade distribution at Harvard, 2004–05

Grades	A	A–	B+	B	B–	C+	C	C–	D+	D	D–	Fail	Pass
%	23.7	25.0	20.5	13.2	5.7	2.1	1.4	0.7	0.1	0.3	0.1	0.4	7.0

By contrast, Table 5.2 shows the grade distribution for 2004–2005. Honors grades are certainly far more frequent now than they used to be, but they were never rare. In short, there never were any good old days of stable grading.

Why grades rise

Rising grades in the academy signal to some critics a collapse of standards. But even in the world beyond the academy, giving more good grades need not mean that those doing the grading have grown soft. "Inflation" can be the result of complex social forces. It was once possible to buy Grade B eggs in markets, but the egg industry responded to consumer expectations and raised the quality of the eggs on the shelves. Today's supermarkets carry only Grades AA and A, and few consumers notice which they are buying. The same dress sizes correspond to larger measurements today than they used to, because both consumers and manufacturers prefer it that way—so much so that in 1983 the federal government gave up on setting standards for the sizes of women's clothing. Rising grades in academia are not a canary dying in the mine of Western civilization any more than higher-grade eggs or smaller dress sizes signal a looming collapse of societal standards. Then why have students' grades risen steadily for more than a century? There is no one answer, but several explanations are germane.

Pressure from students

From time to time, the university administration monitors grades and applies pressure when they are too high. Grades then tend to stabilize for a while. At other times, the pushing comes only from students whose complaints are always about grades they think are too low, not too high. Not every student complaint results in a grade change, and when it does, only one grade changes out of tens of thousands given each year. But the cumulative upward pressure from thousands of individual students exceeds the much more sporadic and half-hearted downward pressure from deans and presidents. Even if those giving the grades never respond to student complaints, the memory of students' distress may translate, a term or a year later, into more lenient grading practices. A colleague noted to me that sales clerks make mistakes both by overcharging and by undercharging, but only the ones who overcharge get punished because the customers complain. For professors the "punishment" is the vague sense that they have failed to maintain good relations with their students.

The imperative for better student-faculty contact is the enemy of stable grading. Of course it is wrong to change a grade just to make a student happy, and equally wrong to give everyone high grades so they will not complain in the first place. But professors *do* want to make students happy—not every student all the time, but in the main, they prefer happy students to unhappy ones. Furthermore, presidents and deans *expect* professors to make students happy. If many students complain to a professor about their grades, the professor's grading scale is likely to shift over time, unless there is equally steady pressure in the other direction from faculty colleagues or the university leadership. Professors hate grading and see little benefit in arguing about it when they have more important things to do.

Student evaluations and tenure decisions

Junior faculty members are in a vulnerable position. When a junior professor comes up for tenure at Harvard, the professor's teaching ratings from the undergraduate Course Evaluation Guide may be the only appraisal of teaching when promotion is discussed. Even though courses are evaluated before students know their final grades, the pressure for good ratings tends to make junior professors reluctant to become known as hard graders. Favorable evaluations and higher grades have been shown to go hand in hand. To alleviate this source of upward pressure on grades, student evaluations in tenure decisions would have to be replaced by peer observations and other forms of teaching assessment—a move that would also, with somewhat greater effort, produce better information.

Students are better

Although the academic quality of college students in general has declined as more American high school graduates attend college, the
academic quality of Harvard students has improved as the university
has expanded its applicant pool and heightened its selectivity. In 1996,
on the basis of correlations between Harvard grades and test scores in
admissions materials, Harvard's Dean K. Whitla estimated that 40 percent of the increase in grades during the prior decade could be explained by improved academic aptitude as measured by rising test
scores. I did my own analysis for the period 1988–2000 and concluded
that higher test scores could explain about 30 percent of the increase
in grades over that period. Thus the amount increase that can be explained away as the result of better students is probably only a third or
so, but it is entirely reasonable to suspect that Harvard faculty members perceived the generally increasing academic preparedness of
their students and overshot the quantitative adjustment of their grading practices—and that the same thing happened many times in the
past, with similar results.

Improvement in the student body may have contributed to rising
grades, but the amount grades have risen is disproportionate to the
amount by which students have improved. Without a sharper analysis,
it is easy for deans to exaggerate the importance of this factor, or even
to yield to partisan sympathies. Richard Brodhead, then the Yale dean
who described the inflation at Harvard as "hilarious," had a different
explanation when Yale also posted high grades: "Modern students take
classes much more seriously, and that accounts for a large part of it."

More small courses

The shift toward small courses also explains some of the increase in
grades. Every study of grading practices shows that grades are higher in
smaller courses—perhaps because students and faculty get to know
each other better. Harvard has made a concerted effort to reduce the
number of large lecture courses and introduce more seminars and
small conference courses. My analysis suggests that 5 percent of the increase in grades in the period 1988–2000 was due to the fact that of the
grades being given, more were grades in small courses; this was in addition to the 30 percent due to improvement in students' objective cre-

dentials. If the correlation stands for the future, moves to increase the number of small courses should be expected to raise average grades.

Better teaching

There is an old Harvard joke about Crane Brinton, a legendary history professor, who welcomed the members of certain athletic teams and social clubs, always awarding them As. One year's contingent all got Bs, and when one of their number sheepishly inquired as to why, the professor is supposed to have responded, "Oh, I know that has been my practice in the past; but I did such a terrible job teaching you this year."

This tale contains a germ of truth. Good teachers labor to improve their students' work during the course of the term. They write comments on drafts, maybe two or three drafts, of students' papers; they prepare model solutions to mathematical problems so students will not repeat their mistakes; they meet with students at all hours to help them understand how to think, reason, and write. The teachers are not doing a good job teaching if students are not doing higher-quality work at the end of a course than at the beginning. As professors' effort increases, it is natural for students' grades to go up too. Faculty members aren't giving those high grades to themselves, much as it might seem so.

Too many grade-scale categories

The grading scale itself can make inflation more likely because grading requires assigning subjective judgments of quality to fixed categories. When there are too many categories, graders tend to use only a few of them—the highest few, in practice. Because of this counterintuitive phenomenon, allowing plus and minus grades, as became official Harvard policy in 1950, eventually contributed to grade inflation.

The letter grade scale, A, B, C, is an ordinal scale specifying only the order of the categories, not the amount by which one group is better than the next. Having the appearance of measurement, rather than just a scale of comparison, the division into categories is constantly second-guessed by students who think they ought to be just over a threshold rather than just under it, and by critics who think the categories should mean something different from what the professors think they do.

A scale with more categories allows more precise comparisons, but the value assigned to any individual piece of work is also more arbitrary. Is this really a B+ paper, or is it worth just a straight B? If there were no pluses and minuses and A, B, C, D, E were the only possibilities, the question might not even arise.

Some years ago when I was running a computer science course with about twenty teaching assistants, I struggled to get them all to assign the same number of points to similar solutions to a programming exercise. My chief assistant, Larry Denenberg, proposed a brilliantly simple solution: restrict the marks on any paper to 0, 1, 2, or 3, rather than 0 through 10. It was far easier to develop consensus and consistency on whether a submission was excellent, good, fair, or poor, than on whether it was a 7 or an 8 out of 10. With enough evaluations of each student, it was possible to develop confidence about the standing of a student within the entire class of 300, even though twenty different people had done the grading using only four grades.

But this way of improving accuracy worked for me only because all the evaluators were part of the same course staff and worked from a common standard. College-wide grade-point averages are numerical averages of grades assigned by evaluators who may never have talked to one another and have only the vaguest of standards to go by—standards that must be vague, since they must apply to papers about *King Lear* as well as to computer programming assignments.

The fact that even five categories are too many for reproducible evaluation causes grading systems to evolve, over time, to use only three categories or so. They used to be called A, B, C; now they are called A, A–, B+. Our present frustration is that the scale, as actually used, has plenty of categories to distinguish among students in whose exact performance we have little interest (grades of B or lower) but only a few categories in the part of the scale about which we care a lot (A, A–, B+). In practice, the grade scale has adjusted toward pegging a student who is not failing as "excellent," "good," "fair," or one of many flavors of "poor."

To extract more information from students' grades, many grades are averaged together, and the resulting GPAs are calculated to four or five decimal places. But what is being averaged is different professors' assessments of "excellent," "good," and "fair" in different courses, and since the professors grading one student probably don't use these categories the same way as the professors grading another student, it actually doesn't make much sense to compare the averages. This point is widely misunderstood. It seems illogical to say that three or four gradations should be enough, since as individual faculty members we can certainly draw much finer distinctions than that among the students we teach. Our grading spreadsheets routinely record scores to a precision of one point in a thousand or more. At the end of the term we hate to throw that information away; Mary, with 965 points, really was a little better than John with 951 points. Yet when there is no agreement even on what is an A and what is a B, much less on what is a B and what is a B+, it makes no sense to average one professor's As with another's Bs. If grades are going to be used for College-wide rankings, then consistency is much more important than precision, and the illusion of precision created by those pluses and minuses does no good at all.

The special case of the humanities

There are significant differences between grading practices in the three broad disciplinary areas, with the highest grades in the humanities. According to the *Crimson*'s summary of a report to the faculty released in early 2004, "Of the three major College divisions, humanities students trumped their counterparts in the social sciences and natural sciences, posting an average GPA of 13.05 on the old 15-point grading scale, compared with averages of 12.52 and 12.33." Differences at this level raise concerns, if nothing else, about students' misjudging what they are "good at," and honors being awarded or denied to students on the basis of the subject they have chosen to study rather than the quality of their work. I have wondered if the relative lack of complaints about grade inflation at MIT is because most grades there are science grades.

The humanities are, I think, in a bit of a mess. What is considered legitimate academic work has expanded greatly over the past thirty years, and judgments of the quality of scholarly articles have not reached a stable consensus. It should come as no surprise that consistent judgments of students' work are also hard to come by, especially when those judgments are made by graduate students who are learning the subjective academic standards of their disciplines. When Harvey Mansfield turned over to the *Boston Globe* an e-mail I had sent him laying "part of the blame on lax humanities professors," I received several e-mails from humanists saying I was right. But the story with humanities grades is more complicated than that, since grades in the humanities were higher than those in other areas even in the days when there was a greater critical consensus within the humanities.

A second possibility is that two effects combine uniquely in the humanities. On the one hand, almost all professors, regardless of field, tend to forgive an isolated low grade. If a student pleads that her poor performance on an individual exercise was due to the fact that her father had just been diagnosed with cancer or she had been up all night with her roommate's alcohol poisoning, we tend to throw out the grade without asking more questions and to base the final grade on the rest of the student's course work. Without making it an announced policy, I tend to award a higher final letter grade when the component grades are rising over the course of the term than when they are falling, even if the average is the same. On the other hand, humanities courses tend to have the fewest pieces of work to evaluate, often only a paper or two and a final exam, so forgiving one component grade as an outlier on the low side tends to make humanities grades rise more than they do in fields where the final grade is based on a larger number of "measurements." This may happen in an informal and impressionistic way, without any special pleading by the student, by simply giving the student the benefit of the doubt when the aggregate grade is near some borderline and one piece is inexplicably worse than the rest.

There has also been, humanist colleagues tell me, a tendency to separate quality of writing from quality of thinking, and to assign grades based on judgments of the latter independent of the former. Teaching assistants grade most of the papers, and some are reluctant to grade a well-researched paper harshly because it is badly written. The confusion over evaluation of humanities papers has grown during a time when Harvard has welcomed more students from poor high schools, where the quality of high school writing instruction is also poor.

And there is also the simple fact that no part of the humanities has anything close to the standard of objective truth that exists at least occasionally within all sciences, and across the board in some sciences. The combination of subjective judgment and human empathy of teacher for student may well result in a systematic upward bias in grades in the humanities.

Mixed signals

Harvard's leaders sometimes scold the faculty for soft grading, but they also sometimes suggest that harsh grading practices are scaring students. Professors welcome any opportunity to be compassionate and any signal that a prior campaign against high grades has been suspended.

In fall 2001, Harvard's dean of Undergraduate Education cautioned all professors that their soft grading practices might not be "motivating students to do their best work." Under a new president and a new dean of the Faculty, the sixty-six-page review issued in 2004 covered every aspect of undergraduate education. Strangely, grading practices, which had seemed such a critical issue two years earlier, were barely mentioned. The report offered but a single grading recommendation—a proposal that half of freshman-year courses be ungraded on the basis that freshmen should be able "to take courses free of the burden of letter grades." Freshman year, the report advised, "should be a time when the possibility of low grades is not a constraint on intellectual exploration," even though we had been told not long before that low grades were almost impossible to find on Harvard transcripts. Grading practices that in 2001 were so soft as to be unmotivating were now seen as so harsh as to be intimidating, in spite of having gotten more lenient in the interim. No wonder professors have a hard time taking grading standards seriously. Our leaders can't keep their story straight on whether our grades are too gentle or too tough, and on whether they help students or oppress them.

CHAPTER 6

Evaluation Is Educational
Why Grade Inflation Isn't Very Important

[T]he marking system of the College . . . made too fine distinctions, and undertook to compare results which were in reality not comparable. The Faculty last year did away with the minute percentage system of marking, and substituted classification of the students in each course of study in five groups. . . . [T]his grouping system . . . diminishes the competition for marks and the importance attached by students to College rank in comparison with the remoter objects of faithful work.

—Charles William Eliot, 1886

Amid all the furor over grade inflation, there has been little debate about why professors give grades in the first place. Critics thunder their criticisms with confidence, but after decades of thinking and talking about grading, there still is no consensus about what purpose they serve. Without agreement on goals, adherence to a consistent scale is impossible. Fixing the grading system would do nothing to improve undergraduate education, and unless professors agree that they will do their main business better if grades are held down, they will continue to give "grade inflation" a backseat to more consequential educational problems.

Over the years, four distinguishable rationales have been implied for evaluating students. Giving students marks makes them work harder and keeps them out of trouble. Giving students marks makes it possible to recognize and to reward excellence and to get the very best work out of the very best students. Giving students marks makes it possible to rank students for those outside the university who want to know which students are better than others. And giving students marks makes them learn more.

These four threads have been interwoven over time, more visibly at some times than others. Every one of them has a downside, and depending on the temperament of the time, the downside has seemed more or less important than the upside. Or the downside may simply be forgotten, to be rediscovered again only long after some old idea about evaluation has reasserted itself.

Though some of the remembering and forgetting has been cyclical, one event changed the landscape forever. The elective curriculum caused a fundamental shift. In the days when all students took the same courses, direct comparison among students was easy, at least in principle. Once different students took different combinations of courses, it became all but impossible to compare meaningfully grades given by different teachers in different departments. Grades are useful within a course, but collegewide grade-point averages are meaningless, especially when calculated to four or five decimal places so that distinctions can be drawn between students whose averages differ by a hairsbreadth.

Over time, most professors came to regard evaluation of students less as certification than as education. For the faculty, grading is a motivational device by which teachers get their students to learn as much as possible by judicious use of rewards and punishments. The subjectivity of grading judgments, the preference of rewards over punishments to motivate students, and actual improvement in the quality of students combine to produce a steady upward drift.

Because grades are educational tools, they should not be used mainly as credentials for external consumption. The pressure to calculate GPAs and collegewide rankings is largely external to the academy. Many professors hate grading not because they are reluctant to give feedback to their students but because they know that their small contributions to detailed but meaningless statistics will have consequences unrelated to their educational value. The pressure for "meaningful" and stiff grading is antieducational, a moralistic imperative revived by contemporary culture but echoing from a time long ago, before education became the main business of college.

Each of the four rationales for grading—that grades motivate harder work, recognize excellence, certify student achievement, and improve education—has its own historical and philosophical foundation and its own upsides and downsides.

The nose-to-the-grindstone rationale

During Harvard's first two centuries, education consisted of daily recitations in required subjects. The system was designed not to prepare unschooled youth for useful roles in society, but mainly to certify members of the hereditary elite for their rightful places in society. Attendance was mandatory and regulations were strict, but academic excellence was not an articulated value; the constant examinations were meant to keep students' noses to the grindstone. In the words of the earliest records (and with original spelling retained), examinations were given "To the Intent that no scholar may misspend his time, to the dishonor of God and the society or the greif and disappointment of his freinds, but that the yearly progresse and sufficiency of Scollars may bee manifest." Until 1772 academic rankings did not exist, and graduates were listed at Commencement not by academic distinction but according to their social rank. Beginning in 1777, simultaneously with larger social developments of the time, the top scholar in each class was identified at Commencement.

In 1825, in the aftermath of the dreadful student riots of 1823, President Josiah Quincy instituted a rigorous marking system known as the Scale of Rank (Figure 6.1). Students received daily marks in each of their subjects, with demerits for absenteeism and bad behavior. The formulas for the accumulation of marks grew complex, and the resulting numbers had the look of great precision. For example, in 1830, one could get 1,600 marks in freshman mathematics, 1,760 marks in freshman Greek, and so on; the maximum total possible over a four-year career was precisely 27,493.

Steadiness, rather than academic excellence, was the cherished value. Freshmen were barely out of boyhood, and the college needed to keep them focused. As President Quincy wrote in 1831, "the best assurance for the continued and unremitted attention of students to their exercises, will be found in the certainty that at every recitation each individual will be examined; and that the estimate of scholastic

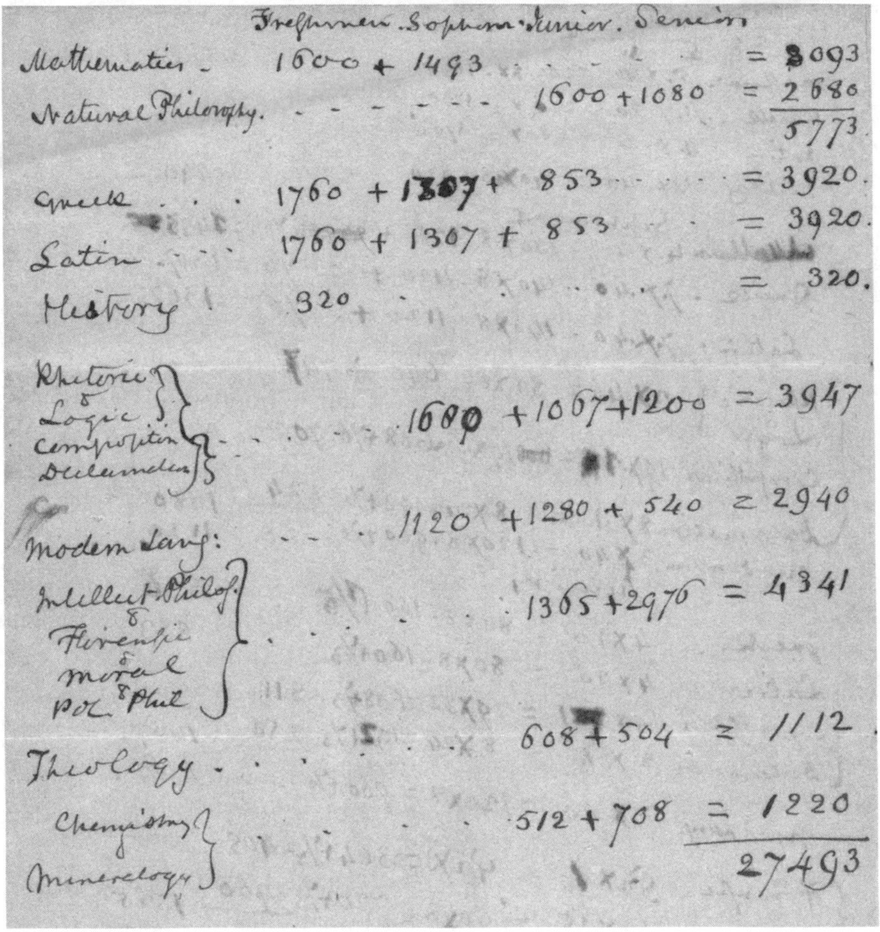

Figure 6.1 Scale of Rank marking system at Harvard, 1830, showing the number of points that could be earned in each subject in each of the four college years.

rank must depend, not upon occasional brilliant success, but upon the steady, uniform, and satisfactory performance of each exercise."

Modern-day critics sometimes confuse encouraging excellence with holding noses to grindstones. "It is difficult for students to work hard, or for the professor to get them to work hard," wrote Harvey Mansfield, "when they know that their chances of getting an A or A– are 50–50."

Downsides of the nose-to-the-grindstone rationale

The problem with the nose-to-the-grindstone theory of evaluation is that students hate it—not because it makes them work hard, but because it makes their work so pointless. Uncompromising systems of evaluation readily become divorced from learning. When students lose confidence in both the purpose and fairness of the work they must do to succeed, the class becomes a game played between mutually mistrustful adversaries, and students may react as a mob. That is what happened at Harvard in 1834. A student, Mr. Dunkin, refused to obey his tutor's demand that he recite a second page of a long list of Greek proper names. Mr. Dunkin's defiance and the tutor's insistence set off a week of riots worse than those of 1823. Students stoned professors and destroyed College property. At the end, almost the entire sophomore class was dismissed. Something similar happened at Dartmouth in 2000, when students lost confidence in the fairness of the computer programming assignments they were expected to do but their professor seemed incapable of doing himself. Students responded at first by rudeness and disorderliness. The professor subsequently accused seventy-eight students of cheating on a single homework assignment, and then resigned. Dartmouth ultimately dropped all charges, on the grounds that officials couldn't sort out who did what. But in both 1834 and 2000, the students would not have misbehaved but for the poor judgment and harsh demands on the part of their instructors.

Defenders of uncompromising toughness ridicule appeals to students' feelings about their grades. Mansfield argued:

> Grade inflation has resulted from the emphasis in American education on the notion of self-esteem. According to that therapeutic notion, the purpose of education is to make students feel capable and empowered. So to grade them, or to grade them strictly, is cruel and dehumanizing. Grading creates stress. It encourages competition rather than harmony. It is judgmental.

But the pathologies associated with the use of the grading system as a buggy whip have been documented for nearly two centuries. Today's grading system at its worst is not much different from the old Scale of Rank as the *Crimson* described it in 1885. Grading to make students work "encourages an unscholar-like tendency to work for marks, and prevents the establishment of high motives for study. Students are dwarfed by it, to the low stature of grinds for marks. Injudicious selections of courses are encouraged by it. Cribbing thrives under it." Today, cheating occurs in nose-to-the-grindstone courses because students realize that the game they have to play is meaningless, and their commiseration emboldens them to dishonesty.

Whatever they would say about it, most professors today do not consciously follow the nose-to-the-grindstone theory. But there are exceptions. Witnessing a student memorizing just enough chemical formulas or dinosaur cladograms to survive a critical test reminds me of those accounts from the 1800s—what was described in 1869 as "that spasmodic and unhealthy industry which is commonly termed *cramming for examinations.*" Mnemonic tricks and efforts to outsmart the professor's exam-setting strategy replace any substantial education. The student is not learning to swim, but only trying to gulp enough air to stay afloat.

Every now and then a dean legitimizes this theory. Harvard has for many years ended fall-term classes before winter break and scheduled exams for late January. In recent discussions about changing to a more common schedule of exams before winter break, one of the principal arguments advanced has been improved student mental health. Under the revised calendar, winter break would separate the terms, and, the argument goes, students would not be stressed about exams over vacation. The deans so readily accepted the representations of the burdens of studying that they agreed the time spent doing it should be minimized. In an age-old comic drama of deans and students, the deans usually preach that study is enlightening and students should do more, and the students complain that it is misery and the College should expect less. Both postures are exaggerations, but in today's Harvard, the deans have switched roles and portray studying as punishment. In a discussion with faculty, a dean offered an even more cynical argument—that students forget the material from their fall-term courses over winter break, so they should be examined in December while they still remember what they were taught. What education can Harvard possibly think it is providing, if a dean thinks that what we teach is forgotten in weeks? By that analysis, we are mere residential custodians of students, keeping them out of trouble until we can give them their degrees, and not educators at all.

The fundamental argument against the nose-to-the-grindstone rationale is simply that it is antieducational. Reliance on grading to make students work hard is bad teaching. Students at colleges like Harvard do not need to be persuaded that learning is important and that studying is worthwhile. If the only way to get students to study hard in a course is to threaten them with bad grades, something is wrong with the way the course is being taught. The professor should try to make it more interesting, more fun, more exciting—or more connected to some part of human knowledge or experience beyond the narrow walls of the disciplinary slot into which the course falls. If that is impossible, the course is probably about what the teacher wants to teach and not what the student wants to learn—or else the student is being forced to fulfill a curricular requirement for which no convincing rationale has been offered.

The excellence rationale

Who could be against excellence or its pursuit? I am as proud of my Harvard *summa* as other *summa* holders surely are of theirs (though my Roxbury Latin School *summa* means more to me). But as an important rationale for grading policies and strategies, the power of grades to encourage or discourage excellence is fraught with harmful side effects that have been discovered and forgotten over the centuries.

Exceptional academic achievement was little recognized at Harvard until the mid-1700s. The first academic prizes were the Detur Prizes, books awarded to meritorious students under the terms of the bequest of Edward Hopkins. *Detur digniori* means "let it be given to the more worthy." Sophomores whose freshman-year academic records were outstanding still receive these prizes in a dignified ceremony each winter.

In 1825 the Scale of Rank was instituted, and until the practice was discontinued in 1887, the top ten scholars were publicly identified, with their rank. The old Quinquennial Catalogues, which until 1935 listed all who had ever graduated from Harvard, reveal that President Charles William Eliot graduated second in his class, behind a gentleman who became a professor at City University of New York. In spite of all efforts to remove ambiguity, a tie for first place occurred at least once.

For a time Harvard publicized not only the names of the top graduating seniors but also the names of all students who received As or Bs in their courses. Celebrate excellence, went the theory, and all will try to achieve it. The competition will raise the performance of all.

The excellence rationale lies behind much of the modern critique of grading. In Mansfield's words, "Surely a teacher wants to mark the few best students with a grade that distinguishes them from all the rest in the top quarter." Ensuring that only the top 5 percent of Harvard students received *summa* degrees—even though the restriction required drawing a line between grade-point averages that did not differ meaningfully from those of students twenty positions higher or lower on the scale—was another example of the faculty becoming enslaved by the details of a system that had been created with every good intention.

Downsides of the excellence rationale

Downside 1: Course selection becomes a game of strategy.   Ranking systems always have unintended consequences. A worthy abstraction—academic excellence, in this case—is given concrete form as the result of a particular numerical computation. But once the terms of the computation are set, students take advantage of loopholes to improve their scores. What started out as a *recognition of* academic excellence, and became an *inspiration to* academic excellence, becomes instead an empty game of score maximization. And the rougher the measure, the greater the opportunities for gamesmanship.

Already by 1885, President Eliot's elective curriculum was under attack for allowing students to get As by choosing courses strategically rather than by doing superior work. According to Eliot, defenders of the old prescribed curriculum claimed that "students who are free to choose their studies will, as a rule, select the easiest studies simply because they are easiest, or put themselves, by preference, under the instruction of easy-going professors who give high marks for little work." Eliot countered those claims, though not very convincingly, and the student who works only for grades rather than learning became a standard type in the demonology of the academy. At the turn of the twentieth century, Dean Briggs referred to the "'mark-fiend' who never comes to anything in [later] life."

Nobody likes the student who is toiling just for grades, but professors, not students, must be held responsible for so honoring the scale on which those students are trying to rise. The sad side effect of the excellence rationale is that its downsides afflict the very best students. Because graduation honors are determined by grade-point averages, students on target for *summa* degrees grow increasingly reluctant to risk taking courses in which they may not do extremely well. It is exactly as a Harvard president described it in 1869—that "a department is not unfrequently chosen because it is supposed that, in the College phrase, 'the marks run higher' there than in the collateral departments." Given that we tend to learn the most by studying things about which we know little, the excellence rationale has antieducational results.

Downside 2: Excellence doesn't motivate students who know they won't excel under the terms that define "excellence." It is well and good to inspire the best students to excellence, but by definition most students are not exceptional. For those who are out of the running for the top academic honors, the glorification of those at the top is at best irrelevant, and at worst alienating.

Back in 1856, the Faculty recognized this downside of ranking students on the basis of marks aggregated over an entire college career. So many points were accumulated over such a long period of time that a student who did not start off well had little to gain from applying himself later on.

> In such cases, the student is held back by arrears which have been accumulated against him during the earlier part of his college course, when his conduct and application to study were less satisfactory. He has now reformed, but no sufficient motive appears for him to continue in well-doing, because he finds from experience that he can rise only very slowly from his former low position on the Scale, and that the higher honors of the class are absolutely beyond his efforts.

Over the past century and a half, the Harvard Faculty forgot that honors have to be achievable in order to provide motivation. Professors tried to restore honor to honors degrees in 2002 by capping their number at about half the class. Yet if a student now recognizes after a year or two that he or she is unlikely to be in the top half of the class by graduation time, what incentive will the student have to do more than passing work during the junior and senior years? Academic distinctions motivate, and a realization that they are unattainable deprives the student of motivation.

With honors degrees at Harvard now scarcer, the quality of the education pursued and attained by the bottom half of the class is declining. The new rules took effect for the Class of 2005, but the *Crimson* reported that their discouraging effect on advanced work was already being felt in fall 2004. Some seniors elected to drop their thesis projects, knowing that their GPAs would not be sufficiently high to qualify them for honors regardless of what they achieved academically during their senior year. One faculty member, Anya Bernstein, defended the new standard on the grounds that "honors do not mean as much when more than 90 percent of the students receive them," but another, Ken

Nakayama, reported that dropped theses would "happen more with the new college rules." The opposition of these two perspectives presents a bottom-line question: If the purpose of a college is education rather than ranking, is the gain in significance for recipients of honors degrees worth the lowered academic achievement of those who know they are ineligible?

I suspect that the most serious unfairness in the raised standards for honors is one that has never been mentioned by any of those who have moaned about grade inflation. When most grades are As and Bs but only half the class can graduate with honors, students who are less well prepared for college because of their poorer socioeconomic backgrounds will find it especially difficult to achieve honors. Freshman-year grades are lower than grades in the last three college years, because most students need a term or two to learn the ropes of college-level work. Consequently, much of the spread in the GPAs of graduating seniors results from variability in freshman-year grades. The transition to college is hardest for students who are least well prepared; they can catch up to their more fortunate peers, but they don't start out with the same academic performance level. For this reason, Harvard's *summa* rules used to have a mercy clause for one or two low freshman-year grades, but that waiver was dropped in 1996 when the *summa* category was capped at 5 percent of the senior class. The combined effect of the fixed number of *summa* degrees, the inexorably rising pattern of grading overall, and the lack of any forgiveness for isolated low grades is to make it extremely hard for a student to get a C or a couple of Bs freshman year and still graduate with a cumulative GPA high enough to qualify for *summa*. Now that the numbers of *magna* and *cum* degrees are also capped, the sensitivity to a few low grades will affect those categories as well.

If the students receiving *summa* degrees were grouped by financial-aid status, scholarship students would almost certainly be underrepresented. To my knowledge this analysis has never been done, but it would be astonishing if the facts proved otherwise. Students from poorer secondary schools simply cannot hit the ground running their freshman year as can students from independent schools or good public high schools. And in general, students with higher family incomes attend better secondary schools. Thus it seems likely that the wealthier half of the class will garner a disproportionate share of graduation honors.

It would be a sad outcome to the much-heralded restoration of academic standards at Harvard if it were to discourage from the pursuit of excellence disadvantaged students who got a low grade or two their first term—students who have lifted themselves by extraordinary exertions from poor academic backgrounds to be seated at Harvard next to students who have had greater educational advantages. This possibility casts significant doubt on whether the whole exercise of academic honors is worth the unfairness that comes with it—especially at a time when Harvard is reaching out more than ever to talented and ambitious students of very limited means. The opportunity to compete for honors is probably not an important stimulus to excellence in any case. MIT grants no honors degrees, and yet its graduates reap more than their share of distinctions and awards after graduating.

This socioeconomic bias may also affect the racial distribution of honors. Anyone who has attended the Detur Prize ceremony comes away feeling that the number of black students receiving the very highest freshman-year grades is disproportionately small. To the extent that race and socioeconomic status are correlated, the phenomenon of low freshman-year grades for more poorly prepared students affects the distribution of honors across ethnic groups. As the academic standards for honors become more unforgiving, the disproportion of honors by ethnicity will likely become more extreme. So will the demotivating effect on minority students of recognizing early on that after stumbling slightly their freshman year, they will never be able to raise their records enough to gain high honors.

Downside 3: The excellence calculations are inaccurate to the point of fraud. There are so many problems with treating GPAs as measurements that it is remarkable they are taken seriously.

At first glance, GPAs appear to be scientifically objective measurements. All students have to take the same number of courses, and the number is large enough that no one professor's grading style can bias the results very much. Even if only four or five grades are assigned with any frequency today, averaging thirty or so grades together for 1,600 graduating seniors spreads them out on a linear scale rather effectively. The various degrees of honors can be determined by drawing lines: Those above the line get honored; those below do not. Those lines are drawn between students whose GPAs differ only in the fourth or fifth decimal place. Precise, hard-nosed, and reassuringly mathematical.

But precision is not the same as accuracy. Under an elective system, different students' GPAs are averages of grades in different courses.

Graders in different courses use the letter grades to mean different things. A committee chaired by A. Lawrence Lowell just before Eliot retired as president described the situation well.

> [Students'] marks in individual courses may be compared, but that means very little. Each course covers so small a part of the total work that rank in it is not a strong incentive, while the lists of courses chosen by different men are so little alike that they are incommensurate. The men are not running side by side over the same road, but over different roads of different kinds, out of sight of one another.

Even when grading practices are most scrutinized, only the feeblest attempts are made to align the grading practices of different professors. An enforceable consensus on a metric scale is unimaginable, especially when the very concept of a string theorist and a romantic-poetry expert "grading the same way" is hard to grasp. In a largely elective curriculum, grades are inevitably comparative and can never be yardsticks that are accurate across different disciplines.

The reality is that even within a course, grades are inaccurate. Professors typically assign grades by converting a numerical score into a letter grade, assigning the same grade to students whose scores are in the same range. Calculating GPAs to four or five decimal places reintroduces precision that was discarded when the A, B, C grades were assigned. The result is precision without accuracy. The irony is that the five decimal places to which GPAs are now calculated to determine graduation honors are the same number of places used in the old Scale of Rank, with its maximum value of 27,493. The entire reason that the old Scale of Rank was eliminated in favor of the A–E grading scale was to blur fine distinctions, which caused too much myopic grade grubbing and discouraged true pursuit of excellence.

The introduction of the letter grading scale in 1886, the use of broad "grades" rather than ranks based on precise point totals, was the culmination of more than a decade's misgivings. But having instituted the system of "grading" rather than recording precise point totals, the Faculty gradually felt the need to re-create some overall numerical measure by which it could compare students to one other, a measure that had the appearance of objectivity and precision. Not all the reasons were academic; by the time of World War II, draft boards used precise rankings of students when deciding whom to call to service. Yet a major consideration, which has continued to the present day, is the need for objective standards that can serve both as targets at which students can aim and impersonal rationales faculty can use to explain why one student is honored but not another. We find ourselves right back where we were in 1885, with students caring too much about "competition for marks" and too little for "the remoter objects of faithful work."

Another problem with honors based on GPA is that they recognize only one kind of excellence. Like the ideal President Quincy described in 1831, GPAs favor consistency over brilliance. Awarding honors by grade-point average disadvantages the student who makes an extraordinary contribution in one area and favors the drudge who does well in all areas but is exceptional in none. This was recognized only a decade after the letter grading system was instituted. The Faculty moved away from the award of honors based only on accumulated grades for a reason: "High attainments in a special line of study in their judgment constitute a claim for distinctions at graduation, not less valid than that which rests upon uniform excellence of college work." The idea was to "encourage effort among that large class who have a certain degree of aptitude for special lines of study, but are hopeless, or not ambitious, with respect to high academic rank." But because a straight numerical system is simpler and less arguable, Harvard returned to it, and it is essentially what we use today.

The GPA is not the only possible academic metric for comparing students. Valen Johnson, in his book on grade inflation, described a failed attempt to introduce a more accurate system at Duke University. Because college students take only a few dozen courses out of hundreds offered, opportunities are few for comparing students in the same course, especially if the students' majors are different. Thus meaningful statistics tend to be incomprehensible because of their computational intricacy. Designers of the "Bowl Championship Series" ranking system in NCAA football face the same problem: There are so many teams and so few games per team that head-to-head matchups, and even games against common opponents, are rare nationwide. Football fans regard BCS ranking formulas with the same skepticism the Duke faculty gave Johnson's sophisticated GPA substitute. The simple GPA is a numerical soup of unreliable ingredients. Colleges do not use a scientifically superior system because they recognize the limited importance of accurate calibrations.

If our goal is an objective assessment of excellence, those doing the teaching should not evaluate how well the student has learned. Professors would not be allowed to grade their own students any more than athletes' coaches hold the official stopwatches at track meets. The reason professors grade their own students with impunity is not that they are more capable than others of setting their hopes aside from their judgments, but because grades should not be viewed primarily as measurements, a use for which they are ill suited. A psychology professor described the letter grading system to me as "a psychometric nightmare that opens the door to every kind of scaling error and psychological bias known to science." As an objective calibration of students, the letter grade scale is hopeless.

The credentialing rationale

According to the credentialing rationale for evaluation, we grade students because we are creating a product, and the world to which we deliver that product expects us to certify who is better than whom. In this theory, students are rather like cars, and grade inflation is akin to shipping Chevrolets with Cadillac nameplates. Even if students have gotten better, goes the argument, medical schools are not going to admit everyone and Citibank is not going to hire everyone. Thus if our grades lose credibility, our students will ultimately pay the price.

Downsides of the credentialing rationale

The credentialing rationale has most of the downsides of the excellence rationale and a few of its own. Ranks do not become less bogus when they are used for professional-school admission than they are when used for determination of honors. But more is at stake when the outside world becomes a player.

The anxiety about the use of grades as credentials is highest among premedical students. Grades are thought to be so important for medical-school admission that Harvard's career service office publishes a booklet showing, for each medical school, what percentage of the students have been admitted with each possible combination of GPA and MCAT (Medical College Admission Test) score. The pressure to score well in a few critical courses—organic chemistry, most famously—can devastate a fragile student. Doing as well as possible in those courses can become an end in itself, and can smother introspection about whether the student even wants a medical career. One of the saddest disciplinary cases with which I dealt as dean was that of a student who had committed a gross and obvious plagiarism after accumulating a stellar academic record and being admitted to a good medical school. It was the only way, it seemed, that she could tell her parents that she was not ready to become a doctor.

Law-school admission is similarly competitive, but lacks the "roadblock" courses that medical-school applicants must get past. Of course, Ph.D. programs expect good grades, but students experience little of the anxiety about Ph.D. admission that other students do about medical-school admission. Students tend to realize that if their Harvard grades were not good, they are unlikely to be happy pursuing a Ph.D. anyway. And they suspect that the worst they can expect if they don't go for a Ph.D. will be lower debt and better financial prosperity.

Beyond that, I have been struck by how little attention prospective employers pay to Harvard grade-point averages, inflated or not. They look for particular skills, evidenced, perhaps, by grades in particular courses. They certainly look for the ability to communicate and to work in a team. But a statistic that averages a grade in a general education course on the Samurai with a course in the student's chemistry major is meaningless. Many employers seem to believe that Harvard course grades aren't the best way to choose among Harvard students and use nonacademic criteria instead. The Harvard Business School until recently took an extreme position against the use of its grades as credentials. It prohibited companies recruiting on campus from asking for students' grades, and prohibited students from revealing them. The Business School rescinded this policy in December 2005, although most students wanted it retained.

A recent study by the American Academy of Arts and Sciences, while bemoaning grade inflation, showed how unimportant college grades are as employment credentials. The study acknowledged there is "no large body of writings in which, for example, employers or graduate schools complain about lack of information because of inflated grades." Instead it merely reported that employers ask for student transcripts less than they used to.

The truth is that employers pay less attention to Harvard grades than Harvard does. Employers have long placed limited weight on Harvard grades, for reasons having nothing to do with grade inflation. A technology employer gave me an interesting explanation of his hiring strategy: High grades from places like Harvard confirmed the judgment of the college admissions offices of these schools. Admission to Harvard and other top colleges was already a strong indicator of quality, and getting good grades, or at least not getting too many bad grades, in his view confirmed that the student was not only smart but had worked steadily for four years without disruptive personal difficulties.

Why, then, does the credentialing rationale have such currency among students? They embrace it because they have been taught it from an early age. Most students who are admitted to Harvard have been trained by their parents and schools to think of grades as nothing more than credentials they will need to get into a place like Harvard.

I tell my advisees that they should do as well as they possibly can in the courses that mean the most to them and not worry about their grades in the rest. I usually receive one of two reactions to this advice: Sometimes it seems to lift a burden from their shoulders, as though I have just said something they wanted to believe but never expected to hear from a grown-up. But sometimes students react with alarm, as though I am bent on knocking out the foundations of the only world order they have ever known.

The educational rationale

Most professors prefer to think of grades not as buggy whips or instruments of excellence or certificates for students to brandish to the outside world. The hundreds of grades assigned to individual pieces of work or at the end of a course are simply part of the educational armament that we use to teach. We encourage students with rewards of high grades and show our disappointment with lower grades. We fail students in the hope that they will learn something about the cost of negligence (very few Harvard students fail courses because they can't do the work). Teachers who don't assign enough graded work during a course or are too slow in grading and returning it are missing key educational opportunities.

Thinking about grading as an educational tool has consequences. It requires assigning grades in a way that students understand them. It requires a commitment to educate not just the A student or the student who could be an A student but all students equally. And it means that grades have most significance within the orbit of the class being taught. That is, grades have significance mostly in the relationship between the teacher and the students in the course, rather than through comparison to other students in other courses or in the way they are interpreted by the outside world. When Eliot rolled out the letter grading system in 1886, he explained that

> students have . . . learned to look upon a course of study not as a mere series of lessons, but as an opportunity for attaining a desired end,—a certain kind of training or the knowledge of a certain subject. . . . This broader spirit and more manly conception of the student's opportunities . . . is to be encouraged in every legitimate way, and it is because the percentage system of marking, with its minute distinctions and the exaggerated importance which it appears to give to marks in comparison with the real objects of study, was felt to be an impediment to this growth, that the Faculty was led to the conclusion that a simpler method of reporting on the proficiency of students was desirable.

The educational rationale for grading is rarely stated as such but resonates with a more fundamental principle: Students are human beings, and no one measurement should define them. Academic excellence should be celebrated but not overvalued among students, few of whom are bent on academic careers. At a time when the bottom of the Harvard class was far less talented than it is today, acting president Andrew Preston Peabody commented wisely on the glorification of class rank, noting that

> every student who maintains a blameless moral character, attends College exercises regularly, and is not culpably negligent in the preparation of his lessons from day to day, should be permitted to remain undisgraced and unmolested. There are many cases in which there coexists with an average capacity of liberal culture an irremediable deficiency as to the memory of words and details. We have had among our students of this description many persons of high respectability,—some of surpassing excellence. . . . Their defect of memory will always keep them near the foot of the class; and by occupying that position they sustain the self-respect and ambition of those next above them.

Peabody was Harvard's minister and Plummer Professor of Christian Morals, so he may have had a professional disposition favorable to human redemption. He was, in any case, a beloved figure there, "ever the incarnation of simplicity and of kindness, of generosity and of love," in the words of one alumnus. And apparently he was not a tough grader himself. "Among the myths which gathered about his name was that of a student who inquired what mark he had received in examination, to which the kindly doctor is said to have replied, 'A very good mark indeed. By the way, what is your name?'"

The reason Harvard abandoned precise numerical marking was to recognize that other forms of merit were more important than marks. "It is well also," an 1886 report to the Harvard Overseers advised, "that young men in college should become used to the standards which prevail in the world outside, where a man's rank among his fellows is determined by many different considerations, and anything approaching the mathematical inaccuracy of a college rank list is unknown."

Although most Harvard professors would individually subscribe to that view, Harvard acts as though the opposite were true. Measurements are good, even if no meaning can be ascribed to the quantity being measured. Even faculty hiring is infected by the urge to quantify. Increasing importance is being attached to citation counts—that is, counts of how often a professor's works are cited in the papers of others. It does not take a genius to see the flaws in that metric: Being cited by one Albert Einstein should be worth more than being cited by a thousand Alfred E. Newmans.

One evening, President Summers was arguing that too many As were given in chemistry; if you wanted a doctor, he said, you would want to know which one was the best. But perhaps there was no one best doctor, a Tutor countered; deciding which doctor was best for a particular patient might require considering human qualities, such as personal rapport with the patient. When Summers pressed the point that there had to be a best doctor, a student offered a wiser analogy. "President Summers," he said, "that is like saying there is a best book."

❧

There have been many more predictions and worries about the evils of grade inflation than demonstrated consequences. The leading charge about the cost of grade inflation is the one Susan Pedersen made in the fall of 2001: Students won't do their best work if they are graded too softly. Occasionally students report the same thing, but I wonder how true it really is.

The principal reason students don't work hard is that the work they are asked to do is not very interesting and has not been made to seem very important. When the work is interesting, students at selective colleges will do it even without the potential reward of a high grade or the punishment of a low grade.

For example, I put a "challenge problem" on each of my problem sets, worth only one point out of a hundred so that people won't tackle it unless they have done the rest of the problems first. Students spend enormous amounts of time on these challenge problems. The trick is to design them to seem easy enough to be approachable, but seductive enough that students don't want to stop working on them once they withstand a first assault. The contribution to students' grades is almost irrelevant. Likewise, I have found that a free-form project of the student's own design can produce far more learning than any prescribed set of exercises. Not every student comes out of the course knowing the same things, but most are better off than if they had been subjected to work in which they had no interest.

College professors use grades to force students to do work for which the students cannot see an educational rationale. If the professor has not been able to show the importance of the issues under analysis or the significance of the theories being expounded, the related homework and term papers will seem pointless, and students won't do the work unless grading practices force them to. Even then, students are likely to resort to shortcuts, from "bullshitting" to outright cheating. Academic dishonesty arises in part from students' ambitions, but the breakdown in the social contract between students and professors precipitates the worst cheating contagions. When students stop believing that professors are demanding sensible work for educational reasons, they respond in kind.

Reliance on grading practices is a poor substitute for expecting professors to justify their choice of course material. In the worst case, professors can't account for the importance of what they are teaching. That can happen for several reasons. It may be that the course is part of a mandatory requirement whose rationale no one takes seriously. Teaching can also become empty because the material being taught not only seems but is unimportant—it is just what the professor has made his or her reputation writing about. A professor late in his career may have lost confidence in the importance of a lifetime's research, or a younger professor may be clinging to the subject of her Ph.D. thesis when it is time to move on. In these situations, students should not bear the brunt of faculty failings.

The most credible alarms about the effects of grade inflation on undergraduate education relate to differential grading standards in different fields—a problem not, strictly speaking, of inflation but of inconsistency. This is troubling, since grades tend to be lower in the sciences. If large numbers of students are avoiding science and engineering fields simply because the grades in those fields are somewhat harsher, it is possible that a large social cost will be paid in the long run for the varying grading standards.

It is certainly possible that some students are driven out of the sciences because their science grades are lower than their nonscience grades. But the greatest loss results when students avoid risky courses in any field because they opt to protect their grade-point average rather than to learn something new. The ultimate solution to both problems is the same: Lower the significance publicly attached to grades and honors. In my rogue's gallery of problems with undergraduate education, the grading scale does not figure prominently.

It would be possible to hold grades down by requiring faculty to distribute their grades according to a specified grading curve, say no more than a quarter As, and so on. This was suggested at Harvard in 1910, and Princeton officials in 2004 adopted just such a system. Described as an "expectation," Princeton's rule is that the aggregate of all grades given in an undergraduate department cannot include more than 35 percent As. (So one course could have more if another had less.) The limit is set higher, at 55 percent, for upper-level independent-work courses.

These limits seem rather gentle, and on the face of it unobjectionable. More than 35 percent of the students can't be doing indistinguishably excellent work, can they? But such quotas and rationing systems suffer from a logical flaw. They imply, as one letter writer put it, "the existence of conservation of knowledge: there is only so much knowledge among a group of students, and if one student acquires more, it means, *ipso facto,* that another acquires less." This tendency to turn grading into a competition for scarce resources explains why many professors do not like to use grade "curves" in their courses. It would be very hard to look a student in the eye and say words to the effect, "Yes, you are right that if you had taken this course last year you would have gotten an A–; that's the grade I gave your roommate when he took the course and did equally good work. But this year the four guys across the hall from you were in the course too, and I used up all the A-level grades on them. You should have taken the course last year, or waited till next year, to avoid having so many really smart people in the course with you." Everyone learns more when there are more smart students in a course, and it doesn't make sense that under a curved system, the grade of an individual student will tend to fall when the quality of students rises.

This example underscores a crucial question. Should grades be assigned on a comparative basis, with high grades being a scarce resource to be allocated by competition to a fixed percentage of the class, so that the meaning of an individual's grade changes as the class changes? Or should high grades describe work of a certain absolute quality, so that the grade assigned to a student's work is independent of the work of others? Almost all complaints about high grades refer, at least implicitly, to a comparative standard, but almost all descriptions of how professors should assign grades refer to an absolute standard. Pundits and critics love the competitive model; most of those inside the university family—the professors assigning the grades and the students receiving them—find logic only in the absolute model.

The lack of scientific objectivity in our grading system is usually harmless, because the system evolved to serve its primary purpose, which is to educate rather than to measure. The fact that grades in some areas are now so consistently high as to compromise their motivational purpose does not mean that the system is entirely dysfunctional, only that certain fields need to have self-critical conversations about the purpose and practice of grading.

The most effective way to combat rising grades would be to initiate serious conversations, at the departmental level, about what constitutes A, B, and C work—"therapy," as a colleague called it, rather than regulation. The Faculty-wide discussion in the 2001–2002 year slightly depressed the grades given that year, though the effect disappeared when the conversation did. But such conversations almost never happen at the departmental level, even when media scrutinize our grading practices and deans send memos about the problems we are causing. In almost thirty years of teaching in a department that is unusually devoted to undergraduate education, I do not recall ever participating in a faculty meeting where an effort was made to coordinate grading practices. To make departmental conversations concrete and specific, there would have to be an exchange of information among professors that would breach one of the sacred barriers of professional academic courtesy: Harvard professors do not criticize each other's teaching or grading. We may have come to accept students evaluating our courses, but we are not used to our colleagues doing the same.

Yet it would be very healthy to have our faculty colleagues examine how we grade. Having the department chair or the dean provide the feedback, the way Lowell did shortly after 1910, might produce even better results. A more centralized or encompassing exchange of views and standards would be needed to address the variation in grading standards across different fields of study, though getting a broad consensus between the physicists and the literary critics on the meaning of a B or C grade would be a truly daunting project—and one that once done, would have to be redone every few years as practices drifted and new faculty arrived. On the other hand, since most of the faculty concern focuses on A-level grades, a concerted effort to press back on the increasing number of As, leaving professors to distribute B- and C-level grades as their consciences dictate, would be an easy place to start.

We must remember that grading is not measurement and can never be an exact science. Grading is part of teaching, and is thus a human activity, subject to all the imperfections of other human judgments. A distinguished British academic talked to me about the experience of his daughter, a student at a major British university. I asked him how her work was evaluated, and he said there was very little feedback; the system still was driven by high-stakes exams at the end of the year. His daughter did get comments and evaluations of some of her work, but she and her father were disappointed because the written remarks were "highly impersonal." What did he mean by that? He meant that the papers were sent off somewhere and critiqued by a person who was unknown to the student, and who also had not taught and did not know the student. I noted that what he was calling "impersonal" might also be described as "objective," but that did not seem to make the system any better in his mind. He wished for his daughter something like the level of personal interaction he observed, at least occasionally, in the American system, where faculty work closely with students and then evaluate their work, with all the biases of judgment that result when the teacher does the grading.

Ultimately, the problem of grading has to be kept in perspective. There is no reason to think that better grading practices would improve the quality of the education we offer, so grading reform is less important than other educational reforms: better advising, smaller courses, more effective teaching, and a more inspiring curriculum. Universities should apply their energy to these goals, which would have clear educational rewards.

CHAPTER 7

Independence, Responsibility, Rape

The End of Moral Development in College

*The educational experience of coming to terms with one's actions, their conse-
quences for others, and their significance for oneself, is the most intense form
of moral education provided by the College.*

—John B. Fox Jr., 1981

One of the oldest ideas about college is that it is a place where children become adults. Especially in residential colleges, students
were out from under the thumb of their parents once they left for college. Colleges set rules both to keep order and to provide a framework
for students' behavior during the years of transition from parental control to personal independence. Colleges offered ideals of good character, counseled students individually about what was expected of them,
and meted out discipline to transgressors. In these ways they helped students learn responsibility for their lives and for the consequences of
their actions. Much of this has been lost today, through the combined
effect of the consumer culture and the drive for perfection. Because we
strive to make students happy, we cannot say that they are wrong. Because students' vision is crowded with immediate demands we try to satisfy, we do not tell them to lift their eyes toward distant horizons. Because students—and their parents—struggle for flawlessness, we do not
make them responsible for their mistakes. As a result, colleges now are
holding students in childhood rather than helping them to grow up.

Some of the consequences of our failures to help students grow, personally and morally, are foolish and comical; others are more deeply

troubling. When students are late turning in homework, the explanations Harvard students offer are more often medical mistreatment than personal negligence—and Harvard responds with elaborate and forgiving protocols for medical excuses. The same students who rarely take the eight-minute subway ride into Boston's entertainment district want Harvard to spend tens of thousands of dollars to bring concerts to Cambridge—and Harvard accommodates in an effort to create a campus "social life" in a bubble separate from the lively urban surround. More consequentially, Harvard indulges students' belief that they should not bear any responsibility for their genuine misfortunes. Where they have unwanted sex under murky circumstances in which they have unwisely placed themselves, Harvard supports students in regarding themselves as victims rather than helping them to move on and avoid similar mistakes in the future.

In the days before telephones and inexpensive transportation, parents living at a distance had no choice but to let go of their children when sending them off to college. While at college, a student was to grow in mind and soul—to become, in the emphatic phrase of an eighteenth-century father to his son at Harvard, "*a youth of learning and virtue.*" By the mid-nineteenth century, when students were matriculating at age eighteen rather than fifteen, they were readier to leave their parents behind. The rigid regulation of behavior, which had never worked very well anyway, gave way to a simpler set of college rules and a more dignified range of expectations. Charles William Eliot saw this relaxation as consonant with the goals of the elective curriculum. Students would have the freedom to choose their courses and the freedom also to make mistakes in their personal lives. College provided a sanctuary where mistakes, either academic or personal, would be educational and not costly. In Eliot's view,

> young men of eighteen to twenty-two should best be trained to self-control in freedom by letting them taste freedom and responsibility within the well-guarded enclosure of college life, while mistakes may be remedied and faults may be cured, where forgiveness is always easy, and repentance never comes too late.

This view of the college world no longer exists, a victim of the collision between the pursuit of excellence and consumerism. Parents no longer want their children's flaws corrected; they want them hidden.

Students coming to Harvard no longer have significant independence from their parents, and do not seem to want it. The College is more interested in making students happier than in making them better.

The objectives of parents, students, and college officials all point in the same direction—towards restraining rather than encouraging the natural development of children into adults. But what lies at the end of that road? Will graduates know what to do with their lives, and how to take responsibility for the society they will inherit? They do not know even what it means to be responsible for their own behavior. They have made few choices for themselves, and yet they have not embraced the choices that others made for them. They have not grown up, and that is the way everyone seems to want it.

How did Harvard—and other universities—get from the days of "don't trust anyone over thirty" to the "helicopter parents" of today, so called because they seem to be hovering over their children's every movement?

Some attribute the change to technology. Instantaneous and essentially free communication has radically altered students' sense of privacy and independence. I had lunch not long ago with parents who had four phone conversations with their son before lunch ended—two calls in each direction—about nothing more important than buying textbooks and passing a routine test. Because they pay their son's phone bill, they receive a monthly record of the hundreds of phone calls and text messages made and received. The information enables them not only to track whom he has been talking to, but gives them a pretty good indication of when he gets up in the morning and goes to bed at night. This way of going to college I find simply incomprehensible, yet it seems perfectly natural to many families. It is a continuation of the way they conducted themselves when their children were thirteen.

But communication technologies simply satisfy demands that already existed. I recall my first meeting with a group of freshman parents in fall 1995, back before the World Wide Web was a household word. During the question-and-answer session, I was assailed with standard complaints. "It's November and my daughter has yet to meet her advisor." "Why must the cafeteria food be so unhealthy?" And so on. Finally I called on a gentleman in the back of the room whose hand had been up for some time. "People are complaining too much. I think you are doing a great job," he said. "You should be congratulated for putting so much information on the Web so I can see it, from my office in California. Every day I can check where my son's classes will be, look at the schedule of seminars and public lectures, and locate all the buildings on the campus map. Then every night I e-mail him a list of events he can attend in the free hours in between his regular classes. It's a great service and I just wanted to thank you and to urge you to keep up the good work." I smiled weakly, but if I had been able that afternoon to get to the physical connection of Harvard to the Internet, I would have pulled the cable out of the wall.

Hovering parents are part of a large retreat from the liberation of the 1960s. This shift has been abetted by the competitive drive for excellence, by consumerism, and by socioeconomic changes in the student bodies of the great universities. But the universities themselves bear the ultimate blame. Since they are unable or unwilling to explain what education they are offering, their customers substitute and act on their own agendas.

By the early 1970s, Harvard, like most colleges, "had withdrawn from the last vestiges of the regulation of the personal lives of students," in the words of former dean John Fox. Parents were no more authoritative over students' lives than was the College. The old expectation that students should develop a sense of responsibility for their own actions remained, but neither the College nor families—nor, by this time, the schools from which most students came to Harvard—provided much structure in which students could learn to come to terms with those responsibilities.

By 1984, Fox observed a shift. The language of "loving" and "caring" that had come out of the 1960s had gradually been translated into an institutional value, replacing the language of regulation and self-sufficiency. Fox observed "increased expectations that the College should adopt a more 'interventionist,' even 'protective,' role vis à vis its students." College advisors were being called on for personal advice that would have come from families a generation earlier. As the divorce rate rose in America, families themselves became more complicated than they used to be. When parents remarry, complex rivalries entangle students, and students may hope that the college can be a neutral source of counsel. Some of the most overly involved parents are those attempting to show their new spouses how very much they care for their newly acquired offspring.

A pediatrician who has seen several generations of students pass through college traced the sharpest increase in dependency to the arrival of the first children raised mostly in daycare. Daycare centers, she theorized, institutionalize obedience to order and ritualize dispute resolution more effectively than happens in most families, and the effects of that early training were still visible years later. Many students raised in daycare do not react to personal reversals in college by seeking authority figures to straighten things out. Still, the daycare experience, for our more dependent students, was likely the first step in a childhood of scheduled, regulated, and planned activities that have left them unskilled in working out their problems, or even finding joy, without adult supervision.

By the mid-1980s, the professors who had been students in the late 1960s began to assume significant power in universities. Being a professor after experiencing the chaotic breakdown of institutional values in a university is like being a chef in a restaurant where you ate when you used to think it was trendy. You can't forget the old feeling now that you are in charge of the menu, but your customers aren't interested in what the place was like in your day. It is a sad spectacle to see professors, deans, and presidents gravely proclaiming freedom, flexibility, choice—few rules and no standards—to today's students, apparently unaware that their point of reference is their own undergraduate education during the 1960s. The moaning by professors who have never left the ivory tower about the careerism of today's students and their lack of revolutionary zeal can be simply embarrassing. The echoes of the sixties are there in the speeches of Harvard's leaders in more nuanced forms. When President Summers said in his inaugural address, "Our most enduring tradition is that we are forever young," he was expressing a view of tradition that was a product of the 1960s. And when he set a goal of "assuring that the academic experience is at the center of the college experience," he was reacting against the degradation of academic standards that occurred in the 1960s.

Most families today are practical about what they want from Harvard. Those who are paying full freight, $41,675 for the 2005–2006 academic year, expect the university to treat them like customers, not like acolytes in some temple they are privileged to enter. Parents who have interceded for their children all through school are disinclined to accept the superior wisdom of the university when they see things they do not like—even though Harvard may have been the place they desperately wanted their children to attend. In an extreme example of parental entitlement, a mother moving her son into his freshman dormitory room a few years ago encountered the boy's roommate, who had already arrived. Discomfited by the roommate's dreadlocks, the mother offered him thousands of dollars to vacate the room. Having invested as much as she had to get her son this far, I suppose she was thinking, why not invest a few thousand more to get him off to a good start?

Students from the other end of the economic scale bring a different perspective to their freshman dormitories. Their families have made enormous financial sacrifices to enable them to attend Harvard. Even though the neediest of these families need not pay Harvard a single dollar, their children work during the academic year to send money home. The well-to-do may see Harvard as a shopping mall, but low-income students see it as a lifeboat, a vessel on which to escape the shortage of money that is all they and their parents have ever known. They consequently see their educational opportunities in terms of the careers they will follow and the connections they will make.

Of course, there is nothing inevitable in either of these economic perspectives on the university. In fact, neither is irrational; they are simply not the whole or even the principal story of the relationship between the student and the college. Students and families cannot be blamed for thinking of undergraduate education in consumerist terms if the university does not offer an alternative vision. When Harvard's ambitions for its College are limited to making students happy and letting them do as they please, students and their families unsurprisingly think it is the university's responsibility to give them what they want.

On March 29, 2005, the *Boston Globe* reported that Harvard students were less satisfied with their college experience than students at almost all of the other COFHE institutions, a group of thirty-one elite private colleges. The data, which were supposed to be confidential, came from an internal Harvard memorandum that had been leaked to the newspaper. So not only were students unhappy with Harvard—Harvard knew it.

The reaction of the Harvard administration was to declare that it was aware of student dissatisfaction and was working on it. Indeed, the data on student dissatisfaction had been driving the entire College agenda. "That's exactly what we've been focusing on for the past three years," dean of the College Benedict H. Gross explained.

This effort extends back to 2002, when Dean Kirby advanced "freedom" for students as an important curricular objective. Faculty tend to go along with clarion calls for freedom by university leaders. The more freedom there is for students to study what they wish, the more freedom there is for professors to teach what they wish. The fewer required courses there are for students, the fewer students there are to whom the professors must teach things the students do not wish to learn but should. This is a limited view of freedom. True freedom is not the freedom to do as one wishes without consequence, but a balance between choice and responsibility, between self and society. Those making plans for today's Harvard College use words such as "freedom," "flexibility," "choice," and "opportunity" all the time, but they have forgotten what freedom is. Their goal is simply to raise the satisfaction numbers on the surveys of student life.

Excellence and the consumer culture

Harvard students are used to excelling, and most have gotten where they are because their parents have both pressed them and supported them. Parents and students alike have become accustomed to focusing on tangible goals and proximal wants. In the absence of rigorous thought about what is best for students in the long run, the development of the college into a shopping mall will go unchallenged.

I do not favor feeding students bread and water. Cultivated human comforts nourish the life of the mind. The problem with focusing on physical amenities, on parties and on which bands come to concerts on campus, is that doing so validates students' myopia. When the university speaks to them more about social diversions than about the purpose of an undergraduate education, it encourages students to be petty and cynical about their dissatisfactions. It also enables the faculty to continue ignoring students, since the administration is so visibly devoting its energies to satisfying them in other ways.

When I became dean, I did not expect that the College would be so involved in students' personal relationships and intimacies with their peers. I was surprised that both parents and students would expect the College to structure students' private lives and also to refrain from passing judgment on them, and surprised that I would follow in the footsteps of other deans in overseeing a lot of talk about sex but would break new ground by writing a *Crimson* column about love.

I well remembered being left in Harvard Yard by my parents in September 1964 and realizing that I was, at last, free from their oversight.

I remembered also the fights, sometimes bitter and sometimes petty, by which my contemporaries wrested control over their private lives from the college administration. I could never have imagined that the modern Harvard student would demand institutionally structured social life, complete with detailed rules of personal conduct, laid down by the Harvard faculty and enforced by the dean.

Student drinking provides vivid illustrations of the tension between universities' educational mission and their customer-satisfaction practices. In the realm of alcohol policies, societal forces push back against the principle that students should be given what they want. Drunken students are problematic at most colleges, and Harvard is no exception. Most nonacademic misbehavior at Harvard—fistfights, destruction of property, sexual assaults—is fueled by alcohol. The possibility of accidental death is always real, especially since Harvard does not control the private Final Clubs* where some of the most serious drinking takes place. Local bars and restaurants have done their risk-reward calculations and have a relaxed attitude about serving underage Harvard students; the Cambridge police usually have more serious problems than breaking up consensual relationships between moneyed Harvard students and taxpaying Cambridge businesses. But the university's risks are much greater, because the media and local politicians love to make an example of Harvard, and Harvard is always dependent on the goodwill of the city. So Harvard tends to discourage underage drinking at its own parties, whatever may be going on behind the closed doors of dormitory rooms.

On the other hand, "inadequate social life" as defined by students today is synonymous with "nonalcoholic parties." Student leaders take any attempt to moderate drinking as an insult to be countered by even harder drinking. The closest I came to starting a riot as dean was when I ruled that only cans and bottles, and not kegs, could be brought to the Harvard-Yale football game. I could not have excited more controversy if I had banned crosses from the Memorial Church.

---

*These old all-male clubs used to operate in coordination with the College administration, but Harvard severed relations with them in the 1980s over their refusal to admit women. One is the Owl Club, from which Senator Ted Kennedy resigned in early 2006 in the midst of the Supreme Court confirmation hearings for Samuel Alito, whose association with an all-male Princeton organization Kennedy had challenged. The term "Final Club" has nothing to do with final examinations; there used to be "Waiting Clubs," which students might join before being admitted to one of the more selective Final Clubs.

Given the panic over student complaints about social life, Harvard decided in 2005 not only to hire a "fun czar," a special assistant to the dean in charge of social programming, but to open a pub. Indeed, the order came down from the top, or close to it. The deputy dean of the college explained, "Bill Kirby wants a pub, we've got to give it a try."

There is a fine tradition of rulers calming their citizens by providing entertainment and alcohol, but most emperors did not have to go up against Cambridge bars. Of course, with an endowment of more than twenty-five billion dollars, Harvard is in a position to compete with the local public houses, and the inaugural "pub night" made plain that it would not be undersold. Beers were a dollar.

Still, underage drinking is illegal. Desperate for approval by its students, Harvard now comes very close to saying that underage drinking is acceptable as long as you don't get caught—rather like jaywalking. School officials decided to situate the pub among the freshman dormitories and at a distance from the Houses where students live after their freshman year. It even put Pub Night on the calendar of freshman events, with a disclaimer that only those over twenty-one would be served beer. There are, each year, one or two twenty-one-year-old freshmen; the other 1,648 students reading the freshman events calendar are underage. Buried in the freshman handbook are more cautions to students "to take reasonable measures to prevent underage guests from obtaining alcohol at parties," but the real message is the winking one in the freshman events calendar. Faced with such ambiguous signals about alcohol, students have trouble knowing which university regulations and exhortations to take seriously.

Harvard students are used to being excellent, and Harvard parents know, or think they know, what it takes to make them that way. They should have no visible flaws; any recorded test score should be as high as it can be made; and information about them should be controlled, either promulgated or suppressed, depending on whether it is positive or negative. The Harvard admissions office is commonly blamed for these parental behaviors, though anyone familiar with Harvard students knows that there are plenty of students whose defects must have been known in advance, along with their extraordinary merits. High school guidance counselors, under pressure from parents to make students seem perfect when they apply to college, obscure students' weaknesses and create expectations that colleges will be similarly artful in their record-keeping in order to help students along the next step of their careers.

Whatever their origin, parents' expectations that students will continue to be flawless undercut the larger objectives of a college education. If the purpose of a Harvard education is to turn out graduates who are as perfect coming out as they were coming in, only at the next rung up the academic ladder, injuries and disappointments are inevitable. I used to tell freshman parents, when I met them as a group during move-in weekend, to be prepared for the fact that fully 50 percent of their children would graduate in the bottom half of their Harvard class. They laughed in September but probably found the thought less funny when the first grades were reported.

Students have always complained about grades; they may do it more today, and more insistently, but student complaints are not novelties. What is entirely new is that parents now routinely call professors about their children's grades. Sometimes they want to take up the cudgels on their children's behalf; sometimes they want to provide excuses and explanations that ought to be provided by the students themselves, if at all. A dispute about whether a B+ paper should really be an A– can quickly turn into a family melodrama, with the professor drawn unwillingly into a conspiracy about who is supposed to be keeping secrets from whom. There are right and principled ways to handle such situations, which give dignity to students and help them learn to take responsibility for their own affairs. But the right way of doing things is much more likely to make students and their parents unhappy and to precipitate appeals to higher authorities.

Parental involvement in grade-grubbing is obnoxious and saddening, but manipulation of students' emotional lives in pursuit of the flawless transcript can be destructive. The perfect children described in college applications may turn out to be deeply troubled in the flesh. Parents intimidate teachers and schools from revealing aberrant behavior if it can be attributed to a psychiatric condition. Mental disorders, it is argued, constitute disabilities that should not affect admissions decisions and should therefore be invisible in college applications.

Parents don't trust college admissions offices to ignore signs of serious emotional instability, so they go to great lengths to see that nothing of their children's fragility is revealed—even if hiding emotional conditions causes them to go untreated. Parents tend not to reveal such problems even in the letter Harvard invites parents to send after the child has irrevocably been admitted. "We wanted to give her the opportunity for a fresh start," such parents typically say, when called by a dean dealing with a student who has broken down in a way that, it turns out, the student had broken down many times before. A student once collapsed within hours of being delivered to Cambridge, and the parents, called on their cell phone while they were yet driving home, had little more to say than "We never knew what to do with her. You admitted her—she is your problem now."

In the saddest cases, parents trying to obtain advantages instead cripple their children's development of personal agency. A student who turned in a plagiarized paper provided as an excuse a novel variation on the old "I turned in my notes by mistake" argument. He suffered, he said, from a disabling inability to write. The student's typist must have typed up his notes rather than his actual paper, and he turned in what the typist gave him without checking it. The typist, known only by her first name, had disappeared from the face of the earth. The processes meant to accommodate this young man's disability had instead victimized him. His family assured us that they would take the College to court for failing to accommodate his disability if he were found guilty of plagiarism. It was not his fault that the paper the professor received, delivered by the student's own hand and with the student's name on it, was the work of others.

There are so many levels of indirection in this young man's escape from responsibility that I wonder what he has learned from the experience. His family and his college may have taught him how to make the system work for him, but did they teach him anything about character?

Even in students' leisure time, the College is expected to coddle students when they should be learning about life by trial and error. In my first term as dean, the mother of a female student called me to complain about the formal dance being planned in her daughter's House. It was an outrage, the mother thought, that Harvard would expect her daughter to buy a formal gown so she could go to the dance.

The first thought that flashed through my mind was how bizarre it was that a mother would call the dean about her daughter's formal dress. I wouldn't have spoken to my own mother for a year if she had called the dean to complain that I had no clothes to wear. "Mrs. Hovering, please don't blame me," I felt like telling her. "I don't plan those dances—they are organized by the House Committees. It was *my* generation that rebelled to end the coat-and-tie rule in the dining halls. If your daughter doesn't want the dance to be formal, tell her to talk to her elected representatives, whose idea this was."

I didn't actually say this. Maybe the student really did have no money and was embarrassed in front of her friends who did. Maybe I was being hard on the mother. After all, she was not my charge, her daughter was. Maybe the daughter was just as embarrassed as I would have been, and my efforts should go toward helping the daughter deal with her mother.

As I came to realize, the mother and daughter were more likely conforming to standard types. Probably the daughter called the mother to ask her what to do, and the mother replied that she would take care of it, just as she had taken care of her daughter's problems since the first day of kindergarten. The daughter may have had no idea how to speak up for herself. She may not even have been able to ask her fellow students what to do, from fear of revealing her incapacity. The institution should solve her problem, and her mother would intervene on her behalf.

Discipline parts ways with education

If a child is viewed as flawless, or at least as having no flaws that anyone should know about, the most that can be hoped for in terms of personal development is that no blemishes will be added or uncovered during the four years in Cambridge. Freshmen, in this Rousseauian view of adolescent development, are perfect pre-adults. Moreover, they and their parents know what they should look like when they graduate. Their ontogeny is deterministic. They will come out as first-year law or medical students or investment bankers, depending on plans already laid down, but a larval doctor should not turn into a mature novelist, even a good one. College is not about self-discovery, not about openness to a fundamental re-creation of self. It is about execution of a prior design.

Since students are perfect as freshmen, they should not be imperfect as seniors. They should graduate with the same clean transcripts as the ones with which they entered, but one notch higher up the ladder of academic degrees. Any flaws discovered along the way must be the result of misunderstandings or unfairness or sabotage. Instead of taking responsibility for their actions, students shift responsibility to others. Efforts to press students to look inward to understand the source of their behavior meet stout resistance. Character growth and moral education are all but impossible under these circumstances.

Parental protectionism is not a new phenomenon. LeBaron Russell Briggs, dean of Harvard College in the late nineteenth century, complained of it:

> To the dean of a large college . . . it soon becomes clear that parents are accountable for more undergraduate shortcomings than they or their sons suspect. . . . "I have spent an hour today with Jones's father," said a college president in a formidable case of discipline. "I have conceived a better opinion of the son after meeting the father,"—and the experience is repeated year by year. Five minutes, or two minutes, with a father or a mother may reveal the chief secret of a young man's failure or misconduct, and may fill the heart of an administrative officer with infinite compassion. . . . "I told my boy," says a father, "that I did not myself believe in [vice]; but if he went into that sort of thing, he must not go off with the crowd, but must do it quietly and in a gentlemanly way."

Parents accustomed to keeping their children's high school records unblemished have the same agenda for their college records. I am disheartened to see the members of my generation going to such lengths to mistrust their children's instincts to be honest. While I was chair of Harvard's disciplinary board, a student was charged with changing some of the answers in his already-graded exam paper before submitting it for regrading. The professor, already suspicious for some reason, had photocopied the exam before returning it to the student, and the student seemed to have been caught red-handed. But a few days later, he produced a letter from his father, swearing that it was the father who had, in an idle moment of intellectual fun, erased and corrected some of the answers on his son's paper. The father, we were given to believe, made the alterations while the son was not around, unaware that his son would be having the exam regraded. He used indistinguishable handwriting and did not tell his son what he had done. This experience caused my soul to reach out across the years to Dean Briggs's.

But the fault lies not just with the consumer culture of Harvard's families. The university has lost, indeed has willingly surrendered, its moral authority to shape the souls of its students. Harvard wants students to be safe and to be healthy, but security and therapy are the limits of its ambitions. Harvard articulates no ideals of what it means to be a good person, as opposed to a well person.

Harvard retains a unique structure for student discipline, a holdover from the end of the nineteenth century. Called the Administrative Board of Harvard College, it oversees the administration of all College rules—the rules about showing up on registration day, the rules about plagiarism, and the rules about fistfights. Its members are mostly young deans who live among the students, together with a few more senior deans and a professor or two. Students tend to think of it as the court where they will be tried and sentenced for serious offenses. For most of its history, however, it has seen itself as Harvard's agent of practical moral education, the College's best chance to see to it that students who lie or cheat or try to settle arguments by physical force will, in later life when the stakes are higher, pause before trying something similar—pause to consider not just the consequences but also what their actions say about who they are.

Seen in this way, college discipline is only incidentally about punishment. It is mainly about responding to the circumstances of individual students in the way that will do them the most good during late adolescence and early adulthood while they are in the relatively protected environment of the college. The disciplinary system is not there to weed out bad apples, though it has to do that every now and then. Almost all Harvard students graduate and go on to lead productive lives. The Board is, as Dean John Fox described it in 1981, "an integral part of the educational enterprise." It evolved to maximize its impact as an agent of an educational community, not to mimic the adversarial process of a criminal proceeding. Students who come before the Board are not generally viewed as enemies of the College, even though there is good reason to think they have violated its standards of behavior. They are viewed, rather, as future members of Congress, business executives, teachers, doctors, scientists, and lawyers. Harvard expects that its alumni can be saved from committing dreadful misdeeds in the future, when they will have far more power, if as students they are pressed to take responsibility for the impact and meaning of their actions.

Dean Fox explained the two basic assumptions supporting the Administrative Board's old educational theory of College discipline.

The first is that any student enrolled in the College belongs here. In many other institutions, a primary task of discipline or academic standard-setting is to decide whether a student should be allowed to continue in that college, or whether he should be removed and not permitted to graduate. In contrast, at Harvard we view a student who comes before the Board as someone who needs the Board's assistance on the way to attaining a degree that he will, in due course, complete. The Board's business is fundamentally educational, to help the student make progress toward his degree.

The second assumption is that students will be honest and forthcoming at all times with respect to their own behavior and will account for that behavior when asked to do so. The assumption of honesty helps students understand that accomplishments have meaning only insofar as they are achieved honestly.

There are broader senses in which the Board carries on the educational enterprise of the College. In most of its weekly business, the Board is engaged in a task that some might refer to as moral education. Obviously, the Board's objective is not to instill specific moral beliefs. Rather the Board provides a process through which the College reaffirms the very general institutionally sanctioned practices, procedures, and rules that provide a framework within which different moral values and goals can be acted upon and pursued. Honesty, and fidelity to agreements, are among the fundamental expectations of this framework. . . . The educational experience of coming to terms with one's actions, their consequences for others, and their significance for oneself, is the most intense form of moral education provided by the College.

Today's consumer culture, in which the college's job is to make its students happy rather than to educate them, threatens the old idea that the disciplinary system should make students into better people. It is easier to respond to students based on how unhappy they will be, and how far reports of their unhappiness are likely to spread, than on what they need to learn. Because the Administrative Board has always done its best to understand the origins of students' behavior, their schooling and family history and prior behavior have always been used to inform decisions about what students need to learn and how best they can learn it. But with so much personal information available to the members, it is easily misused to provide excuses that will bury underlying problems rather than solve them. A Chinese student might be excused of plagiarism because it is endemic in his native culture; a *Crimson* editor might be sanctioned less sharply than another student for the same malfeasance because of the power the press can bring against the university administration. When only the short run is considered, many undergraduate offenses become victimless crimes.

The University is losing its moral authority over undergraduates in another way—by failing to respond to faculty malfeasances with the same high-mindedness with which it treats undergraduates. In 1997 the federal government charged Harvard and certain individuals, including star economics professor Andrei Shleifer, with fraud. The government alleged that Shleifer and others had made improper private investments in Russia while advising the Russian government on the establishment of a Russian capitalist economy, under a contract between the United States and Harvard. For years the charges were stoutly contested, but in 2004 a federal judge handed down a decision that Shleifer had, in fact, conspired to defraud the government. As a trial loomed on the penalties the defendants owed, they settled the claim in August 2005 without admitting anything by agreeing to pay the U.S. government more than $30 million, including $26.5 million from Harvard and $2 million from Shleifer.

Harvard had an opportunity to settle more quickly. Noted economic columnist David Warsh tied the last years of delay to the close personal relationship between President Summers and the professor at the center of the controversy. The *Crimson* reported that Summers had stayed with Shleifer when he came to Cambridge to interview for the presidency. They remained close as the case became more serious. Around the time Summers became president, after the investigation had been under way for several years, Summers pressed Jeremy Knowles, dean of the Faculty, to see that Shleifer did not leave Harvard because of the tempest swirling around him. Shleifer was reported to have broken the fast with Summers on Yom Kippur, the Jewish day of atonement, three months after Shleifer had been found to have defrauded the government in his Harvard role.

The Administrative Board's expectation of openness and honesty did not seem to have been met—and the cost in dollars to Harvard probably rose significantly as a result. President Summers recused himself at the beginning of his presidency; his only public statements on what the judge called Shleifer's "apparent self-dealing" came when he was deposed during the government's civil case. As to whether Shleifer's investments had been improper because of his conflict of interest, Summers suggested that Shleifer's actions would not have been problematic under "Russian mores and Russian practices"; the Russians "would have, in part, valued advisers more extensively if they were more involved in actual private sector activities." Localizing ethics in this way seems rather akin to excusing a Chinese student's plagiarism at Harvard because plagiarism is endemic in China. Pressed on his own views about whether it was "a conflict of interest or otherwise improper to make investments in a country just because you're providing advice to the government of that country," Summers recognized no ethical yellow lights. Reflecting on his own experience in government, he said "there was no aura of wrongness of any kind that would be associated with providing advice on a financial issue in which one had an interest."

As of early 2006, Harvard itself has had nothing to say about Shleifer, and he remains in good standing on the Harvard Faculty. David Warsh, a former *Boston Globe* columnist whose economics newsletter followed the affair closely, put the question squarely to Harvard once the legal case had been settled. "Why not acknowledge obvious wrongdoing? Why prefer intelligence to integrity?"

Harvard professors' reputation for integrity has taken other blows in recent years. For example, Charles Ogletree and Laurence Tribe, both law professors, allegedly misused the words of others in books they had authored. In response to the charges, each man promptly acknowledged making an inadvertent mistake and apologized. In each case a university committee investigated and reported its conclusion that the professor had made a scholarly transgression, but that the error was inadvertent and did not rise to the level of plagiarism. And in each case the dean of the Law School—with President Summers joining in Tribe's case—issued a formal statement noting the seriousness of the professor's scholarly error.

It is not known what punishment, if any, either Ogletree or Tribe received, beyond the humiliation of having their work revealed as not entirely their own. Harvard's actions did not satisfy some critics but on balance seem appropriate. In both Ogletree's and Tribe's cases, the offense appears to have been what would be called "misuse of sources" in an undergraduate case, not the more serious transgression of "plagiarism." It is certainly not what is hoped of Harvard professors, but their acknowledgments of their mistakes, their apologies, and the fact that a high-level university committee was delegated to conduct an investigation and came back with a conclusion in line with what the professors had already acknowledged, all support a sense that some kind of due process and responsible justice was carried out.

The Shleifer matter is strikingly different. A federal judge found that Shleifer had conspired to defraud the government, but Shleifer has not acknowledged doing anything wrong. In fact, he stated after the case was settled that he was sure he would have won if he had the resources to continue his legal defense. Harvard has given no indication that any response is under consideration. The Faculty of Arts and Sciences Committee on Professional Conduct would seem to have interest in such a matter, but a former member of that committee described its role to me as limited to determining the facts. The facts already being known, it would fall to Dean Kirby, dean of the Faculty of Arts and Sciences, to "take whatever action he . . . considers appropriate," as the committee's charge states. Dean Kirby has made no statement about Andrei Shleifer at all. It would not be unusual for the university to treat personnel matters in confidence, but the Tribe and Ogletree cases, which involved offenses far less serious than Shleifer's, establish the principle that a dean and even the president will sometimes publicly express disapproval of a professor's conduct, and in advance of such a conclusion may signal that the university is concerned and is investigating.

A year and a half after the fraud finding against Shleifer and five months after the settlement, Harvard remained silent. Observers wondering how to account for the difference in the treatment of Shleifer, Ogletree, and Tribe concluded that Harvard, if it was planning to respond to the Shleifer affair at all, was considering its words and actions with reserve it had not used with Ogletree and Tribe. None of the plausible explanations for Harvard's long silence puts the university in an honorable light. Perhaps defiance is a better way to escape institutional opprobrium than are confession and apology. Perhaps being an acknowledged young star (Shleifer won the Bates prize, for the foremost economist under age forty, while the case against him was working its way through federal court) provides protection not available to scholars who are older and past the peak of their careers. And being a close personal friend of the president probably doesn't hurt.

The relativism with which Harvard has dealt with the Shleifer case undermines Harvard's moral authority over its students. As President Derek Bok said in 1987:

> If campus authorities are reluctant to explain their policies and unwilling to answer critics, they will only seem morally callous and leave themselves all the more vulnerable to those who seek to discredit their actions and charge them with shabby motives. In this event, any effort to emphasize the importance of moral education will soon fall prey to cynicism and distrust.

The Administrative Board emerged from a tradition of direct faculty oversight of all student affairs. Until the late nineteenth century, the Faculty as a whole acted to discipline individual students. There were, of course, many fewer students and many fewer faculty members than today, so the Faculty could act as a committee of the whole. The body took up matters as petty as a student's loud music in the same meetings in which it debated great educational policy questions.

On October 21, 1890, Harvard was reorganized; the separate Faculties of the College and of the Graduate School were unified. At the same time, the governing boards changed the statutes of the university so that the "Faculty might delegate any of its powers relating to ordinary matters of administration and discipline to administrative boards consisting of members of the Faculty." The Faculty of Arts and Sciences did in fact delegate all disciplinary matters to its Administrative Boards, "subject, however, to the statutory limitation that no student should be dismissed or expelled from the University except by a two-thirds vote of the Faculty itself."

The Administrative Board technically remains a subcommittee of the Faculty, but the professors are less and less involved with the administration of college affairs. On the rare occasions when they are called on for one of those two-thirds votes on a student disciplinary matter, they are all but incapable of judging an individual student on the basis of their past experience; they have to construct a theoretical framework first.

Since 1953 the officers with immediate responsibility for the welfare of students have been deans resident in the various dormitories and Houses. Traditionally Harvard has required those deans to have Ph.D.'s and sufficient academic stature so that they could teach their specialties within the regular academic departments. Fox noted that he had "made a steady effort to attract academics to [these resident dean positions], largely in order to preserve the character of the Board as a committee of the teaching Faculty."

Harvard College has gone through a drastic reorganization since I left the dean's office in 2003. Having found his responsibilities to be "just too much," the Dean of Harvard College delegated many of them to a deputy dean, whose degrees are in business and who had previously run a business school. A dean of residential life, formerly the director of "Greek Life" at another university, was brought in to supervise the dean of freshmen and the Masters of the Houses—while finishing a degree in education. Several other experienced administrative deans with Ph.D.'s in arts and sciences have left Harvard College for senior roles in other universities. While Harvard was searching for an advising dean in 2005, two long-serving Harvard hands departed to head advising programs at other colleges. Harvard instead hired as its own advising dean a former private-industry education consultant with less university experience than either of those who had left.

In a little noticed but deeply significant shift, Harvard has dropped the Ph.D. requirement even for the deans of the residential Houses. Deans no longer need to be academics to interpret and explain college rules to students and to help confused students come to grips with their place in the academy. "Experience in student affairs" has become an alternative qualification to a Ph.D. A faculty member explaining the change cited experience with "issues of wellness, issues of race, and so forth" as the sort of expertise that would qualify deans in the future. The implication is that there are not enough Ph.D.'s who are competent to address such issues, and that in the new vision of Harvard College, professionals in "student affairs" can provide guidance to students as well as teachers and scholars can.

So here is where Harvard finds itself: The first "fun czar" moved on to a position planning the campus pub. A new fun czar replaced him, and the 2005–2006 academic year at Harvard began with "the 'Harvard State Fair,' complete with carnival foods, bluegrass bands, a mechanical bull, games, pie-eating contest, and a dunk tank." Both fun czars have been joined by a new alcohol czar. The Harvard administration that began with President Summers's promise that "we will assure more of what lies at the heart of the educational experience—direct contact between teacher and student" has instead created a nonacademic bureaucracy to manage and entertain the student body. The pediatrician who wondered if daycare was responsible for the dependency of today's college students may have had a point. The new way to run Harvard resembles a daycare center for college students.

Rape at Harvard

There remains one reality of college life for which the daycare model does not work well. When one student is accused of raping another, the College cannot make everyone happy. The crime of rape is not victimless, and society has an interest so compelling that the legal system can intervene. In its handling of rape cases, the educational failures of today's Harvard are glaringly evident. Instead of teaching students to take responsibility for themselves, the College indulges their dependency on adult authority and creates an atmosphere of irresponsibility.

Until the 1970s, the term "rape" was almost never used to describe a sexual incident involving a man and woman voluntarily alone together. In the absence of witnesses or serious injuries, women had little recourse against innuendos that they had consented to sex and then changed their minds, or had entrapped men from whom they sought vengeance or money. If a woman had consented to be alone with a man, society showed little interest in what happened to her afterward. The women's movement drastically shifted the discourse of responsibility, and college campuses, where sexual exploration so often begins, experimented with progressive thinking about rape. Universities took up the challenge of advancing social justice in this area as they have successfully done in many others, and as in the case of efforts to advance racial equality, universities responded under the influence of politics as well as principle.

During the 1990s, the date-rape issue interacted in unexpected ways with universities' increasing paternalism toward their students. Universities are expected simultaneously to care for their students and to fix their problems, to leave them alone to do what they wish, and to adjudicate allegations that male students have raped female acquaintances. The college is expected to give the woman a fair chance of success in such complaints; no one wants the old world in which women were nearly voiceless and men could walk away from almost any incident involving a female friend.

The cost of trying to meet all these expectations simultaneously is to turn the old assumptions about women's responsibility for their sexual misfortunes upside down. Having advanced beyond the presumption that women have no one to blame but themselves, colleges now treat women as weaklings who should bear no responsibility for what befalls them rather than share responsibility for what happens during sexual encounters. Like many colleges, Harvard backed up its theory of acquaintance rape with carefully negotiated regulations paralleling but not duplicating those of the criminal-justice system. Despite its good intentions, Harvard has failed all its duties in this area. It does not help students grow up and learn to take responsibility for their lives. It does not protect the innocent, and it does not create realistic expectations for its institutional competence to define, ascertain, and punish guilt. And it fails to insist on honorable behavior by both men and women.

Anything at Harvard that involves either violence or sex provokes media attention. But I did not appreciate the explosiveness of the combination until the summer of 2002. My wife and I were on vacation at our place in northwest Montana, on the edge of the largest wilderness area in the lower forty-eight states and about an hour from the spot where the Unabomber had holed up. Having run low on conversation partners after a week or so, we dropped in on the fellow who made the antler chandeliers that hang in our house. I'll call him Buck. Buck is a fine craftsman and is always good for a story about the past year's trends in the antler business.

Buck talked for a while about how hard it was getting to find six matched moose antlers, when he stopped and said, "Oh yes! You're from Harvard, aren't you?" I didn't remember telling him that, but it is hard to keep secrets in Montana townships. In any case, I am sure he had no idea what I did there. "Yes," I acknowledged, expecting to hear next about some distant relative who was applying to college. "Well," he went on, "you should be very proud of your university. Those new procedures you are using for rape cases are a big improvement over the old ones."

"How did you hear about *that?*" I gasped. "Oh, it was on 'The Abrams Report' last night," he answered. Buck had a satellite dish on his house in the woods. I remembered that I had let pass the invitation to appear on the show, but apparently the producer had found individuals on both sides of the issue, neither from Harvard, to fight it out on TV. I recall feeling two contrary emotions. The first was, *There is no place to hide.* The other was, *I'm so glad there are sensible people left somewhere in the world.*

Acquaintance rape was the most difficult issue I faced as dean. Intense emotions surround every case. First impressions of the principals might produce profound sympathy for either or both but little reliable guidance in determining the truth. Confidential hearings might reveal the most personal kinds of information in clinical detail, and the students involved and their friends and lawyers might report incomplete versions to newspaper and magazine reporters. Reports of Harvard's response might surface on national television for all the world to judge, while the university remained determined not to attack or discredit its own students in public. Far more than in any other area of student life, students and parents resorted to manipulation and anger to influence the course of Harvard's procedures.

Yet these cases were uniquely troubling for another reason. Rape cases were the only ones for which it could be impossible to find a "correct" course of action. In other domains disinterested parties usually could help determine a just if imperfect way of proceeding, or at least a compromise that could not be far wrong. The problem was then to face or to mute the hostility of those disappointed with the resolution. In rape cases there was often no middle ground and yet no plainly correct answer. For example, a Harvard student accused of rape should not have his education interrupted unless he is known to be guilty; but if he remains housed on campus until his guilt can be adjudicated, Harvard might be allowing a rapist to endanger other students for months. Even if the university can find a wise balance of rights on some issues, on others Harvard is not a free agent to decide what it thinks best. Laws of the state overlap with Harvard's rules, and they are not necessarily the same where both apply.

The state has found rape a difficult crime to prosecute because it is rarely witnessed by anyone but the principals. Advances in criminal forensics have made it easier to be certain that a suspect was the one who committed the act, but in college rape cases identity is usually not in doubt. The problem, rather, is to ascertain whether the intercourse was consensual. The ambiguities of consent have played out in a political surround in which some of society's structures have progressed faster than others. Some colleges have tried to accelerate society's evolution toward women's equality, and to make the question of consent less uncertain, by promulgating rules about sexual conduct that go far beyond the legal code. Most famously, Antioch College required in 1992 that each individual sexual act, from kisses to intercourse, had to receive "willing and verbal consent" or be punishable by the college judicial system. Harvard has been, for better or worse, behind the times. But that is nothing new; Harvard has long been a follower in women's education.

At the time of Charles William Eliot's installation as president of Harvard in 1869, there were stirrings elsewhere about women going to college, but Eliot found the idea of women at Harvard scandalous. "The difficulties involved in a common residence of hundreds of young men and women of marriageable age are very grave," he opined. "The necessary police regulations are exceedingly burdensome." It would take several generations of social equality, Eliot thought, before it would make sense even to begin the conversations about women's "innate capacities." Thirty years later, at the inauguration of the president of Wellesley College, Eliot laid out his theory of female frailty in more detail. "It would be a wonder, indeed," he said in the major address at the inaugural, "if the intellectual capacities of women were not at least as unlike those of men as their bodily capacities are. . . . Everybody knows that the influence of women depends more than that of men on bearing, carriage, address, delicate sympathy, and innocent reserve." Even in 1899 the time for such condescension by a Harvard president had passed. Carey Thomas, the president of Bryn Mawr College, seethed as she listened in the audience.

With such leadership at Harvard, it is little wonder that women's education got off to a slow start. In 1872 a group of determined Boston and Cambridge women opened an "Annex" to Harvard College for the education of young women. Harvard professors earned extra income by repeating their lectures to women students under an arrangement that continued even after the Annex became Radcliffe College in 1893.

I remember the wife of the great mathematician Garrett Birkhoff telling me that Radcliffe was once a "gravy train" for professors, because of the money they could earn by walking a few blocks and repeating what they had just told their Harvard students.

Harvard remained stoutly opposed to coeducation well into the twentieth century. While my mother was attending the University of Michigan Medical School in 1935, Harvard Medical School was still a decade away from admitting women. Radcliffe women were finally allowed to sit in the same classroom with male undergraduates in 1943 not because of a more progressive spirit at Harvard but through economic necessity: World War II had emptied Harvard classrooms. The secondary status for women students persisted at Harvard while every other Ivy League college was normalizing their circumstances. My wife remembers seeing ambiguous signs of progress in 1967 while she was a sophomore at Radcliffe. Because of a policy change the previous year, she was able to study in the same library as men undergraduates—but only study. Harvard had neglected to install women's rooms.

The last formal vestige of the second-class status of women undergraduates finally disappeared from Harvard in 1999. But the old view that women are the weaker sex is kept alive—now advanced by women, with the acquiescence of men. Running against the educational ideal that a college should help students mature, instilling in them a sense of personal responsibility for their actions, are well-intentioned forms of support for women that tend to infantilize them. In the 1970s, a movement began that was intended to empower and protect women and to bolster their independence; now, it teaches them that in matters sexual, they cannot control what happens to them.

Like everything else, the devolution of personal responsibility for sexual misconduct has a history—a short history by Harvard standards, but one with a few important milestones.

From a murder to a definition of rape

In 1973, a Radcliffe Fellow and wife of a Harvard professor was brutally murdered on a street near Harvard Square following an attempted rape. A Harvard committee to propose methods of improving security had been formed before the murder in response to several other incidents of violent crime, and it assumed new importance in light of this terrible event. The committee found that the crime of sexual assault had been "heavily under-reported" in the Harvard community, and the University Health Service established a facility to treat the victims of sexual assault. Some found a larger and more political meaning in this murder, arguing, for example, that the way to reduce the incidence of such crimes in the future was "to build a society in which social and sexual equality are complete and taken for granted." Only a few voices connected this crime directly to the experience of women undergraduates with their male peers, as expressed in this letter to the *Crimson:* "I shudder to think of the number of rapes that probably occur on this very campus every day, to think of the numberless forced into submission, thereby making 'actual,' 'overt,' 'illegal' rape by their partners unnecessary." The Radcliffe Office of Women's Education sponsored a conference that spring on assaults against women, inviting legal, medical, and police experts, but the focus was on street crimes.

The first "Take Back the Night" march at Harvard occurred in fall 1980, three years after similar events had started to occur on other campuses. The Harvard march rolled out a sweeping manifesto, with as much political as practical content: "Although men have always had and will continue to have the capacity to rape, women need not eternally accept the violation of their autonomy that rape represents. Now is the time for us to take back the night." "Men will never be liberated until every woman is autonomous." "Only with help will a woman come to see that she bears no responsibility for her rape, that she can turn her anger outward and effect social change." The broadside characterized rapists as strangers, not fellow students. The victim feels guilty because she feels that "[i]t is her fault that she was sleeping in her bed when a man broke in or that she walked home from the library alone." Matina Horner, the president of Radcliffe College, declined to fund the rally, reportedly stating that "she didn't think the march 'solves the problem.'" Short of the "permanent solution . . . to alter the power structure and attitudes that lead to violence against women," the rally's organizers proposed practical defenses against external assailants: floodlights, police patrols, female officers, self-defense courses, all of which appeared on campus in the subsequent years. The event became annual and, after Harvard assumed full responsibility for women's education, gained the support of the Harvard administration.

From this point on, the issue of rape flared up on a schedule approximating the four-year cycle of college generations—sometimes emerging after three years in the background, sometimes after five, but not every year. Different circumstances bring the issue to the fore in different years, and each time the college community starts from a different place in responding.

But always the question of who is responsible for what is not far in the background and is liable to spring to the foreground at any moment. In the beginning, responsibility was clear. When a stranger surprised a woman, she bore no responsibility for being raped. There were things she and others could do to help prevent recurrences, some practical and some political, but there was no doubt that the man was to blame for the actual event. The College could provide security and education, prerequisites for women's self-determination.

The first public recognition at Harvard of the fact that a rapist could be the victim's acquaintance, friend, or even lover came in 1983. Harvard's health service had published a booklet on rape since 1978, a year after Harvard assumed full responsibility for women students from Radcliffe. The 1983 edition included for the first time the notion of "acquaintance rape" and stated that such incidents were often unreported. Calling rape both "violent" and "political," those involved in producing the brochure endorsed shifting its viewpoint to that of the victim, now called the "survivor" to emphasize that "Someone who has been raped is 'no longer helpless after the crime.'" Legal proceedings were suggested as recourse, but no internal disciplinary process was mentioned. Because "acquaintance rape" and "date rape" have never been terms of the criminal-justice system, prosecutions take place under the same procedures that apply to other rapes in Massachusetts and can lead to the same penalties, including lengthy imprisonment. However, no criminal case of this kind seems to have been successfully prosecuted against a Harvard student during these years.

By 1986, Response, a peer counseling group formed three years earlier, stated that it was receiving "one to two phone calls a night" about date rapes and other forms of sexual misconduct against Harvard students. The counselors, "often themselves survivors of rape or sexual harassment," reported that "the majority of calls concerned rapes, and . . . the majority of rapists were other Harvard students." Commenting on the difficulties of using the College's disciplinary process to seek redress, one student counselor said, "Unfortunately, most of the time it's not worth prosecuting because the incident happened too long ago, and there's no proof." Ellen Porter Honnet, the responsible assistant dean of the College, described the problem as being that "two students with different interpretations of the same series of events make it very difficult to determine blame, even though one's sympathies lie with the victim."

Responding to a student petition, Harvard offered the first freshman education program in fall 1986, with a lecturer warning attendees against passivity in sexual relationships. "Most of us don't come up with assertive responses in sexual situations," she told an audience estimated at two hundred. "In a situation where you don't say anything about [sex], you contribute to your vulnerability." A college disciplinary process existed, but neither students nor deans thought it could solve many problems. There was only so much the College could do if students lost control of their sexual relations.

1990 was a watershed year. In September a *Boston Globe* story reported that date rape was widespread at Harvard and other colleges. The piece said that educational and preventative programs were universal, but so were dismissive responses from men. Some of those working on prevention continued to point to communication as a central issue. A women's peer counselor at Brown University said, "People need to be taught how to communicate during sex. This is the thing that's going to change it." The role of alcohol in date rapes was highlighted in a vignette printed in the *Globe* story—an early example of a story line heard many times since.

> A male and a female student were attending a party together. Both were quite drunk and both smoked pot. The woman's roommates heard her invite the man to her room. Some time after entering the room, the woman said she blacked out or lost her memory. What she next remembered was the man on top of her, engaging in intercourse. For some time the woman contended it was date rape. The man said she had consented during the period in which she was blacked out. The woman's roommates said they were appalled she called it rape and said they have many times gotten drunk and had sex with a man they wouldn't have touched if they were sober. After a while, the woman decided to drop the whole thing.

On October 26, 1990, a *Crimson* feature on date rape set off a firestorm. A quotation from the dean of Harvard College, L. Fred Jewett, was singled out for protest in the subsequent days. Jewett said, referring to some cases that had been heard by the Administrative Board,

"When people are drunk, they may not remember whether they said yes or not. The person that's drunk is not always clear, is not articulate, and that's why you get these cases." This statement, and one by another male dean citing the "confusion" that women can create when they "find it difficult to say a forceful no," were decried as evidence of an "archaic, blame-the-victim attitude" on the part of members of the administration. The deans were accused of lending "credence to the vicious view that saying 'no' can, 'in subtle ways,' really mean yes."

Jewett protested that his quotation was taken out of context. Neither remark was out of line with statements made by activists trying to enlighten the Harvard community about the nature of the problem. It didn't matter. Posters appeared urging students to "Attack Jewett," and a candlelight vigil and a building occupation ensued. Jewett wrote to the entire College community to clarify his views. But the blood was in the water. Jewett formed a committee to make recommendations. Known as the Date Rape Task Force, it was charged to propose reforms in the disciplinary process in allegations of date rape, as well as to plan educational and "sensitivity training" programs for members of the College administration.

The Date Rape Task Force was cochaired by Dean Honnet and one of the students responsible for the "Attack Jewett" posters, and included thirteen women and four men selected by the chairs. In February 1992, after more than a year's deliberations, the task force submitted its recommendations. It proposed to define rape as "any act of sexual intercourse that occurs without the expressed consent of the person, or is accompanied by physical force or threat of bodily injury," thus echoing a key element of the Antioch College rules: Sexual intercourse would *always* be rape, *unless* the parties had expressed their consent in advance.

The "rape unless" nature of this definition set off considerable campus debate. The student government, the undergraduate Civil Liberties Union, and the Administrative Board itself all favored a "rape if" definition, something like the legal concept—that intercourse would be rape if it occurred "despite the expressed unwillingness of the victim," in the student government's proposed language. The task force protested that such a definition put a burden on women that victims of any other crime would not be expected to bear. The "rape unless" definition would, its advocates hoped, remove all ambiguity about where responsibility lay. Future campus judicial proceedings could then be not about the cloudy question of the woman's willingness but simply about whether she had said words that would release the man from his responsibility.

Harvard's top legal scholars got into the act. On the question of whether Harvard could define rape more broadly than the state, law professor Arthur R. Miller said, "It's not irrational for the University to come up with a different definition of date rape than the state. [The school and the state] operate within different spheres." Law professor Alan Dershowitz was more cautious, noting that "The legal definition of rape is very much in flux, and very complicated. When you're drafting things like this you need professionals. [The discussion] bears all the hallmarks of enthusiastic amateurism."

The debate raged on for another year. In the end a "rape if" notion, something like that favored by the student government and the Administrative Board, won out over the version favored by the task force and the campus activists. Dean Jewett assured the Faculty that the language it was adopting was simply the legal definition of rape. As the *Crimson* described this outcome, "[T]he bureaucratization of the date rape question has . . . defanged the grass-roots campus debate and exhausted its momentum. . . . The issue goes out not with a bang but a whimper."

Rape occupies a unique position among campus offenses. It is the sole crime likely to be committed by a student that has both of two characteristics: It is an extremely serious crime, one likely to result in a significant prison sentence if proven in criminal court; and it usually cannot be pursued in court without the cooperation of the victim.

When two students embezzled almost $100,000 from the Hasty Pudding theatrical group, Harvard did not ask the organization for permission to inform the state authorities. Harvard just called the police. If a student were to commit an armed robbery, Harvard would not ask the permission of the victim before notifying the police, and the court would probably not care very much if the victim wanted the robber to get off the hook. But the College will not attempt to have a rape case taken up by criminal authorities unless that is what the victim wants, and a district attorney usually is reluctant to prosecute a rape case if the victim won't testify against her assailant.

So a victim has a choice about how to pursue an allegation of rape against a fellow undergraduate. She can take it to court, or she can take it to the Administrative Board. One choice does not preclude the other, though if the Board knows that a case is going to court, it defers consideration of the matter until the court has finished with it. People sometimes suggest that complainants should be required to forgo court as a condition for having a case taken up before the Board, but the College could not ask a student to waive her legal right to seek redress through the criminal-justice system as a condition for anything. The statute of limitations in Massachusetts for rape cases is fifteen years. For all practical purposes, therefore, it is never certain that a matter will not wind up in court; a victim's intention not to pursue a criminal action cannot bind her not to do so.

I learned early on that advising women about the choice between criminal and Board processes was one of those no-win situations of which deans' lives are full. If we steered a woman toward the Board process, we were accused of trying to hush up a terrible crime to protect the rapist's name and the University's. If we steered a woman toward the court system, we were accused of sending her into a hostile judicial environment alone and of failing to discipline a rapist we were housing under our own roof. So I directed that women who sought counsel on this question should be carefully advised of their choices, given as realistic a description as possible of the Board process and its range of possible outcomes, and referred to experts who could advise them on the nature of the criminal process of prosecuting a rape case in Massachusetts. They should then be given as much time, with as many follow-up conversations as necessary, to decide on one of these options, or neither. But they should not be pushed in one direction or the other, beyond being given realistic advice about the toll taken by the processes and their likelihood of success. That middle ground did not fully satisfy anyone.

The delicate balancing of interests—those of the accuser, the accused, the Harvard community, and the state—creates many opportunities for anger against the university. What it rarely provides is any opportunity for education, which is, after all, what the disciplinary system was designed to accomplish. Victims and their advocates want retribution, which the College cannot mete out on anything like the scale available to the state. The accused, unsurprisingly, cares most about vindication, or at least escaping punishment—especially, of course, if he is not guilty. When the college has to adjudicate a rape case, the old ideal of honesty within the college judicial system runs into matching brick walls—mistrust of the judiciary by the innocent, and reluctance to self-incriminate by the guilty. The more deeply the College becomes embroiled in sorting out who did what to whom, the more it becomes the enemy of both students, and the less both of them learn about responsibility for their own welfare.

Honesty meets self-incrimination

In the spring of my first year as dean, I commented on an assault on a woman undergraduate in a well-lit and well-traveled area, by asking rhetorically, "What can one say except that students, women in particular, should try to travel with someone?" The remark drew a furious response from women's groups. "Calling attention to the student's behavior in this way," said a representative, "implies that it is the student's behavior that needs to be changed. This suggests that the assault was, in some way, her fault." I was, like Dean Jewett, accused of blaming the victims.

My goal was to reduce the number of rapes, so I urged women to protect themselves. But this was taken as shifting responsibility to where it did not belong. Women should be able to walk alone at night; therefore I should not advise them not to. Such advice takes responsibility off the shoulders of rapists. My effort to encourage campus safety was seen as a distraction from the task of bringing criminals to justice and as an attempt to hold victims responsible for attacks against them.

In February 1999, two rape cases came to light in anonymous interviews in *Perspective,* an undergraduate publication. One of the women, identified as "N" in the publication, said that a fellow student had raped her the previous spring. The man, she said, "took advantage of the fact that [she] had been drunk and sleeping." N reported that she took her complaint to the Administrative Board, which required the male student to withdraw and recommended to the Faculty that he be dismissed. N described herself as "furious" that the recommendation was for dismissal—which could in theory be reversed by a subsequent readmission vote by the full Faculty—rather than expulsion—an irrevocable separation. She told the interviewer, "I left the office crying and I went straight to my room to my phone, picked up the phone and began the process of going to court, that very second." A plea bargain with the district attorney quickly ensued. N's assailant pled guilty to one count of indecent assault and battery and was sentenced to five years' probation, the first eighteen months to be served with an electronic monitoring bracelet. He must register as a sex offender if he returns to Massachusetts within twenty years.

The interviews set off a firestorm. The Faculty had not come to a final resolution on either case. The *Crimson* said that "for the women involved in these cases, the lack of official action has been both astonishing and frightening." Nor was there any doubt in the mind of that year's *Crimson* editorial board that only one administrative response to rape was appropriate, and that was expulsion, a sanction not used in response to any disciplinary case for more than sixty years.* I suggested that the Faculty may have stopped using expulsion for the same reasons of irreversibility that had caused many societies to stop executing criminals, but not everyone found this analogy persuasive.

In March, Professor William Paul disclosed to the *Crimson* that the motion to dismiss N's assailant had in fact been discussed at the October 20 Faculty meeting but did not reach a vote. "Lots of issues were brought up. None were resolved. The conversation flew in all directions." He reported that some faculty members were concerned that the student who had committed the assault "may have made incriminating comments before the Ad[ministrative] Board." He also explained that he and other faculty members favored not dismissal but a requirement to withdraw for a fixed term as the appropriate response in the particular case of N's assailant. The eighteen-member Faculty Council had split on the issue of the penalty when it considered the case before it reached the floor of the Faculty. The minority, five professors including two women, agreed that a rape had occurred but was the result of the man's confusion. They also noted discrepant testimony about the woman's passivity or responsiveness, and evidence of the man's candor and contrition after the fact. "Rape is not an undifferentiable single act," they stated in explaining their opposition to the dismissal motion. "Rather it is a category of acts that vary dramatically in their causes and consequences. It is easy to imagine rapes that warrant the most severe penalty we can confer, if not more. It is our belief that this case does not fall in that category."

---

*Expulsion had occasionally been used in modern times for admissions fraud, on the basis that the individual being expelled was an impostor and the individual who had been admitted never existed.

But the sentiments for leniency did not prevail. When the Faculty vote was finally taken, N's assailant was dismissed. Later in the year, the Faculty also dismissed the assailant in the other case, which lacked the murkiness that some saw in N's circumstances.

The Faculty was troubled by the entire business and happy only to be done with it. But the two cases had put the entire date-rape issue back into debate, with opinions and comments on date rape voiced by Harvard counselors, local columnists, and national publications. Much was said about date rape that was sensible, and some was nonsense. But none of the published reports describing the actual circumstances of the two incidents, nor any of the court records, suggested that either couple was dating the night of the assault or had ever dated before. I gradually began to appreciate the subtle politics of language. The widely used term "date rape" did not necessarily mean that a couple had been dating—it was used as a reminder that "rape" covered more than the acts committed on darkened streets by strangers taking women violently and by surprise. The language shifted to "rape" and "rapist" to emphasize the enormity of the crime by linking it to the darkened-street variety, even if it had been committed following social intimacy. As the *Boston Herald* reported, some students took the decision to dismiss rather than expel N's assailant as evidence that "Harvard was not taking date rape as seriously as other forms of rape."

Following the dismissal of N's assailant, concern turned to the possibility that he might have incriminated himself in the criminal-justice system by cooperating with the College in its process. If he confessed to the Administrative Board, the confession, in the form of his statement to the Board, would have been given to N for her response; and N might have given it to the criminal-justice authorities. Even if this had not occurred (a newspaper account said that he had written an apology directly to N), the sequence of events N had described in her published interview raised the possibility that statements to the Board could be used to incriminate students in the future. Professor Miller's description of the College and the state as operating in "different spheres" had been shown to be wrong.

A Faculty committee studied the issue, and new procedures for rape cases were put in place for the following year. As explained by the Secretary of the Faculty, "deans will now take an active role in encouraging students who may need a lawyer to hire one and will also have a memorandum available to give students accused of 'very grave crimes.'"

Because the Board can never be sure that a criminal case will not be initiated, Harvard now uses an awkward amalgamation of procedures when a disciplinary complaint is brought against a student. Ordinarily, a dean calls the student in and asks him what happened, advising him to be open and honest. But if the matter might result in a serious criminal charge, the dean calls the student in, outlines the matter at issue, and tells the student to say nothing until he has consulted a lawyer. The process then goes forward in the normal way but with the shadow of a lawyer in the background assisting the student in preparing his statement to the Board and coaching him on any personal appearance he may make to account for his actions. Not surprisingly, women who bring complaints began to feel they should hire lawyers too, so they would be on equal footing with the men they were accusing. The result is that both parties to a peer sexual assault case within the Board are advised to hire lawyers—at the same time as they are told that honesty and openness are cherished values of the university.

The trial becomes punishment

The two cases handled by the Faculty in 1999 were troubling on many different scores: that the assailants were being punished either too severely or not severely enough; that the College bore responsibility for a male student winding up with a criminal record he would not have had if he had not been encouraged to confess; that the College bore responsibility for assaults against women that might not have happened if better educational and preventive programs had been in place. Still, peace ensued on campus for a time, and Harvard rapes dropped out of the media.

The wide publicity of the dismissal of two Harvard students for rape had an unexpected side effect. During the single academic year 2000–2001, the College disciplinary process heard seven cases of sexual misconduct—in the entire previous decade it had heard only thirteen. Apparently the word had spread that the process was not inaccessible after all.

In most of the new cases, it was impossible to determine what had happened. As is typical, the only witnesses were the principals, and more often than not, both had been drinking and had only vague or partial recollections of the events. In the process of adjudicating the complaints, much of the arguing concerned not whether sex had taken place but how drunk the woman had been when it happened. Complainants pointed to the statement about alcohol in the 1993 Faculty vote: "Rape may also include intercourse with a person who is incapable of expressing unwillingness or is prevented from resisting, as a result of conditions including, but not limited to, those caused by the intake of alcohol or drugs."

Several complainants declared that they had been so drunk as to justify application of the "incapable of expressing unwillingness" standard. The alleged assailant typically countered that although the complainant had been drinking, she hadn't been coerced into drinking and at all times she had been *capable* of expressing unwillingness to have sex. If the woman was just drunk, it wasn't rape. If she was very, very drunk, passing-out drunk, maybe it was rape. Harvard's job became determining how drunk the woman really was, and deciding accordingly whether to throw the man out.

Something had gone dreadfully wrong, not with our disciplinary system but with the entire context in which sexual behavior and misbehavior had been cast. A movement that a few years earlier had used as a call to arms the right of women to control their own bodies had wound up encouraging women to argue that they had lost control of themselves.

Bertrand Russell once said that men are born ignorant, not stupid; they are made stupid by education. Now women, it seemed, were validating Russell's quip. No one could have arrived at Harvard thinking that the way to handle a rape was to try to prove how drunk she had gotten herself. Women had been taught to think this way by the industry organizing itself around date rape in colleges. And Harvard was accommodating them.

The "incapable of expressing consent" standard wasn't met in any of the seven cases brought in the 2000–2001 school year, often because the complainants had capably expressed other things. In some cases, the complaint came so long after the event that the testimony of witnesses, already of doubtful value since they had been drunk at the time, had frayed with time and become distorted by the endless retellings while the complainant was deciding whether to formalize her charge. In one case, a woman accounted for her lengthy indecision about charging her boyfriend with rape by explaining to a dean, "If I do that, he'll *never* marry me."

Given the murkiness of the evidence, most of the cases brought in the 2000–2001 year were irresolvable; in fact, after dozens of hours of testimony, the Administrative Board established nothing more than could have been ascertained from the original complaint. Deans were reluctant to discourage women from pressing cases, fearing that they would be pilloried as insensitive or worse. Men, if any of them were guilty, weren't confessing, on advice of their lawyers.

The Board was overwhelmed with the sense that the trials it was conducting were worse than pointless—they were destructive. When one complainant said of her ex-boyfriend that she wanted "to see him squirm" even if she couldn't prove that he raped her, it was clear that something had to change. In the world of criminal law, prosecutors don't make charges they think can't be sustained, but there was no such step in Harvard's process—under the protocol established by the Date Rape Task Force, a complaint automatically started the judicial machinery. The process itself was being used as punishment, even though the Board's inability to establish fault made the complainants even unhappier at the end than they had been in the beginning.

Rape at Harvard goes national

I explained the problem in my 2001 annual report on the College, which was on the Harvard website and was widely distributed. A committee of senior faculty was appointed to recommend procedural changes and proposed that a full Administrative Board hearing should not be initiated unless "the case presents the type of evidence that might permit the Board to arrive at a reasonable evaluation of the facts." The *Crimson* ran a news story accurately stating: "Starting in September, the Board will evaluate sexual assault cases earlier to determine whether an investigation is likely to result in a resolution." The Faculty Council, an elected committee that screens all faculty legislation, approved the proposal. No questions were raised when I explained this proposal to the Faculty in May 2002. It passed on the routine voice vote reaffirming the rest of the College rules.

The next morning's *Boston Globe* ran the front-page story, "Harvard to Require More Proof in Sex Cases," and another firestorm was ablaze. A demonstration was quickly organized against the new policy, and flyers began circulating around campus "informing" the community about the great leap backward that Harvard had taken. Faculty members from whom I had never heard about a single case of sexual assault came forward to report that students sought them out about it all the time. Others claimed that the Board was trying to wash its hands of its responsibilities and to leave its women students to fend for themselves after they had been raped.

Not all the opinion pieces in the press were negative. "Alert: Disturbing Evidence of Common Sense Found at Harvard," wrote columnist Kathleen Parker in the *Orlando Sentinel.* Cathy Young wrote in the *Boston Globe,* "Blatant disregard for the rights of the accused is shockingly unfair, even if it is legal. If the new policy at Harvard signals a turning of the tide, it will be a victory for true gender equity." My favorite, even though it missed a crucial point and was intended to be harshly critical, was a piece by Pulitzer Prizewinner Eileen McNamara linking Harvard's struggles with date-rape cases to the Catholic Church's failure to treat sexual abuse by priests as a crime.

> Crimes are the jurisdiction of police departments, not campus disciplinary boards or church leaders bent on protecting the reputations of their institutions, sometimes at the expense of their student or communicants. They are missing the point at Harvard. The university's method of handling sexual assault cases is not the problem; the problem is Harvard's presumption that it is qualified to handle them at all. The law's reach does not stop at the gates of Harvard Yard any more than it does at the door of the rectory. The minimum we've learned from the crisis in the Catholic Church is the folly of internal policing in criminal matters.

All true, if only we could figure out how to get complainants to go to court. Still, the gap in logic in this piece was more than made up for by the thought that someone believed I might have the kind of sway over Harvard and its students that Cardinal Law had over the Roman Catholic archdiocese.

As the academic year wound to a close, the inevitable happened. I received word from above that given the faculty objections, another committee was being established to study the problem of sexual assault. With that, faculty members ended their threats to try to rescind the new policy about evidence.

But that was not the end of the story. Over the summer a Boston lawyer filed a complaint with the U.S. Department of Education's Office of Civil Rights, claiming that the new policy was in violation of Title IX, the law prohibiting discrimination on the basis of gender. Describing Harvard as "the first school to put in writing that the word of a woman is not good enough," the lawyer implied that in a crime generally committed by men against women, a presumption of the innocence of the accused until he is proven guilty creates a systematic bias against women.

The Office of Civil Rights agreed to investigate the claim, tying up Harvard's legal department, several College officials, and heaven knows how many federal lawyers and administrators in a consideration of whether Harvard should be required to have a full hearing on every date-rape case, even if it could tell from the beginning that it would be impossible to determine with any confidence what had occurred. Harvard parents paid twice for this investigation—as taxpayers for the federal bureaucracy's time, and as tuition-payers for the time of the Harvard bureaucracy. The story made national television, including the MSNBC program seen by the antler craftsman on the edge of the wilderness.

The matter boiled in the feminist press throughout the year. In April 2003, the Office of Civil Rights gave the prescreening policy a clean bill of health. "OCR found that, as currently described by the College, these changes do not deny a student with a complaint of sexual assault access to a prompt and equitable process for resolving the complaint. . . . Title IX does not prohibit the use of due process." Describing it as a "victory for fundamental fairness," defense attorney Harvey Silverglate posted the full text of the OCR letter on his organization's website. The lawyer who had brought the complaint also found a way to announce victory. For once, everyone seemed happy.

But not really, of course. The online newsletter *Women's eNews* described Harvard's policy change as part of a national cover-up effort. And immediately after the sexual-assault study committee issued its report, including recommendations for extended educational programs and the creation of an office of Sexual Assault Prevention and Response with 2.5 full-time-equivalent staff, student leaders called for "a complete review of [Harvard's] disciplinary procedures for adjudicating sexual assault cases." That has not happened yet, but who knows what the future may bring.

Harvard is at the moment in a period of calm on the issue of campus rape, but the position it has reached is neither good nor stable. Harvard is teaching women that they are not responsible for their own well-being. And it is trying—and failing—to create a better system of courts and laws, forgetting that its business is education, not criminal justice.

Teaching irresponsibility

In the politically charged campus environment of today, responsibility is a zero-sum game. If a woman alleges that she has been raped, the smallest implication that her actions were contributory is met with a barrage of resistance. It is impossible in the current climate to place the blame for a rape fully on the assailant, and also to urge other women to take easy precautions that might have prevented the attack. Even cautioning women against disrobing and going to bed with a man with whom they don't want to have sex can be painted as a cruel attempt to shift attention away from rapists' acts and onto the behavior of the victims.

I did not fully understand this zero-sum game until a meeting I had with students who were drafting a proposal for enhanced educational programs surrounding the issue of date rape. I expressed surprise that there was no mention of alcohol in the draft proposal, given that in my experience virtually every allegation of date rape involved at least one drunken participant. Sober Harvard students were very rarely involved in allegations of rape, and it seemed to me that it would be helpful to say something along the lines that sex and alcohol don't mix well, with the evidence to back it up. I was told that the reason alcohol was not addressed was that for an act to be rape it didn't matter whether the woman was drunk; being drunk didn't mean she deserved to be raped.

It dawned on me that the old rallying cry of "take back the night" had developed a very generalized meaning: Women should be free to go anywhere and do anything and should be immune from sexual assault *no matter what.* Of course they should be. But that approach is not very useful if the objective is to reduce the number of assaults. How can colleges teach women that there are things they must do for themselves, simple things, and the failure to do them may have undeserved consequences no institutional response can reverse?

One aspect of the calculus of responsibility is the question of whether all rapes are the same. It is regularly argued that rape by a friend is no less traumatic, and can even be worse, than rape by a stranger. For example, two clinical social workers wrote, "There are many misconceptions about date rape. Perhaps the most flagrant one is that victims of date rape have an easier recovery than those who have been sexually assaulted by strangers. This is usually not the case." The idea that a rape that begins with terror, blows, and tearing off the woman's clothes is no harder on the victim than one that begins with consensual petting and voluntary disrobing is certainly counterintuitive. This view of equivalency of consequence happens also to be essential to the political position that all rapists should receive the maximum punishment. As Professor Daniel Gilbert argued in urging the Faculty to adopt less than the severest punishment for N's assailant, "Any offense—rape, assault, or plagiarism—is not a single act but a whole category of actions. Nobody would contend that a single penalty is appropriate for all acts within a single category." All rapes should be treated the same way only if they are all equally bad.

When a rape has occurred in the course of some prior intimacy, Harvard's latest report on the subject says, women "express confusion about their own sense of responsibility." The report continues, "[W]e must instill students with a clear sense of boundary setting and boundary acknowledgment, thus turning the tide of these self-blaming behaviors." Certainly a protocol of permissions requested and permissions granted or denied might—if it could be implemented—reduce rapes and make their circumstances less ambiguous. Yet as Harvard continues its struggle to educate students about rape, the hardest question remains: Will the lessons it teaches about personal responsibility serve students well in their later lives?

The support given to women in pursuing complaints of sexual assault teaches that the way to cope with an assault is to exercise one's right to seek justice, at all costs and to all ends, rather than to get help coping with it and then to move on. It is dangerous these days to say that there is dignity in overcoming adversities over which you had no control. The issue has become politically charged in the same way that the politics surrounding childhood sexual abuse (CSA) eclipsed the relevant science. Clinical psychologist Richard McNally described a disquieting scientific study establishing that victims of CSA did very well psychologically in the long run; they were "nearly as well-adjusted as their counterparts who had not been

abused." An adult's mental health depends much more on other
variables, such as how generally dysfunctional a person's family was,
than on whether childhood abuse had occurred. This finding ran so
counter to prevailing opinion that it produced a violent reaction
from both professional scientists and political conservatives. "Rather
than interpreting the article as documenting the resilience of children," McNally noted, "they saw it as a defense of pedophilia." The
matter boiled all the way to the floor of the U.S. Senate, which unan-
imously condemned the research. Yet it stood up to subsequent scientific review just as it had passed prepublication review.

The variability in the way survivors remember trauma is pertinent to
the question of whether all rapists should be punished the same way.
The argument that victims of date rape and stranger rape are, in the
long run, equally traumatized by their experiences may not imply that
the two kinds of rape should be punished the same way. It may simply
mean that in the long run, the impact of the rape on the survivor, like
the impact of childhood sexual abuse, depends on characteristics of the
survivor as well as on the specifics of the rape. The rational conclusion
in that case would not be that all rapes should be treated the same, but
that the degree of long-term post-traumatic stress is a poor indicator of
the heinousness of the particular criminal act that had been committed.

By encouraging rape survivors to seek retribution and justice even
when the chance of achieving it is slim, and by failing to help victims
realize that sometimes the best thing to do about an injury is to put it
behind them, victims' advocates have unintentionally shifted the terms
defining good character. What used to be admired—a capacity to rise
above severe trauma—is now discouraged. Respect for women's capacity to recover is seen as deflecting attention away from the need to punish the perpetrators. Urging women to move on is seen as insulting, a
failure to comprehend the depth of the trauma they have experienced.

I now wonder whether the verbal shift from rape "victim" to rape
"survivor" was really a good idea. "Survivor" was meant to be empower-
ing: There is something you can do for yourself after the event, even if
you could not have prevented it. But the usage has now been turned
on its head, to emphasize that you are a survivor forever, in a state from
which you are powerless to escape. I wonder if it is good for the individuals involved to have such support for not getting over their trauma.
It cannot be good for women as a group to be seen as vulnerable to ir-
remediable emotional injuries.

Through our ever more elaborate systems of procedures and ac-commodations, we are unintentionally training our students to be brit-tle, to expect that everything will work for them and to find fault with the system if anything goes wrong. In an effort to be compassionate to victims of sexual trauma, we foster a protracted and unproductive process. In real life, resilience in the face of the unexpected, the un-just, the imperfect, is more useful than paralysis. If higher education is to create strong, competent, and self-reliant adults, colleges need to encourage and admire victims' resilience without being accused of protecting rapists from responsibility for their crimes.

Harvard tries, and fails, to outsmart society

Rape cases are hard to prove. The most strident calls for reform of Harvard's disciplinary procedures have come because the conviction rate was low. Proposed "improvements" of extremely doubtful fairness have all been devices to make it easier to convict a rapist—easier than it has been at Harvard in the past, and easier than it is in criminal court. Take, for example, the frequent proposal that members of the judicial body "be trained to recognize symptoms of having survived sexual violence," as a *Crimson* staff editorial put it. Such professional-sounding verbiage fails to acknowledge that the entire field of post-traumatic stress is itself under great strain. No fair process could use the recognition of symptoms of post-traumatic stress as a substitute for real evidence that a crime had been committed. As McNally said in his critique of research on post-traumatic stress disorder (PTSD):

> Forensic psychologists have sounded the alarm about the abuse of the PTSD diagnosis in civil litigation. . . . [L]awyers have been coach-ing litigants on what symptoms to mention when they are being as-sessed by clinicians prior to bringing suit for psychological damages linked to PTSD. Faking these symptoms is easy, and there is no ob-jective standard test for the disorder as there is for many serious physical injuries that figure in litigation.

In addition, only a minority of trauma victims experience PTSD, and those who do have PTSD remember their trauma as having been worse than do those who experienced the identical trauma but do not suffer from PTSD.

The point is not just that this idea is deeply flawed. More generally, it is risky for Harvard or any university to develop a legal system of its own, when the one that the Commonwealth of Massachusetts has provided, imperfect as it may be, has evolved through a long process of experience and compromise that the university cannot duplicate.

Almost a century and a half ago, a Harvard president made a crucial point about the limits of Harvard's authority.

> The College Faculty is not a body that can well investigate [serious infractions of the law]. Its members have no power to place witnesses on the stand, or to administer an oath; and if they had, they cannot inflict punishment upon conviction of the offender. The highest penalty they can impose is expulsion from the College.

Depriving someone of a Harvard degree is not an appropriate response to a crime to which society responds with imprisonment. Why, then, are victims' advocates so eager for Harvard to take up these cases, when there is so little that Harvard can do to the accused? They hope that convictions will be easier to obtain in the College than in the courts, and they hope to draw attention to the larger cause by focusing attention on the response of the College rather than simply on the act of the assailant.

A faculty advisor to student activists on the peer sexual-assault issue explained to me that it was common knowledge that the court system is stacked against rape victims, and the university has an obligation not to duplicate it but to develop a better alternative. It is the height of hubris to think that a group of smart professors sitting around a seminar table could, on the basis of little actual experience, draft a better legal system. But excessive humility has never been a particular weakness at Harvard, and the fear of failure does not prevent us from trying.

No better example of academic foolishness about legal matters, the "enthusiastic amateurism" of which Professor Dershowitz wisely cautioned, can be found than Harvard's struggles with the definition of rape. After two years of debate leading up to the adoption of a particular definition in the 1993 vote, Harvard got it wrong anyway.

There was no need to write a new definition of rape if it was supposed to have the same meaning as in the criminal code. It would have been easy to say, in so many words, "Rape is what the Commonwealth of Massachusetts says it is, and it's a violation of Harvard's standards of conduct as well as being a crime in the Commonwealth." "Anything that is a felony in Massachusetts is against Harvard's rules too," as Harvard's rules once provided, would have been elegant and encompassing. Instead, in 1992 Harvard tried to improve upon the state's words defining the particular crime of rape. While struggling with the question of whether sexual intercourse would be "rape if" or "rape unless," it overlooked another detail.

Harvard's definition of rape begins:

Rape includes any act of sexual intercourse that takes place against a person's will or that is accompanied by physical coercion or the threat of bodily injury.

Massachusetts law reads:

Whoever has sexual intercourse or unnatural sexual intercourse with a person and compels such person to submit by force and against his will, or compels such person to submit by threat of bodily injury, shall be punished by imprisonment in state prison for not more than twenty years.

The two definitions have the same elements—that the victim is unwilling and that the perpetrator used force or the threat of force. But the elements of unwillingness and forcibleness are joined by "or" in Harvard's definition and by "and" in the state's.

There is a big difference. As a legal matter, in a rape case, the prosecution needs to establish separately both the unwillingness of the victim and the use of force by the assailant. "Force" has its own legal parsing; if the victim is too drunk to resist, the amount of force need only be minimal. But the requirement that the assailant use force (or the threat of force) means that for the act to be rape, the man must have had some way to know that the woman was, in fact, unwilling.

The difference between Harvard's definition and the state's was there to be seen from the beginning. But no one seems to have noticed the discrepancy until someone on the Administrative Board, trying to apply the definition to an actual case, observed that neither force nor threat of force was required under Harvard's definition. It would be rape if the woman were unwilling, even if the sexual intercourse was without force or threat of force. In the case in question, the woman said she performed oral sex on a man even though she didn't want to do it. He was an authority figure because he had been the leader of an outing group on which she had obeyed his instructions. So when he asked her for sex, she reluctantly went through the motions. He had pressured but not forced her to do it, and she had not said anything either agreeing or refusing to do it. Surely what he did was wrong, but was it rape?

I told the Board to go by the legal definition, not the definition the Faculty had voted. I did that in part because I knew the Faculty had been told at the very moment it voted for the definition that it was the legal definition. But I advised the Board to go by the legal definition also because I was aware of the decision in *Schaer v. Brandeis University*, which put an end to any notion that universities operated in a universe parallel to state law and could do what they wanted with rape policies. That case involved a student accused of rape at Brandeis. The charge was upheld by Brandeis's disciplinary board, the finding was challenged in court, and the complex details of the outcome need not be of concern here. But the decision of the appeals court in the case makes clear that where rape is at issue, the conventions of the legal system must be observed.

> [A] court is most unlikely to adjudicate whether an examination has been graded fairly or a student has been fairly placed on probation by reason of poor academic performance. Plagiarism is more an academic than societal offense. If a student is disciplined for defacing college property or postgame brawling, the degree of deference will still be very considerable because this involves concerns peculiar to the educational institution. Should the student, however, be suspended or expelled for misconduct, such as theft or—as here— rape, the subject matter is not only familiar to courts but mars the record of the student in a manner that is likely to have serious consequences for the student in admission for graduate study or competition for a job.

Given this, I was unwilling to prosecute a case using a peculiarly Harvardian definition of rape, which had mistakenly been represented to the Faculty as the legal definition.

I don't know how Harvard got the definition wrong. Members of the Date Rape Task Force thought the definition finally adopted was the legal definition. The senior cochair of the task force is no longer alive. It may have been simply a drafting error, committed in an attempt to reorganize the elements of the legal definition into plain English. Old-timers have suggested to me that it was not an accident and someone might have wanted to sneak the Antioch-style "rape unless" definition past the Faculty. There seems to be no way to know for certain.

I was troubled by the discrepancy, which allows two categories of actions to be rape at Harvard that would not be rape in the legal system. The first is of the kind that brought the matter to our attention: non-forcible sexual intercourse with a woman who does not wish to have sex. But there is another category covered by the "or" version that is excluded from the "and" version: consensual sexual intercourse involving the use of force. Bondage, for example, also seems to be against the rules at Harvard.

I brought the problem to the attention of the Faculty Council and asked to substitute "and" for the critical "or." The matter was discussed at length and noted in *Harvard University Gazette*. The professors didn't know what to do—narrowing Harvard's definition of rape could cause another firestorm, and deciding to leave it alone might invite a complainant to claim rape on the basis of her unexpressed unwillingness to have sex. Gender and sexuality theory entered into the argument—what about "psychological force," and why shouldn't Harvard hold men to a higher standard than does the state? In the end, no decision was taken, one way or the other.

Thus the erroneous "or" remains in the student handbook to this day, a tiny—but consequential—monument to the folly of academics operating in realms beyond their expertise. Confident of the superiority of its wisdom on matters of both justice and sex, the Harvard Faculty refused to acknowledge its incompetence to be fair, wise, or even logical in coping with rape.

CHAPTER 8

Students and Money

Educational Excellence for the Rich and the Poor

The student in a polytechnic school has a practical end constantly in view. . . . This practical end should never be lost sight of by student or teacher in a polytechnic school, and should seldom be thought of or alluded to in a college.

— Charles William Eliot, 1869

More than ever before, policies, curricula, and salaries no longer follow what an institution thinks students and citizens need to prepare for life . . . rather, they increasingly follow the voting feet of students from class to class . . . . This practice can be rationalized as respect for student opinion, or meeting consumer demand. . . .

— James Engell and Anthony Dangerfield, 1998

In the absence of any credible educational principles, money is increasingly the driving force of decisions in universities. Students' best interests get lip service, but profitable enterprises get attention. Harvard professor James Engell and his coauthor Anthony Dangerfield have called the resulting educational system the "market-model university." The ultimate source of this cultural shift is the replacement of education by research as the university's principal function. Research costs money and, increasingly, produces money. The tale is told in full in several recent books: David Kirp's *Shakespeare, Einstein, and the Bottom Line;* Jennifer Washburn's *University, Inc.;* and Engell and Dangerfield's *Saving Higher Education in the Age of Money.*

Money distorts the curriculum and the pursuit of scholarship. But it also provides direct benefits to students—better facilities and, most of all, more financial aid. The competition among universities for the best students can only make life better, it would seem, for the students who win that competition. Even if there is more money for research, don't students at the great universities get their fair share of the benefits?

Sadly, students experience the use and misuse of money as so incoherent that no consistent educational message is heard.

2004 was a milestone year for Harvard College. For the first time in its history, the entering class included a significant number of students whose parents would pay nothing at all for their children's Harvard education.

In a major speech delivered February 29, President Summers presented compelling statistics about the rising income gap in America and its consequences for higher education. Today, he explained, the top 1 percent of the population earns more than the bottom 40 percent. Twenty-five years ago, the top 1 percent had earned less than half the share of the bottom 40 percent. The increasing income stratification has serious consequences for universities. In the most selective colleges and universities, only 3 percent of the students come from the bottom income quartile and only 10 percent come from the bottom half.

Summers argued that because our national competitiveness is at stake, and because "excellence in education depends on diversity," students at the low end of the income scale must not be excluded from places like Harvard. "I think of a young woman at Harvard who came from a refugee camp on the border between Cambodia and Laos when she was two, and whose parents worked in an L.A. laundry," Summers said. "In the summer before last, she went back to that refugee camp to help."

Summers put Harvard's money behind his commitment to socioeconomic diversification. Henceforth, parents earning less than $40,000 would not have to contribute anything to the cost of their children's education. Since the early 1960s, Harvard had admitted students without regard to their ability to pay and had provided enough financial aid so those wanting to attend would be able to do so. Under this system of "need-blind admission" and "full need-based financial aid," even families with very low incomes had been expected to make at least a token contribution to their children's education. Now Harvard would no longer expect them to pay anything. For many of these families, this move would have the practical effect of shifting a burden from the students themselves, since they often took extra jobs to pay the parental contribution rather than ask their parents to come up with the money from their meager incomes. Still, the main point of the initiative was to signal to families of modest means that Harvard was open to them.

Harvard's initiative prompted stories in the *New York Times* and in *USA Today*. The response to the new policy was almost uniformly positive, though officials of some other universities worried that the program would enhance Harvard's already strong competitive position in the market for students. M. Lee Pelton, president of Willamette University and a Harvard Overseer, noted in *USA Today* that "most of us do not have [Harvard's] resource base." Others murmured that Summers had stolen a bit of thunder from William G. Bowen, president of the Andrew W. Mellon Foundation, who in his Jefferson Lectures at the University of Virginia a few weeks later hit several of the same notes while reporting on an extensive research study he had led. Others speculated openly that Harvard's move was a direct competitive response to Princeton's decision a few weeks earlier to improve its financial aid program by no longer requiring students to take out loans. The Yale dean of Undergraduate Admissions and Financial Aid critiqued Harvard's program: "Sounds to me like they've done some analysis and responded to the competition. . . . This is a very reactive world. You can rest assured that we're paying attention."

If Harvard was reacting to competition, the school was not about to admit it. In the world of higher education today, it is hard to tell the difference between principle and reaction. In 2001 the president of Princeton, which has regularly led other colleges in improving its financial aid awards, explained while announcing an aid increase: "We had not hoped for a competitive advantage here. What we hoped for is what we did would be followed by our competitors so that education as a whole would be open." Students with little money don't particularly care about colleges' motivations for financial support. They like not only the money but also the college's signal that they are the kind of students the college wants to have. A student who chose Princeton because of its generous financial aid package explained, "I wanted a college experience where you end up with an array of students from various socioeconomic backgrounds, where money is not a factor, nor is there a class system within the university."

Harvard got its message across. With vigorous recruitment backed by the new financial aid program, Harvard in one year increased by 22 percent, to 360, the number of admitted students from families with modest incomes. Most of them accepted Harvard's admission offers and arrived in Cambridge in fall 2005.

Yet they arrived to hear a different message. In 2005 for the first time, Harvard allowed those students who could afford it to hire maid service to make their beds and clean their rooms.

Harvard has a long history of maid service. What was new in 2005 was not maids but the fact that some students would have them and others would not.

At its March 1, 1659, meeting, the Harvard Corporation voted to engage a maid dubbed "Olde Mary . . . for to doe her worke, undertake, & to give content to the College & Students." Olde Mary had many heirs to her responsibilities. At Harvard the maids—employees of Harvard, not of individual students—were called "Goodies" (probably from "goodwives"). They became stock figures of the culture of college life. The mock heroic epic *The Rebelliad*, composed in the aftermath of student riots in 1817, invokes the Goody as muse, "Aloft in pendent dignity, Astride her magic broom, And wrapt in dazzling majesty." She is also the object of the kind of college humor that has only lately become unfashionable:

> *My muse was once a virgin; but*
> *'T is no great matter*
> *How, when, or where, the little slut*
> *First broke the platter.*
> *'T is rumor'd that a certain tutor*
> *In her young days became her suitor*
> *One morning, as the story goes,*
> *Before his tutorship arose,*

The Goody entered with her broom,
To make his bed and sweep his room.

The rest of the story is predictable, and true to the roles to which society long assigned women at the bottom of its hierarchy.

Times changed as the student body changed—and changed drastically once the electric vacuum cleaner was invented. In 1954 Harvard eliminated bed-making and soon phased out maid service completely, as most other eastern colleges had already done. Savings were projected to be $150,000 per year, but something more than dollars was at stake. "I object to the twentieth century," lamented Lowell House Master Elliot Perkins, "and the passing of the amenities of life."

A stout traditionalist though he was, Perkins was at least half joking. By the 1950s Harvard was looking less like the domain of American hereditary aristocracy. It was on a delicate path to maintain its old classiness, while genuinely welcoming students for whom those old "amenities" were only the stuff of imagination. To this day, on special occasions the Masters of Lowell House sit at "high table" on a dais a few inches above the rest of the dining hall. Students now join them, and the Masters are now a same-sex couple, but for the moment at least--there are rumors this may change—the Masters are still called Masters. Harvard has long resisted the claims of a few students that they are reminded of the slavery of their ancestors when told they are living in a "House" under the leadership of a "Master." Where it has retained the forms of its old institutions while modernizing their conduct, Harvard has succeeded in becoming new while remaining connected to its roots.

Master Perkins himself initiated an important act of real social leveling: to eliminate different room rents for different rooms. Ever since the Houses opened, better rooms had been more expensive. Students with money, if they lived on campus at all, took the first-floor rooms facing the courtyard; students who were scrimping took the fourth-floor walkups. In 1958 Perkins proposed that Harvard switch to a uniform room rent. In 1963—at the same time Harvard completed its transition to need-blind admission and full need-based aid—the flat rate was finally adopted.

Despite some student objection, on the basis that the University had removed "one of the few remaining flexibilities in a student's budget," Harvard was committed to equal educational access. Over the next four decades, Harvard tried to eliminate one after another of the visible markers of income differences between students. "Glassware fees" are no longer added to the cost of chemistry courses, nor are equipment charges any longer part of film-making courses. Tuition is now charged at a flat rate—courses above the standard four-course load do not cost extra, so students will not be discouraged from academic pursuits for financial reasons.

Of course, these leveling efforts do not change some aspects of students' private lives. Some wear designer clothing, and some do not. Some have large flat-screen TVs in their rooms, and some do not. The College has not required students to wear uniforms or to leave their luxury items at home. As a result, some students have always been ostentatious about their wealth, causing others to feel out of place.

It was into this social nexus that the reinstitution of maid service, now known as DormAid, was introduced. The College had to get involved because the maids would be wandering the halls of locked dormitories; at a minimum, security was at stake. But the real question was one of social policy. Was getting maid service more like getting a courtyard room, which Harvard had decided should not be a privilege of wealth, or more like getting a pair of Manolo Blahnik shoes, which was none of Harvard's business to prevent?

Opinions were sharply divided. The *Crimson* editorialized against the service: "By creating yet another differential between the haves and have-nots on campus, DormAid threatens our student unity." Others touted the value of good hygiene and the benefits to those who would gain their livelihood by cleaning students' rooms. To the service's advocates, the social-class issue was a minor one. "There's so many ways in which on our campus you're able to display wealth in so much more obvious a fashion than having someone quietly clean your room," one student noted. To get in the way of a service that some students wanted and was a benefit to the workers performing it was, said the business's founder, a Harvard undergraduate, "to cut off trade and commerce." The *Wall Street Journal* agreed: "Somehow our eyes remained dry as we read about the plight of the impoverished Harvard student; we guess we're just callous." But a faculty colleague was bewildered. "Didn't we just lower the threshold for financial aid?" he asked me. "It is as if Harvard is trying to bring in more low-income students to even the playing field of a future class war!"

Either allowing or prohibiting maid service would send a message. The two possible messages ran in opposite directions, and there was no middle ground. What lesson would Harvard offer the impoverished Cambodian refugee of President Summers's call to arms against inequality in higher education? The one with maid service for her roommate from Park Avenue in New York, the one where her own sister, perhaps, could benefit from the opportunity to neaten the rooms of Harvard students? Or would the inequalities of American society be artificially and temporarily muted in the interest of a stronger sense of community and student friendship across the lines of social class?

The Harvard deans decided for free enterprise and students' opportunity to choose. The choices for maid service range from Platinum (a two-hour cleaning twice weekly at $1,649 per term) down to Bronze (one hour per month at $175 per term).

I prefer the more egalitarian Harvard, however imperfect, in which the realities of the market do not force economic decisions and misgivings on students every day. Students will, of course, return to a real world after graduating, perhaps different from their world of origin. But college is a time for thinking, not always about who we were and are but who we might become. Modestly utopian conditions of daily college life free students' minds and spirits. Colleges should nurture students' hopes and encourage their ambitions, rather than remind them to be cynical about the future.

The free-market rationale in higher education, coldly logical as it is, knows no limits. Why should Harvard charge a flat-rate tuition, which causes students taking four poetry courses to subsidize students taking five science courses? Because everything the college does is educational and students are youths, not yet fully formed, in transition to adulthood. They are old enough to make their beds but young enough to imagine a different life for themselves. Old enough to be brilliant poets and scientists and young enough to discover a love of poetry or science they did not know they had. The college can signal its support for their open-mindedness, or it can remind them of where they came from and of how different they are.

If students who can afford maids should be allowed to hire them, why should students who want to save hundreds of dollars not be allowed to rent the fourth-floor walkups if they so wish? And what about students who don't want to walk up stairs, or their maids to walk up stairs? Why shouldn't they be allowed to pay a little extra to get ground-floor rooms? Both kinds of students would get what they want. Yet they would miss an important part of their education, whether they realize it or not—for the first student, respect from the institution and the privilege of being treated as a human being in the making rather than as a rational economic agent; for the second student, encouragement to put aside the protection of personal wealth and to regard less privileged but equally talented peers as equals.

The saddest part of the DormAid matter is not the decision itself but the fact that Harvard did not explain it. A teachable moment slipped by. University leadership had a perfect opportunity to address ethical and economic reasoning. Both sides had moral justifications for their positions, and Harvard came down on one side. In favoring the free-market argument, the dean or the president could have used the opportunity to teach Harvard students where jobs really come from, and why the decision supported the greater good in spite of the misgivings some might have.

The decision, however, was made not on principle but out of expediency. No one ever thought, except in financial terms, about what was going to happen to the new cohort of low-income students once they arrived at Harvard. With that, the compelling vision that President Summers put forward at the American Council on Education to the open ears of the *New York Times* and *USA Today* lost a piece of its moral foundation.

In the end, Harvard got the low-income students it wanted, and the low-income students are getting a great education at an affordable price. The student entrepreneurs who started DormAid got what they wanted too—to run their business—and the students who want maid service can get it. By not offering any larger rationale, Harvard avoided provoking any more media scrutiny than it had already received.

And at least, while allowing the cleaning service to operate on campus, Harvard insisted on fighting one source of social inequality: The deans insisted that the name be changed from DorMaid to DormAid so as not to imply that all the floor-scrubbers in the new Harvard would be women.

❧

In the beginning, teaching at Harvard was like going into the ministry. The holiness and the austerity of the life of the mind continue to dignify the academic profession for those who have chosen to enter it rather than more lucrative lines of work. Of course, Harvard professors are not badly paid, but most of them could have made more money by going into business or law. In fields where their expertise has market value, professors have long supplemented their income by consulting. Harvard is now luring faculty toward activities that will profit the university. The new Office of Technology Development has more than ten professionals aggressively helping sell Harvard discoveries to industry, with Harvard and the inventors sharing the profits.

So far Harvard's efforts to profit by faculty inventions seem not to have vastly distorted its research programs in science and technology, though plans to combat looming budget deficits assume that costly science building projects will eventually yield significant revenue. Monetary temptations, however, are largely meaningless to professors in less applicable fields.

Students relate to the university within a shorter time frame. They want careers, and at a minimum, they want jobs after they graduate. Especially as Harvard breaks the barriers of access to higher education, more of its students will enter college with at least one eye on what lies beyond. And the more the professors are left to their own devices, the less of what is taught will be useful.

The careerism of undergraduates has been much lamented, especially by humanists. The humanities, because they are the least obviously useful of the subjects taught in college, are the biggest casualties of the market-model university. Students choosing courses for occupational reasons tend toward the social sciences and the sciences. Those choices are not always based on complete information—law schools love philosophy majors, in my experience, and although medical schools require some science background, more science courses are not necessarily better than the minimum. Parents naturally anticipate in material terms the effect of college on their children and can't be blamed for focusing on their children's employability along with their happiness and self-fulfillment.

In reality the "careerism" rap against students is unfair. Harvard students simply want to be the best, in landing a job as in anything else. They know they will need jobs, so they try to figure out how to get the "best" job, whatever that means. And who will tell them? Not the professors, most of whom have never held a nonprofessorial job themselves.

The old "placement office" that used to exist at colleges has grown, at Harvard as at most colleges, into a more robust career counseling office. It holds an open house for freshmen during orientation week-end, partly because it knows that parents will otherwise flood it with questions about how their children can best position themselves to get into medical school. But it tries, more persistently and gradually through all four years, to get students to think about their personal goals in relation to their academic goals and their career options. Career thinking is part of the process of self-discovery that students should experience in college.

Unfortunately, it goes against the grain of a "liberal education," as it is commonly understood at Harvard, to get students thinking about their whole lives from the day they enter college. A liberal education, in the sense in which professors discuss it with one another, is not about earning a living. In this caricature of a liberal education, college students need no more impetus to look toward employment than they already have been given by the materialistic culture from which they emerged. College, in fact, is not about useful knowledge at all. In the extreme, anything that would help graduates make a living probably should not be in the curriculum. For most students, only the para-faculty, the career counselors, can help them think about their later lives and how their aspirations relate to their academic program. The fortunate exceptions, the students whose professors can provide useful advice about jobs and careers, are those who want to be professors, and those whose professors are involved in the nonacademic world.

The tensions between the objectives of students and the ideals of professors are evident everywhere. The Harvard Economics Department won't teach accounting—it once did but dropped the course even as its faculty and course offerings expanded. Harvard is extreme in its vision of academic purity—even Yale undergraduates can find accounting in their course catalog. Instead, most Harvard students entering business school need a prep course in a subject most of their state-school classmates learned while in college. The introductory life-sciences courses have been reorganized to create an exciting new sequence—exciting at least to the prospective biochemistry majors who have had Advanced Placement courses in high school. But the courses will be less exciting to the history majors who want to earn the science credits required by medical schools and are compelled to take the same course as the biochemists because the new curriculum has no other courses more appropriate to their background and needs.

The career office, on the other hand, operates like any other nonacademic office. It brings enlightenment to those who use it, but the university leadership does little to carry its messages about the nature of life beyond college. Because employers love to hire Harvard students, corporate representatives flood the campus looking for seniors, starting as early as October. These recruiters provide an education to many Harvard students about the world of jobs and money and about the highest goals on the totem pole of postgraduate jobs. Many students go into consulting and investment banking as a result—jobs that offer money, utilize students' social and analytical skills, and have come to be known as markers of success. I have no objection to these lines of work—many of my best friends are in them. But an economy in which all the smart people were consultants or investment bankers would not last very long.

Harvard's diffidence about the practical, the applied, the inventive, the utilitarian—the real sources of invention and progress in our capitalist economy—is not a new phenomenon. Its roots date to a special circumstance of mid-nineteenth-century Harvard: the creation of a technical institute a mile or so down the Charles River.

Even before he became president, Charles William Eliot characterized the ideal of a college education in ivory-tower terms:

> In the college, the desire for the broadest culture, for the best formation and information of the mind, the enthusiastic study of subjects for the love of them without any ulterior objects, the love of learning and research for their own sake, should be the dominant ideas.

College studies were like the amateur ideal of sports: They should be undertaken not for money, not for fame, not out of ambition for some livelihood beyond college, but only out of love.

Eliot, a chemist, advanced this vision to contrast it with the role of the scientific and technical schools that were emerging across America in the mid-1800s. Harvard's Lawrence Scientific School, founded in 1851, was one of the oldest of these. Eliot taught there as a young man and gained a reputation as an excellent teacher if only a competent researcher. By the end of the Civil War, technology was changing the country, and institutions everywhere were responding to the country's demand for education in practical things. The Morrill Federal Land-Grant Act of 1862 had provided generous support for colleges that would "teach such branches of learning as are related to agriculture and the mechanic arts." Visionary educational entrepreneurs whom Harvard viewed as malcontents and castoffs founded the Massachusetts Institute of Technology (MIT) the following year. Eliot was passed over for the distinguished Rumsford chair in the Lawrence Scientific School when it came open in 1863. Having no prospects at Harvard, he joined MIT's faculty in 1865. It was from MIT that he described his vision of the difference between colleges and technical schools.

The technical schools were, as Eliot saw them, the answer to the question a father might ask in the new America:

> What can I do with my boy? I can afford, and am glad, to give him the best training to be had. I should be proud to have him turn out a preacher or a learned man; but I don't think he has the making of that in him. I want to give him a practical education; one that will prepare him, better than I was prepared, to follow my business or any other active calling. The classical schools and the colleges do not offer what I want. Where can I put him?

Eliot advocated practical education enthusiastically but with condescension. It was good, it was important, but it was for boys who did not have the "making" of a preacher or a scholar. It was not for the sort of boy who went to Harvard.

When Eliot returned to become president of Harvard, the grandiose promise that among subjects of learning, "we would have them all, and at their best," gave way to a decided bias against teaching applied subjects. A college should certainly not teach applied science, because students in a fine college should be pensive, undisturbed by the realities of life, ideally in conditions of "quiet and seclusion." "Just as far as the spirit proper to a polytechnic school pervades a college," Eliot theorized, "just so far that college falls below its true ideal. The practical spirit and the literary or scholastic spirit are both good, but they are incompatible. If commingled, they are both spoiled." Harvard would not be MIT, nor verge into MIT's territory.

Eliot was committed to a vision of Harvard as a place for pure but not applied science. Three times he tried unsuccessfully to give Harvard's applied science program to MIT—revenge, perhaps, for Harvard's passing him over for a chair in that program. President Lowell made a fourth attempt in 1914, precipitating a challenge in the Supreme Judicial Court of Massachusetts. Lowell proposed, in essence, to contract its applied science education to MIT. MIT would receive the Lawrence Scientific School and its assets, along with the bulk of a huge bequest for applied science that Harvard had received from the estate of the Civil War–era shoe-machinery magnate Gordon McKay.

Proposals for cooperative arrangements between Harvard and MIT caused discomfort on both sides. Anticipating what many others have thought over the years about striking deals with Harvard, one MIT partisan wrote, "The lamb is always *inside* the lion, when the two lie down together." Harvard alumni, on the other hand, wondered if Lowell's deal would require that Harvard start granting degrees to women, as MIT already did.

The biggest problem with the 1914 proposal was that, as the trustees of Gordon McKay knew well, McKay had been repeatedly urged to give his money to MIT, and he had repeatedly refused. Thus it was improper for Lowell to do with McKay's money what McKay had specifically meant not to do. According to an account written by Nathan Shaler a decade before Lowell's proposal, McKay respected MIT but felt that "the training in schools of that kind lacked the quality of general culture which he wished those educated under his endowment to have." Seeking an alternative where applied scientists would receive an education of greater breadth, McKay went to some length to verify that Harvard was an institution which, having accepted a trust, would "keep strict faith by it" for centuries to come. Having heard such evidence of McKay's intent, the court ruled against Harvard's effort to rid itself of the McKay money and the programs it supported. McKay's capacious imagination about the educational role Harvard might play in the useful arts—and the vigilance of the McKay trustees—are responsible for Harvard having an applied science program and for the endowment that supports my own faculty position.

In spite of Harvard's long ambivalence about teaching subjects like engineering, even during Eliot's presidency Harvard University was not wholly against practical pursuits. The medical school evolved into national prominence that it has never surrendered. Harvard established schools of law and, in Eliot's last year as president, of business.

Harvard became known as much for its professional schools as for its college. But it remained *infra dig* for a Harvard undergraduate to be motivated by practical pursuits.

The wild popularity of practical subjects in American colleges in the late nineteenth century was not difficult to explain: Students were pursuing science degrees in college so they could get jobs afterward. Eliot acknowledged, "The motive of earning a livelihood presses more constantly, and the students feel more distinctly that they are beginning their life work." The result was to leave the "old-fashioned college" bachelor of arts degree "gravely affected." But not at Harvard: "At Harvard University this movement, so general throughout the country, has not been seriously felt." There was little risk of Harvard following the example of Cornell, which opened a veterinary college in 1894, or of the College of New Jersey, which adopted the motto "Princeton in the Nation's Service" when it renamed itself in 1896.

The connection between scientific training and career opportunities is still a fact of life today. Students on financial aid are more likely to declare a major in the natural sciences than students not receiving financial aid (27.9 percent versus 21.7 percent), and less likely to concentrate in the humanities (20.4 versus 23.9 percent). By the time they graduate, the differences have diminished but not disappeared (26.8 percent of financial aid graduates concentrated in the sciences, versus 22.5 percent of those not receiving financial aid; and 20.5 percent of financial aid graduates concentrated in the humanities, versus 23.9 percent of those not receiving financial aid). Such shifting as occurs for the group on financial aid is from the natural sciences into the social sciences; the percentage in the humanities is essentially unchanged from freshman to senior year in both the financial aid group and the no-financial-aid group. Students who have little money do not have the luxury of the old diffidence about learning useful things, the ideal that Eliot set for the college and that is still idealized today for a very different student body.

Harvard has never quite accepted the reality that most students, in need of jobs after they graduate, heed that objective while choosing courses and leading their collegiate lives. Harvard's ambivalence toward practically and occupationally related studies for undergraduates, and even the development of expertise of any kind, was there from the beginning and still exists today.

The 2004 Curricular Review report sets out the purpose of an education in high-minded but abstract terms.

In an era of increasing specialization, professionalization, and frag-
mentation in both higher education and in our wider society, we
reaffirm our commitment to a liberal education in the arts and sciences. We aim to provide students with the knowledge, skills, and
habits of mind to enable them to enjoy a lifetime of learning and to
adapt to changing circumstances. We seek to educate students to be
independent, knowledgeable, rigorous, and creative thinkers, with a
sense of social responsibility, so that they may lead productive lives in
national and global communities.

The "skills" referred to are written and oral communication, foreign
language, and quantitative reasoning. The report later acknowledges
that it does not have a theory of how to teach social responsibility, and
that objective seems to have disappeared in the subsequent elabora-
tion of the report. In spite of the document's stance against specialization, "concentrations" (what other colleges call "majors") would continue to be required, not in order to instill "mastery of a field of
knowledge, but rather as a means by which students can develop a
greater degree of sophistication in their thinking." College studies are,
as for Eliot, about sophisticated thinking, "the best formation and information of mind," not about "ulterior motives," which should be as
far from consideration as possible. The report several times pejora-
tively uses the terms "specialization" and "professionalization" without
explaining why they have negative connotations.* The fact that students go on to careers after graduating is mentioned only twice in the
sixty-seven-page report, once in acknowledging that courses must be
offered for premedical students, and once in a curious list of the roles
that concentrations can play in students' education: "For some students, work in the field of concentration is an opportunity to focus on
a special area of interest, though they plan careers that will take them
in other directions."

Oddly, the surrounding list nowhere mentions the obvious: that students often choose concentrations because they think the courses *will*
help them get a start on their careers. This notion is, perhaps, thought

---

*The report's negative description of students' achieving "mastery of a field of knowl-
edge" stands in contrast to President Summers's insistence that a Harvard education
should assure that not only science concentrators but "all who graduate from this place
[be] equipped to comprehend, to master, to work with, the scientific developments that
are transforming the world" (p. 68).

so naturally repugnant that it need not be mentioned. The purpose of a concentration is not to teach anything in particular of substance but to teach certain "habits of mind": "to educate students as independent, knowledgeable, rigorous, and creative thinkers." It must be wrong, then, to study a subject because it might be useful, as students often do, especially students without a lot of money.

Harvard issued its new vision of liberal education—what it describes as a reaffirmation of an old vision—at the same time as it announced its new program to address unequal socioeconomic access to higher education. Harvard's curricular plan ignores the obvious linkages between where people come from and what they want their education to do for them. Students from poor high schools do not often arrive in college with the same ambition to develop "habits of mind" that their better-prepared peers with college-educated parents may find natural. Students who grow up with little money in the bank and few books in the house are disproportionately represented in concentrations related to career options, because the academic ambitions that have brought them to selective colleges generally are accompanied by financial ambitions, or at least financial obligations.

Left to their own free choice, students with little money tend to concentrate in areas that feed into, or at least are seen as feeding into, business, law, medicine, computing, bioscience, and engineering. Within those fields, ambitious students try to achieve mastery, that expertise to which the Harvard Faculty is opposed on the basis of some supposed antithesis to "liberal education." They will do so in order to win competitions for jobs and graduate schools, for which depth of knowledge is critical. Several times in the course of discussions of the curriculum, Harvard professors have based their arguments on the educational experiences of their own children, as though the Harvard education that would be best for children who have grown up in households full of books and ideas would be the best for other Harvard students as well. The more Harvard and similar colleges do to recruit and admit ambitious, talented, but economically disadvantaged students, the greater the tension that will exist between their goals and the liberal-arts curricula that are defined in terms of an emphasis on breadth and reflection and the disparagement of specialization, expertise, and useful knowledge.

It is, of course, not just the economically disadvantaged students who will need persuading that a liberal education as now construed is right for them. Economics is the largest concentration at Harvard not because most of its students are fascinated by economic theory, nor because it offers one of the better undergraduate experiences, nor because it is a major that is particularly good at developing "habits of mind." Economics attracts many students at Harvard and other colleges because those colleges have a lot of students who want to go into business, and this major seems to them the closest thing to a concentration near their career interests. The economics professors don't like this, and the students may not be correct in thinking that economics will be the most useful undergraduate program for them. Many businesses now look in their new hires for skills in information technology, knowledge of science or foreign languages, or other applicable learning, or simply seek the clear thinking, logical reasoning, and articulate speaking and writing in which philosophy students are trained.

After almost a century and a half of an elective curriculum, Harvard still has not squared its concept of liberal education with the realities of student choice, nor has it even acknowledged that the two are at odds. The course selections made by less-advantaged students reveal the tension between faculty rhetoric about the purpose of an education and students' pragmatism.

Though Eliot's Harvard curriculum was almost anarchic, his Harvard was held together by a set of assumptions about the purpose of a Harvard education. Those assumptions were challenged—the practical spirit could not be ignored in the late nineteenth century—but their cultural dominance was taken for granted. What a younger Eliot had called "the old-fashioned college" remained the gold standard of American education during his presidency and beyond. When Eliot eliminated the required curriculum, he radically changed Harvard and all of American higher education. But in this respect he did not change Harvard at all: Whether the curriculum was required or elective, students were not supposed to go to college to learn practical subjects or to prepare for a career. The social bonds of that Harvard are long gone. No longer is the gentleman, in pursuit of the Harvard watermark but otherwise unconcerned about what he learns, the normal Harvard student. Harvard is a much better institution for being free of the social presumptions that used to unify the College, but it has done little to replace the educational premises that came with them.

A college education is not just about preparation for earning a living. But a good education means something more than one that is broad in some respect and deep in some other, the vague ambitions of the curriculum proposed in late 2005. Of course, the dimensional extremes—an education a mile wide and an inch deep, or a mile high and an inch wide—are unlikely to be good for many students. But choice, flexibility, and distribution are simply the terms available for discussing undergraduate requirements when all discrimination about substance is off-limits and all reference to finding purpose in life has been ruled out.

A college education should provide "freedom from the isolation of one's own self, time and place," as former Cornell president Frank Rhodes put it recently. But inspiring what Harvard's Red Book called a "belief in the worth and meaning of the human spirit, however one may understand it" is not at odds with educating students to be employable. Today's Harvard is uninterested in both. It pays lip service to liberal education, saying that a Harvard education "must provide a broad introduction to the knowledge needed in an increasingly global and connected, yet simultaneously diverse and fragmented world." Yet it declines to offer an opinion on what knowledge is "needed" or on "what that breadth of knowledge should look like." These tattered remnants of the grand notion of general education are the emperor's new clothes; they signify nothing except that Harvard no longer knows what a good education is. Harvard tries to distract attention from its nakedness by disparaging students' motivations when they seek expertise and career preparation in the absence of any other rationale for their education. Harvard can again offer a great education if it recognizes that not everything Harvard professors want to teach is equally worth students learning, and that students should have the opportunity to learn useful things that the professors may not think interesting. Embracing those simple principles would begin to restore the ideal of an education that prepares students for lives as responsible and productive citizens.

CHAPTER 9

College Athletes and Money

Elitism in the Name of Amateurism

The War of Secession showed how much nobler are strength of will, firmness of purpose, resolution to endure, and capacity for action, than are the qualities of the speechmaker and the fine writer, which the nation had once agreed chiefly to admire.

—Francis A. Walker (LL.D. 1883), 1893

When I hear, therefore, the cheering at our great games, . . . I cannot feel that the passion is excessive. Is there not some pent-up energy in us . . . ready to bring us into other arenas, in which, as in those of Greece, honour should come not only to strength, swiftness, and beauty, but to every high gift and inspiration?

—George Santayana, 1894

The bearded, bespectacled young dean of students in one of the Houses stopped me after a meeting of the Administrative Board. "Is it true," he asked, "that they are trying to cut the number of athletes?" It was true; the *Crimson* had reported, correctly, that the presidents of Ivy League colleges were planning to reduce the ceiling on the number of football admittees in the freshman class to at most thirty, maybe twenty-five, from the current thirty-five. I was surprised he was interested; I didn't recall having seen him at any games. "That would be terrible," he continued. "They add so much to the House. They are the only people here who know how to lose."

It was halftime at the football game, and a faculty colleague and I interrupted our conversation to glance out onto the field at the formations of the Harvard Band members. We have both passed the age where the band's jokes make sense to us.

"Pretty small turnout by the band today," I said, wondering if there was another important event out of town that had depleted its ranks. "Good thing they don't have to spell any words longer than three letters. They wouldn't have enough bodies to do it."

"Yes," replied my colleague. "And if the football team had to spell anything longer than three letters, they wouldn't know how."

About 20 percent of Harvard students participate in varsity athletics at some point during their college careers. Many fewer than that were recruited to play sports, and many more than that play on some kind of athletic team, including junior varsity, club, or intramural sports. It is rarely hard to get a ticket for a Harvard athletic event; even the largest contest, the annual Harvard-Yale football game, is not the occasion for campus unity that athletic rivalries spur at many colleges. There are so many different levels and kinds of sports that the athletes are as diverse as the student body at large. Both the dean's and the professor's stereotypes about the worth of athletics are extremes. And both miss a characteristic Harvard athletes share with their less athletic peers: They have many talents and are devoted to the pursuit of extraordinary excellence in at least one of them.

The troubles with college athletics

Big-time intercollegiate athletic programs have been plagued with dreadful scandals—minuscule graduation rates, use of prostitutes to recruit high school athletes, gang rapes by members of athletic teams, and point-shaving schemes. Such scandals in nationally televised athletic programs fuel anti-athletic sentiment as passionate as the loyalty with which alumni support their football and basketball teams. Boosters happily donate large sums so their schools can pay coaches more than professors. No similar horror stories have surfaced recently about any Ivy League school. But as admission to selective colleges has grown more competitive, doubts about athletes' qualifications and the place of athletics have spread from nationally ranked programs to the Ivy League, where the number of beds is small and the proportion of athletes is large.

Harvard has no athletic celebrities. Most Harvard students, faculty, and deans could not name or recognize the quarterback of the football team. In 2004, Ryan Fitzpatrick captained the team during an undefeated season, and within six months of graduation, he was a quarterback for the St. Louis Rams; but while he was at Harvard, he was just another student to most of those who passed him in Harvard Yard.

For no other group at Harvard has the divergence between students and faculty, as both have evolved on their own paths toward excellence, been so consequential. Athletes are the last students for whom contempt and stereotyping are considered fair. A few years ago a field hockey player informed me that a professor had excluded her from his studio art course. He had students fill out a questionnaire listing their qualifications and other commitments, and, as he unapologetically explained, automatically excluded athletes on the basis that they would not be committed enough to his course work. I had the Faculty Handbook amended after this incident to caution against picking among students on nonacademic criteria, but the attitude behind the professor's selection method is not so easily eliminated.

Two facts about intercollegiate athletics are inescapable, and both trouble academics. First, athletics is about competition, about winning. Second, money matters. The history of college sports is a story of the interpretation and interconnection of these two facts.

Critics spin these two fundamental facts into anti-athletic edicts: Athletes care too much about winning when they should be playing just for fun; and athletes are too interested in making money and not interested enough in the life of the mind. The two distortions come together around the notion of athletic amateurism, sport played just for fun and not for money, the base on which the vast regulatory system of intercollegiate athletics is built.

Competition fuels everything at Ivy League schools. Yet only in athletics is excessive competitiveness viewed as a bad thing. As in other competitive domains, athletic success comes to those who are talented and experienced. Competition is an agent of improvement and, if the games are played at a high level, of excellence. In these ways athletic competitions are akin to the competitions in which scholars engage.

On the other hand, Ivy League athletic competitions, for all the work involved, are also a source of joy. Contests are exhilarating for those competing and entertaining for those who may be watching. Even the winners do not take much pleasure in lopsided competitions, because they have not been challenged to improve. Competition itself, not just victory, provides satisfaction.

The impulses to win and to enjoy are not inconsistent but should be in balance. In the Ivy League, athletes do not play *just* for fun, but—because all financial aid is based on need rather than on athletic participation—they can, if they wish, stop playing if playing is *no longer* fun. Some of the most interesting students are recruited athletes who excelled in something else after giving up their sport. One articulate president of the Black Students Association became active in campus politics after he parted ways with the football coach. A basketball player who preferred computer science to ball handling sold her first software company within five years of graduating. The saddest cases occur when athletes sustain injury and lose almost their whole identity. Harvard tries to impose a "broken leg test" when admitting athletes: If she breaks her leg, will she excel at something else? Of course, even athletes who remain healthy in college have nonathletic careers ahead of them—even if they play professionally for a while.

Athletic competitions differ from academic competitions in another important way: In athletics, there is no doubt who is the winner. The certainty and the undeniability of loss help explain why athletes tend to be mentally healthy and to help the mental health of those around them. They are used to sharing blame, not shifting it. They can lose but they are not victims. They are also used to thinking that teams, not individuals, accomplish great things.

Some professors scorn athletes because they care so much about practicing, perfecting, and winning. These same professors want their students to compete for academic honors, as they themselves have done. But—unless they were college athletes themselves—they do not see a connection between the games they have spent their lives winning and the athletic games their students are playing. In fact, they resent having their professional activities portrayed as competitions, even though they never turn down academic prizes when they win them. They are merely pursuing excellence, they believe, and occasionally being recognized for it. In fact, the two kinds of competition are more similar than they think, except that athletic competitions acknowledge what they are, and winning is unambiguous.

The second academic distortion of the nature of athletics involves money. Money spent on coaching, training, equipment, and facilities makes athletes better. In spite of the obvious role money plays in the development of athletic skill, the entire structure of intercollegiate competition is based on the fiction that good sportsmanship, the amateur athletic ideal, requires that money be kept away from athletes.

In the Ivy League, there are few walk-ons in the sports of football, basketball, soccer, lacrosse, field hockey, and ice hockey. Most members of Ivy League teams played in high school and were successful enough to attract attention. Their talent was recognized by a college coach—perhaps by coaches of several different colleges, which then competed for the students' attention. Their skills were developed by good coaching before college, often in special after-school and summer programs as well as in schools known for their good athletic programs. Such coaching and camps and clinics can cost a lot of money.

But money is considered a bad thing in college sports. Athletes must not touch any of it or they will lose their amateur standing. The rules are complex, and inadvertent violations are easy to incur. Every college has a compliance officer whose job is to work with the NCAA (and the Ivy office, in the case of Ivy League schools) to report violations and to assess penalties. The technicalities of compliance can be ludicrous. While I was dean, Harvard had to apologize because a member of the cross-country ski team had parked overnight at the athletic complex since he was driving the team, which had no van of its own, to a practice early the next morning. This was improper because the one night's free parking constituted a benefit of tangible value given to an athlete but not to other students. This benefit was not exactly at the same level as the gift of a golden Cadillac, but it was a violation of the same rule.

Of course, the money donated to support the athletic program, as opposed to athletes personally, does not draw frowns. Outside the Ivy League, universities turn their football and basketball games into national public spectacles in the hope that they can make money (though few actually do). No Ivy League school expects athletics to be a profit center. But Ivy League schools all engage in massive athletic fundraising from their alumni.

Lurking underneath all the ambivalence Ivy League colleges display about athletics and athletes are old questions about character and

about social class. Even in the twenty-first century, anti-athletic sentiments are proxies for misgivings about deeper values. Academics and
ordinary Americans view athletics very differently, and athletes get
caught in the middle.

The standard theory of college athletics

In the early 2000s, William G. Bowen, president of the Andrew W. Mellon Foundation and former president of Princeton University, published with coauthors two detailed studies of college athletics.* The
books, entitled *The Game of Life* and *Reclaiming the Game,* call for restraint
and reform in intercollegiate athletics at selective colleges. Both books
are subtitled *College Sports and Educational Values,* and their basic thesis is
that the one, as presently practiced, is out of whack with the other. The
books received widespread praise—Louis Menand called *The Game of
Life* "one of the most important books on higher education published
in the last twenty years"—and precipitated self-scrutiny in many athletic
leagues. In the aftermath of the books' publication, the Ivy League instituted athletic cutbacks and stronger admissions restraints. Two critical reviews of *The Game of Life* published in a law journal were more detailed and more sophisticated but attracted less notice.

Bowen's books hold the facts of college athletics against a theory of
why sports belong in colleges at all. The theory is the one generally accepted in academic circles, so I call it the Standard Theory of College
Athletics. The Standard Theory argues that sports are good for students, but not as good as athletes and their supporters would like to
think, and good only as long as athletes don't take the games too seriously. Bowen, for example, acknowledges that "by competing one
learns 'life lessons': teamwork, discipline, resilience, perseverance,
how to 'play by the rules' and accept outcomes one may not like." But
he then asserts that the goal should be "for regular students, who have
come to highly selective colleges for the right reasons . . . to learn the
lessons that sports can teach and to have fun in the process." Students
should not aspire to develop or to exercise athletic excellence, which
in a *New York Times* opinion piece he treats as an innate and accidental
characteristic: "With intellectual capital ever more important, how

---

*The books have different coauthors. For simplicity I use only Bowen's name when re-
ferring to the authors of either book.

great a role should hand-eye coordination play in deciding who is given educational opportunity?"

The Standard Theory is attractively democratic. Inclusiveness is universally valued, and under the Standard Theory everyone could be an intercollegiate athlete. In addition, the admissions committees of all colleges would know exactly how much weight to put on athletic excellence: zero. This approach would save a great deal of expense (no need for coaches to recruit if they play anyone who shows up) and would also avoid balancing imponderables (no need to compare a quarterback to an oboist, for example, since being a good quarterback would be irrelevant).

The Standard Theory is also warmly nostalgic. Advocates of the theory rue the changes that have occurred over the years in college sports, conjuring memories of a time when they were not as competitive or prone to excess as they now are. In their preface, the authors of *The Game of Life* sketch themselves as sometime college athletes who were also regular students, unlike today's college athletes. We are led to imagine the climate of college athletics in their day as the state of innocence they wish to reclaim.

Appealing as it is, the Standard Theory has negative consequences. First, most people who are not professors don't subscribe to it. Americans love sports, Americans are loyal to their alma maters, and Americans want to see their college teams win. Not everyone feels this way, of course; every year there are righteous editorials written about the disgrace of colleges prioritizing athletic talent in their admissions practices. But most of the colleges' constituents, aside from the professional academics, don't accept the Standard Theory, and that is why few colleges adhere to it.

If the Standard Theory were merely an imaginary ideal, it would not matter. The damage comes because some professors, and some reformers, believe that it could be realized. When they observe variations from it, they disapprove and generalize, and all athletes become targets of the disapproval. The art professor with the exclusionary enrollment policy assumed that athletes wouldn't devote long hours to working in the studio along with other students. If athletes were adhering to the Standard Theory, they would be playing just for fun and their course work would always come first. The professor felt justified in excluding the student because he was confident the student would not adhere to the Standard Theory.

When an incident like this occurs, word gets around that professors don't like athletes, and athletes become reluctant to let anyone know they are athletes. They stick together—they are inevitably together with their teammates for many hours anyway. They are then accused by adherents of the Standard Theory of not being real students, of having their own distinctive "jock culture."

It doesn't matter who started this vicious cycle. Anything students do that betrays the consequences of their athletic status (fewer hours in the day to devote to course work, scheduling conflicts between academic and athletic obligations, nodding off in class due to physical exhaustion) gives faculty the opportunity to hold students in violation of the Standard Theory. Professors then feel they can respond to athletes' failure to be "regular students," and athletes withdraw to protect themselves. Students may not even need to do anything to get this cycle started—their size alone may give them away.

The only way to repair relations between professors and students is for academic leaders to articulate, as though they truly believed it, that athletics have educational value and that athletes add something other than entertainment to the college community. It never happens at Harvard—only at alumni or athletic department gatherings does one hear of "teamwork, discipline, resilience, perseverance," to use Bowen's list of the virtues of athletics. Athletes, never hearing anyone from the university administration talk of such values, are likely to think the worst of faculty dispositions. The Faculty, not hearing any language to the contrary, may lump together Harvard athletes with the inarticulate football players they see in televised bowl games on New Year's Day.

It is difficult to believe that anyone who knows anything about athletics really subscribes to the Standard Theory. Bowen has fair-minded intentions: "Students who excel in sports have done absolutely nothing wrong, and they certainly do not deserve to be 'demonized.'" However, he elsewhere says—the emphasis is his:

> *Each recruited athlete who attends one of these schools has taken a spot away from another student who was, in all likelihood, more academically qualified—and probably more committed to taking full advantage of the educational resources available at these schools.*

The professor reading this vivid image of an athlete snatching a spot in the classroom away from a more qualified and more committed student might be forgiven for demonizing the athlete.

Explaining a concern about the disproportion of athletes majoring in the social sciences and interested in business, Bowen states: "In an ideal world, we would suppose, schools would like to see a diversity of majors, values, and career choices among all subgroups of students." This is the Standard Theory, extended beyond athletes to all categories of students—what might be called the Standard Theory of Everything. According to this theory, students who grew up in abject poverty should be no more interested in making money than students who grew up in comfortable circumstances. Students who grew up in Beijing should be no less interested in majoring in Afro-American studies than students who grew up in Chicago. And students from arts academies should be no less interested in playing football than students from public high schools in central Texas. Diversity, in the Standard Theory of Everything, would be an instrument of sameness.

The Standard Theory of Athletics is wrong. Indeed it is ridiculous. The idea that there was once a golden age when sports were played just for the love of the game, and winning was unimportant, is a persistent and damaging myth. According to the myth, sports became corrupted by excesses of competitiveness and by money, and colleges need to purify athletics by throwing out the harlots and moneychangers and restoring the purity to which athletics were born. Professional athletics evolved from amateur athletics, the myth says, just as professional baseball players started out as youngsters who played the sport for the love of it. That's what the Latin *amator* means—someone who loves something.

According to the myth, amateur competition can be kept pure only by arresting its development. An impermeable barrier must be established between competitors and money, specialization, training, and other excesses of professional sports. Rules governing both the modern Olympic games and intercollegiate athletics were based on this philosophical foundation. The Olympic games started to relax the pretense of amateurism in the 1980s and dropped it altogether when the U.S. basketball team became an NBA spin-off. In intercollegiate sports, however, the amateurism rules still stand.

But they are built on a foundation of sand. The notion that sports used to be amateur is not just factually false. It was an intentional lie, created in England in the nineteenth century to protect the hereditary aristocracy from having to play against members of the working class. And when carried across the Atlantic to American society, the lie lost much of its rationale. The attempt to preserve it in America has caused endless tension and confusion. Yet down to the present day, the highest authorities on intercollegiate athletics do not acknowledge the obvious fact that the price of staying within the rules of amateurism is vastly greater for people who have no money than it is for the well-to-do. Amateurism is an instrument of hierarchy, not of equality.

Greek athletics were never amateur, wishful thinking on the part of founders of the modern Olympics notwithstanding. The Greek word *athlon* means both a competition and a prize, and an athlete is someone who competes for a prize. The prizes in the Olympics and the other ancient Greek festivals were tangible and enormous, often the equivalent in olive oil of more than a year's earnings. Even when the prizes were crowns of laurels, more valuable rewards awaited the athletes after they returned to the cities that sponsored them. One authority calculates the lifetime earnings of one fifth century B.C.E athlete at more than $44 million. So important were Olympic victories to the prestige of Greek cities that top athletes exercised free agency more than two millennia before Curt Flood challenged the major league baseball owners for the same right. After the runner Astylos placed first in races for the city of Croton in both the 488 and 484 B.C.E Olympics, the city of Syracuse made it attractive for him to switch teams. He won in his third Olympics running for his new franchise. The Greeks saw in athletic excellence a virtuous ideal that payment of money did not sully.

Amateurism did not originate in Greece but in England in the nineteenth century. Intercollegiate competitions between Oxford and Cambridge were well established before 1850, and the spirit of competitive athletics stayed with the graduates when they moved on to their appointed roles in aristocratic British society. The world into which they took their athletic spirit was rapidly becoming industrialized. For the first time in history, laborers had time for leisure. Reformers helped create parks, holidays, vacations, working-men's clubs, and other institutions designed for the betterment of working men.

When the university graduates took their brand of participatory sports into the outside world, they found laborers eager to compete alongside them. Not all welcomed the breach of the wall between the social classes, and none welcomed it less than those who had most recently styled themselves gentlemen. As one contemporary account declared, "nearly all the members of the athletic clubs calling themselves 'Gentlemen Amateurs,' and who exclude tradesmen are, *in reality tradesmen's sons.*" Worse, the manual laborers, being in better physical condition than the upper classes, sometimes won, thus undercutting the premise of innate superiority that legitimized the British class system.

Amateurism was the solution to the problem. Until the late nineteenth century, the word "amateur" described painters and sculptors. As a description of sportsmen it acquired a technical definition that was unapologetically elitist, shutting out the lower social classes from gentlemen's athletic competitions. The British Amateur Athletic Union was formed in 1866 and two years later adopted this definition of an "amateur":

> Any person who has never competed in an open competition, or for public money, or for admission money, or with professionals for a prize, public money or admission money, and who has never, at any period of his life, taught or assisted in the pursuit of athletic exercises as a means of livelihood, or is a mechanic, artisan or labourer.

You could be born to a state of amateurism, if you were lucky enough to have a father who did not have to work with his hands. But if you lost your amateur status, then, like virginity, there was no getting it back. These sweeping definitions are the origin of the current NCAA warnings that if you are a prospective college athlete, you may not "Use your athletics skill for pay in any form" or "Participate on an amateur sports team and receive any salary, incentive payment, award, gratuity, educational expenses or expense allowances."

By long association with the standards of gentlemanly behavior, amateurism became synonymous with good sportsmanship. But as practiced in intercollegiate athletics today, amateurism and sportsmanship have little to do with each other. Amateurism under the NCAA is simply a prohibition on athletes earning money or associating too closely with commercial activities. It enforces the Standard Theory, but now as in the past its strictures bind financially disadvantaged students very differently from students of more privileged backgrounds. And the rules do little to support the educational values college sports can represent.

Amateurism jumped the Atlantic and became doctrine in American colleges because academics longed to restore an athletic purity that never existed. As early as 1893, a Harvard alumni magazine wrote: "The question of purifying athletics is not new." The history of sports in America, as seen through the lens of America's oldest college, explains how the nation imported this legacy of the British aristocracy.

Harvard's Puritan founding fathers were not fun-loving folk. To the extent they had anything positive to say about sports, it was that exercise might refresh students so they would work harder—literally, re-create them. A father sending his son off to Harvard around 1670 advised him to "break off" from his studies every now and then, suggesting that he "recreate your Self a little, and so to yur work afresh; let your recreation be such as may stir the Body chiefly, yet not violent, and whether such or sedentary, let it be never more than may Serve to make your Spirit the more free and lively in your Studies."

Even Cotton Mather of the Harvard Class of 1678, son of Harvard's sixth president and the minister at the center of the Salem witch trials, thought sports could serve a useful purpose, noting that "we suppose there are Diversions undoubtedly innocent, yea profitable and of use, to fit us for Service, by enlivening & fortifying our frail Nature, Invigorating the Animal Spirits, and brightening the Mind, when tired with a close Application to Business." One can hear echoes of Mather's melding of spiritual, physical, and mental refreshment in the advertisements for today's yoga and fitness classes. Though it would be a long time before the Standard Theory was crystallized in words, some of its precursors were forming even in the seventeenth century.

Games and other recreations were allowed in the early days, but not encouraged. In 1781 it was among "the antient Customs of Harvard College" that "The Freshmen shall furnish Batts, Balls, and Foot-Balls, for the use of the students, to be kept at the Buttery." The catastrophic riot of 1823 helped the Faculty realize that students needed nondestructive ways to let off steam. So in March 1826, just when Harvard was looking to Germany for modern learning, a German instructor, Charles Follen, was retained "for teaching a System of Gymnasticks to such members of the society as should choose to practise them." The drills proved to be just another unpopular regimentation, but Mr. Follen should be regarded as Harvard's first athletic director.

In 1839 a student was reprimanded for owning a boat, on the basis "that no student was allowed to keep a domestic animal except by permission of the Faculty, and that a boat was a domestic animal within the meaning of the statute." Rowing began at Harvard in 1844 as a British import—Oxford and Cambridge had been competing since 1829. But rowing at Harvard was curtailed within a few years. As a report written some twenty-five years later explained,

> toward the close of 1850 one of the crews had an "unpleasantness" in Boston with the guardians of the peace, which proceeded from words to blows, and ended by the calling out of the fire department, a very jolly *row*, and the incarceration of the crew. This made great trouble, boating was frowned upon, and new clubs were not allowed to organize.

Faculty disdain of athletics on the basis of what Bowen calls "jock culture" has deep roots at Harvard.

Though there are hints of earlier wrestling matches, the first clearly recorded competition was a football game between classes, already an annual ritual by 1827. A mock heroic poem, entitled "The Battle of the Delta" for the triangular piece of land on which the games were played, described the "shins unnumbered bruised" in the game, which was played less for exercise than for hazing the freshmen. Almost immediately after arriving in Cambridge, they had to face the sophomores, who had the advantage of knowing one another; in some years they had to face the juniors and then the seniors if they managed to win the earlier matches.

Though remembered fondly by the alumni, football games were very rough and eventually alarmed the Faculty. The last straw was when the president learned that "it was a growing custom of scholars preparing to enter college to take lessons in sparring and boxing, by way of qualification for the football match at the opening of the term." Thus when the 2005 Harvard football team arrived on campus August 24, almost a month before Harvard's first classes, the players were following a tradition of preseason practice almost a century and a half old.

President Felton declared in 1860 that "The annual game of football had degenerated into a fight between the Classes, in which serious injuries were inflicted," and on July 2 the Faculty banned the annual freshman-sophomore game. In protest the students staged a solemn funeral. A football dubbed "Foot Ball Fightum" was interred on the Delta in a casket, and the students mocked the Faculty's paternalism. "Exult, ye Freshmen, and clap your hands! The wise men who make big laws around a little table have stretched out their arms to encircle you, and for this once, your eyes and 'noses' are protected." The whole sophomore class then sang in unison, to the tune of "Auld Lang Syne," "Against the Faculty, let not a word be said, / Though we cannot but speak our sorrow / With steadfastly gaze on the face of the dead, / And bitterly think on the morrow./" This was an early student protest against the kinds of athletic regulations that are still resented today. In 2004 a *Crimson* columnist mocked the Ivy League presidents as "the eight grim reapers of the Ivies" for the restrictions they placed on football, accusing them of "seek[ing] to make winning of minimal importance" and challenging his fellow students to "stop giving these presidents a pass." The Faculty always had a different view of sports from the students. In 1860 the Faculty won the battle, but there were many more to come.

The first intercollegiate competition was in crew, not football. And the force that launched all of intercollegiate athletics was commerce. The very first intercollegiate contest would never have taken place had the amateurism rules existed at the time.

By 1849 it was possible to travel by rail from Boston to Alton Bay, New Hampshire, on the southern tip of Lake Winnipesaukee. From there passengers could take a grand side-wheeler owned by the railroad, *The Lady of the Lake,* to the developing resort communities around Winnipesaukee. The Boston, Concord, and Montreal Railroad Company was eager to stimulate interest in travel to the lake. While riding on the train near Lake Winnipesaukee, James Elkins, superintendent of the railroad, proposed to James Whiton of the Yale Class of 1853 that if he could arrange a race against a Harvard crew, the railroad would pay the full costs of both crews, travel and lodging, for the eight-day trip.

Yale issued the invitation only a few days before the beginning of summer vacation, and the race very nearly did not come off. Because the boating clubs had been banned, Harvard had no organized racing crew. President Eliot, who was an undergraduate at the time, later recalled that in those years, when a boat went out from Cambridge, two or three members would act as what we would today call "designated drivers," charged with "bringing home members of the crew who did not propose to return sober from an evening in Boston." Nonetheless, eight able-bodied men were found to accept Yale's challenge, and after several days of preparation, the race was held at Center Harbor on August 3, 1852, before a crowd of about a thousand spectators. Despite having practiced only three or four times before the race out of fear of raising blisters, the Harvard rowers won the two-mile race by four lengths, and American intercollegiate competition was born.

Was this first race an amateur competition, even in the informal sense—engaged in for the joy of the sport? The race was fun for the students and not a professional undertaking from their point of view. Nothing more than a pair of handsome oars was being awarded to the winner. Neither crew had a coach, and the training on both sides was minimal. Yet the entire enterprise was designed as a moneymaker for the railroad. From the beginning, the money involved, the public interest in athletic spectacles, and the less than gentlemanly behavior of the athletes made American intercollegiate athletics unlike anything in England.

Despite the success of this event, Harvard continued to limit the opportunities for racing. After a desultory showing in a race in 1857, the Harvard crew disbanded out of student indifference. Barely five years after America's first intercollegiate competition, Harvard students asked, "Are we to regain our reputation, or has our glory departed, never to return?"

Boating survived because it became respectable. Eliot, who had graduated in 1853 and was by now a tutor, joined a Harvard boat club consisting of graduate students and university officers who rowed for recreation "without aspiring to any great excellence, or taking part in races." Before disbanding, the 1857 crew had ordered on credit a six-oar shell, the first proper racing boat on the Charles River. When the boat arrived, four undergraduates recruited Eliot and Alexander Agassiz of the Class of 1853, later to take over for his father Louis as professor and head of the Museum of Comparative Zoology. In summer 1858 these six, quite likely the brainiest team Harvard ever assembled, rowed in two regattas. What Eliot called "a Boston City committee which had a large Irish element in it" organized the events. Among the opponents was "a crew of young Irish longshoremen called the 'Fort Hill Boys.'"

In letters to his fiancée, Eliot first assured her that he planned to "row just as hard as I comfortably can, and not a bit harder," though already after three days of practice his "fingers [felt] as stiff as any hodcarrier's." But after the race he acknowledged having gotten "tremendously excited" as "in the last half mile the people shouted and clapped, and cheered tremendously, which was a very nice thing to hear, which made us pull all the harder and better." By prearrangement, Harvard split the prize money, $100, with the Irish, and then used its share to pay off the debt on the boat. It was in these races that Harvard first donned red, a color selected by Eliot and one of his fellow oarsmen in preference to blue, orange, green, and yellow alternatives shown them by a Boston cloth merchant. The Chinese silk bandannas helped viewers on the shore to identify the Harvard men, and in the cascade of intercollegiate competitions that occurred during the subsequent decades, the color crimson became the Harvard standard.

Less than twenty years earlier, Harvard considered a boat to be something like a dog and prohibited students from "making or being present at any festive entertainment." And now here were a Harvard faculty member of Beacon Hill pedigree and the son of Harvard's greatest scientist, the one bragging to his girlfriend that his hands felt like those of a common laborer and the other observed from shore by his eminent father, both competing under the benevolent gaze of Boston politicians, exulting in their triumph over "great stout Irishmen, with awful muscles," and grateful to have pocketed enough prize money to cover their crew's debts.

America was changing. The idea was emerging that sports were good for one's character and even good for one's soul. There was something invigorating to spirit and body about athletic competition. What prompted this shift in attitude? Christianity had legitimized athletics.

In 1858 the Harvard-educated minister Thomas Wentworth Higginson published the manifesto of a new religious movement, Muscular Christianity. "Saints and Their Bodies" appeared a few months before Eliot's races in Boston Harbor. Higginson set out to correct the "impression that physical vigor and spiritual sanctity are incompatible." The Christians provided few good counterexamples, he said; one had to go back to ancient Greece to find ideal types, such as Plato, who was a wrestler. "We distrust the achievements of every saint without a body; and really have hopes of the Cambridge Divinity School, since hearing that it has organized a boat-club." Athletic pursuits were particularly important for young people, in Higginson's view. He went as far as suggesting that if more sports meant less study, that might be a good thing.

> Only keep a boy a pure and generous heart, and, whether he work or play, his time can scarcely be wasted. Should it prove, however, that the cultivation of active exercises diminishes the proportion of time given by children to study, we can only view it as an added advantage. Every year confirms us in the conviction, that our schools, public and private, systematically overtask the brains of the rising generation.

Higginson saw athletics as stress-reduction therapy for college students—Cotton Mather in a more progressive form. Higginson preferred contact sports, the red-meat sports. Football, boxing, and wrestling were better than gymnastics and especially walking, which, he said, was "to real exercise what vegetable food is to animal."

Muscular Christianity was in part a reaction to the feminization of religion in the Victorian era. It was also a reaction to the fact that in late-nineteenth-century America, the growth of industry was accompanied by a growth in sedentary desk jobs in finance and administration. Higginson noted in another essay that

> for an average American man, who leaves his place of business at nightfall with his head a mere furnace of red-hot brains and his body a pile of burnt-out cinders, utterly exhausted in the daily effort to put ten dollars more of distance between his posterity and the poorhouse,—for such a one to kindle up afresh after office-hours for a complicated chess-problem seems much as if a wood-sawyer, worn out with his week's work, should decide to order in his saw-horse on Saturday evening, and saw for fun.

Whether the risk was perceived as effeminacy or simple weakness, the reaction was, in the words of historian Clifford Putney, "a new model for manhood, one that stressed action rather than reflection and aggression rather than gentility." Theodore Roosevelt of the Harvard Class of 1880 came to symbolize America itself in what he described as a vigorous battle against the "general tendency among people of culture and education . . . to neglect and even look down on the rougher and manlier virtues."

Muscular Christianity provided a moral justification for the growing interest in "manly sports"—including football, which Higginson described as "the most glorious of all games to those whose animal life is sufficiently vigorous to enjoy it." The movement glorified regulated savagery, of which football was a natural exemplar. Higginson explained:

> There is, or ought to be, in all of us a touch of untamed gypsy nature, which should be trained, not crushed. We need, in the very midst of civilization, something which gives a little of the zest of savage life; and athletic exercises furnish the means. . . . The animal energy cannot and ought not to be suppressed.

These sentiments aligned with a much broader antimodernist sentiment in America, a fin-de-siècle despair that post–Civil War prosperity had softened the well-to-do Anglo-Saxon Americans and left their lives empty of meaning. In the words of the historian Jackson Lears, "For the late-Victorian bourgeoisie, intense experience—whether physical or emotional—seemed a lost possibility. There was no longer the opportunity for bodily testing provided by rural life, no longer the swift alternation of despair and exhilaration which characterized the old-style Protestant conversion." They "somehow had to choose between a life of authentic experience and the false comforts of modernity." For the new caste of office workers and capitalists, athleticism tinted with primitivism promised a path to reinvigoration.

The rise of college athletics also served to accommodate aspects of American populism within academic institutions. In 1828, Andrew Jackson had been elected president of the United States. With the exception of George Washington, all of his predecessors had been college-educated—two at Harvard, two at William and Mary, and one at Princeton (then the College of New Jersey). But Jackson was an unschooled warrior and represented an ideal man of action, a "primitivist hero . . . who brought wisdom straight out of the forest," as historian Richard Hofstadter put it. The type was prominent in American culture for decades, though the award of an honorary degree to Jackson outraged the Harvard Faculty. Late-nineteenth-century Harvard students must have been pained by the dissonance between the rough and ready masculinity idolized in politics as well as in religion, and the urbane sophistication of their collegiate experience.

Not until Theodore Roosevelt was the gap bridged: A Harvard man, too, could be physically vigorous, and proud of his past as frontiersman, warrior—and athlete. Ever since, as Hofstadter noted, "The aspiring politician, suspected of having too gentle an upbringing, too much idealism, or too many intellectual interests, can pass muster if he can point to a record of active military service; if that is lacking, having made the football team may do." The images in the 2004 presidential election of two Yalies, John Kerry giving a military salute to the Democratic convention and George Bush clearing brush in Texas, are tributes to the endurance of Roosevelt's legacy

Adherents of the Standard Theory argue that if athletic values ever had any relevance to the advancement of society, they do no longer. *The Game of Life* quotes a former business school admissions director asking, "Will the same marketing, team-oriented, structure-loving, athletic guy of the past function the same way in the nimble dot-com world?" Bowen suggests his answer to the question by noting that Bill Gates was not an athlete at Harvard. Indeed, Bill Gates's favorite game in college was poker, the game of choice of many an inventive capitalist in days gone by. However, Microsoft's CEO Steve Ballmer was a high school football star, managed the Harvard football team while he was in college, and deeply respects coach Joe Restic, under whom he served. If the games people play are related at all to the skills needed for success in business, the example of Microsoft makes the New Economy look a great deal like the Old.

Adherents to the Standard Theory argue against the value of athletics on the basis that the world of the future is the world of the mind, the world of "intellectual capital," the "nimble dot-com world." But the enormous popularity of intercollegiate sports was *caused by* the change of America from a rural, agrarian nation to an urban society of men whose "overtasked" brains were "a furnace of burnt-out cinders." The unmet longings that caused athletics to become a vast social force in America are, if anything, stronger in the world of office workers staring at computer screens than they ever were before.

President Charles William Eliot, who played a key role in creating the research university, also played a key role in bringing amateurism to America. As president he struggled for forty years to set up lines preventing Harvard students from the kind of interclass competition in which he had engaged.

When the coffin containing Foot Ball Fightum was solemnly interred on the Delta in 1860, the headstone stated *Resurgat,* that is, *May it rise again.* And so it did. In early spring 1871, William R. Tyler, a sophomore from the Class of 1874, accompanied by a junior and a senior, "waited upon" President Eliot, as Tyler described it, to "ask permission to play football." "As was natural, the request was met with some suspicion at first," Tyler reported, "but when, on investigation, our good faith became manifest, the desired permission was graciously accorded." By 1873 Harvard had a University Foot Ball Club—which was driven off Cambridge Common by complaint of some unsympathetic city residents.

Meanwhile, a different kind of football, more like soccer, was emerging at other colleges. Yale invited Harvard to a summit in New Haven where Harvard, Columbia, Rutgers, Princeton, and Yale were to come to a consensus about rules for intercollegiate competition. Counting the votes in advance, Harvard realized that its "Boston rules" version of the game would die if it joined the summit, and so, in a gesture of uncooperativeness repeated many times by colleges since then, politely declined to attend the meeting. The other schools met in frustration, knowing that Harvard would eventually have to be reckoned with regardless of the agreement they reached among themselves.

Instead, on March 14 and 15, 1874, Harvard played two games against McGill. The Delta was no longer available—the grand Memorial Hall had been built on it after the Civil War—so the games were played on Jarvis Field, where the Law School and the engineering buildings, including my office, now stand. About five hundred spectators paid fifty cents each to watch the game. After the second day, the teams went to Parker's in Boston (now the Omni Parker House Hotel) and drank the gate receipts. Intercollegiate football at Harvard, like rowing, was from the beginning a commercial activity.

The first day's game was played under "Boston rules," but with eleven to a side. The second day's contest was under rugby rules, but with ten to a side. An oblong rugby ball was used in place of the spherical ball of the Boston game, though Tyler doubted there were "three men in the college who had ever seen the egg-shaped ball." After a re-

EDUCATION.
Is there no middle course?

Figure 9.1   Thomas Nast's 1879 caricature of the scholar and the athlete.

turn engagement in Canada, Harvard concluded that the rugby rules were superior. Harvard's boycott of the 1873 convention gave rise to the basic parameters of the modern game of football.

Football grew rapidly and outstripped every effort to control it. In 1879, only a decade after the first intercollegiate football game, between Princeton and Rutgers, the divide between academic and athletic types of students was already so notorious that the great satirical draftsman Thomas Nast could caricature the two extremes in *Harper's Weekly* without explanation (Figure 9.1).

In the early 1880s, football games drew crowds of a few hundred and sometimes a few thousand people. A decade later the crowds were in the tens of thousands. In 1882 the baseball team played twenty-eight games, including nineteen on the road, and a professor demanded to know "whether the members of the team could be said to be fulfilling the purpose for which they came to college."

The Faculty finally imposed its authority, decisively and permanently, creating what is known as the Faculty Committee on Athletic Sports. The first regulations prohibited games against professionals and restricted competitions to Saturdays (the latter regulation was soon relaxed). With this, as Eliot reported to the Board of Overseers, "the Faculty . . . assumed for the first time a direct responsibility for the character and extent" of athletic competition. Harvard simultaneously learned the lesson it had taught its peer institutions a decade earlier: Where intercollegiate competition is concerned, if all the contestants cannot agree on the rules, a college may be forced to choose between withdrawing from competition or competing at a disadvantage. In this case Yale, by then an athletic powerhouse, refused to accede to the rule prohibiting college teams from competing against professionals.

Thus Eliot began his crusade to prevent college sports from "losing that amateur quality which should always characterize the bodily exercises and sports of young men who are in training for intellectual pursuits." A "professional standard of excellence" in athletics was for others who might not care so much if the games should "lose a large part of their charm" in the process. Yet the records of the time show clearly that football games were already so violent by the 1880s that they retained little of the "charm" Eliot hoped to preserve.

Along with banning competition against professionals, the Harvard committee also prohibited the hiring of athletic trainers or instructors without the written permission of the committee, which also voted to erect a fence around the athletic field to "protect the grounds and exclude objectionable persons." In 1884 Harvard and other colleges agreed on more stringent regulations. Professional coaches would be banned entirely, on the premise that if one college did it, then "their opponents should have a similar advantage, or the terms would be unequal"—an early gesture against athletic arms races.

Eliot's bottom line on sports was essentially the Standard Theory as we know it today. College sports are healthy recreations for regular students. Competition is good only insofar as it encourages physical exercise; beyond that it is bad. And even the scent of money taints college athletics, a warning he issued in 1882:

It is agreed on all hands that the increased attention given to physical exercise and athletic sports within the past twenty-five years has been, on the whole, of great advantage to the University; that the average physique of the mass of students has been sensibly improved, . . . and the ideal student has been transformed from a stooping, weak, and sickly youth into one well-formed, robust, and healthy. It is also agreed that athletic competitions, though necessary to the maintenance of a proper interest in the general subject, may easily run into excess, and on that account need to be kept within discreet limits; . . . the whole spirit of College sports and contest should be that of amateurs who are amusing themselves, and not that of professional players who are earning a living, and seeking a reputation for its pecuniary value.

Eliot's language grew sharper and more exasperated as athletics surged in popularity and wandered farther from his ideal. In 1888 he reported, "There are still many excesses and evils connected with athletic sports as intensified by intercollegiate competition," but he conceded that "effeminacy and luxury are even worse evils than brutality." In 1893, while praising the work of a reconstituted athletic committee, he complained of "an exaggeration of training and practice, which is caused in turn by an extreme and irrational competition"; of the "extravagant expenditure on athletic sports" at places like Harvard and Yale, which had "always put the things of the spirit above things of sense"; and of "an unwholesome desire for victory, by whatever means." Yet Harvard already honored the rule against professional coaches more in the breach than the observance. It paid its crew and baseball coaches, and the baseball coaches were often big-name major leaguers from the Boston Red Stockings.

Eliot was out of touch with America in his understanding of sports. In attacking football for its pointless dangers, he contrasted it with "other manly sports in which courage, presence of mind, and promptness of decision are to be cultivated, such as sailing, riding, climbing mountains, hunting, and the like"—sports to which few ordinary Americans could relate. He considered any form of deception unsportsmanlike. "To pitch a curved ball seemed to him to be a resort to a low form of cunning," according to Eliot biographer Henry James. Eliot was happy to see a student placed on probation and thereby removed from the baseball team, because "[t]hey boasted of his making a feint to throw a ball in one direction and then *throwing it in AN-OTHER!*" "The manly way to play football," he believed, "would be to attack the strongest part of the opponents' line." After complaints about fans' behavior toward the visiting team, Eliot seriously proposed that instead of "Three cheers for Harvard and Down with Yale," Harvard students should chant "Three cheers for Harvard and *one* for Yale." Even his grandchildren made fun of him for that.

In the meantime, the alumni were increasingly supporting athletics and were ever more persuaded of their virtues. On June 10, 1890, the great Boston philanthropist Henry Lee Higginson gave a large tract of land on the Boston side of the river in memory of six alumni who died for the Union during the Civil War. Higginson donated Soldier's Field "without any condition or restriction whatever," but he hoped "that the ground [would] be used for the present as a playground for the students, and that, in case [the Corporation] should need the ground by and for other purposes, another playground [would] be given to the students." Higginson saw nobility in the pursuit of athletics and hoped that the field would remind those playing on it of the character of the men it commemorated. The lives of those heroes taught

> the beauty and the holiness of work and of utter, unselfish, thoughtful devotion to the right cause, to our country, and to mankind . . . [and] my chief hope [for the field] is, that it will help to make you full-grown, well-developed men, able and ready to do good work of all kinds,—steadfastly, devotedly, thoughtfully; and that it will remind you of the reason for living, and of your own duties as men and citizens of the Republic.

When football games moved from Jarvis Field across the river to Soldier's Field, both their popularity and their roughness continued to grow. The boom in football was a fruit of the big changes Eliot had made to Harvard, the growth in numbers of undergraduates, the deregulation of their studies, and the creation of a research graduate school. The games provided a unifying collegiate experience for students who had no unifying academic experience and were treated as inferior to graduate students. In a report published in 1896, an alumni committee gave a sober assessment of the College in stating that the students do not meet; and the result is what may be expected. Unless a fellow comes from a large preparatory school, or has special advantages, he may never enjoy that good-fellowship which is one of the most important formative influences, as it is one of the dearest memories, of college life. Class feeling . . . is obsolete,—inevitably destroyed by the Elective System. . . . Will College feeling—will devotion to Harvard—go too?

This report laid the premise for another beneficence of Henry Lee Higginson, the Harvard Union, a clubhouse that would be called a student center if it were built today.* Higginson identified the social vacuum Eliot had created and tried to fill it.

By 1905 Eliot was fed up with football. He declared it "wholly unfit for colleges and schools" and "more brutalizing than prize-fighting, cock-fighting, or bull-fighting." He announced that it should be banned.

But football was beyond Eliot's control. The "mammoth new stadium" had opened on Soldier's Field in 1903. It was built in less than six months with the aid of gifts from the Class of 1879 and labor from students of the Lawrence Scientific School. The second game played there, the Yale game of 1903, drew a crowd of 40,000, reportedly the largest ever to witness a football game. Yet Harvard did not score a point against Yale in 1902, 1903, or 1904. Even the athletics committee knew it had to follow Yale's lead and hire a football coach. Abandoning with a vengeance its policy of no professional coaches, the committee offered $3,500 to Harvard athletic hero Bill Reid of the Class of 1901, but it wasn't enough. An alumni group threw in another $3,500, and in early 1905 Reid became Harvard's first paid football coach.

Reid's $7,000 salary was 30 percent more than the best-paid Harvard professor received and was comparable to Eliot's salary after his almost forty years as president. Eliot's personal financial condition had not been secure until he became president. He had been raised on Boston's Beacon Hill in comfortable circumstances, but his father had been bankrupted while Eliot was an undergraduate. Eliot deeply respected the self-denial of the New Englanders who had built Harvard. The extravagant compensation of a coach only in his twenties, the cost of the vast stadium, and football's violence all horrified him.

---

*After the Houses were built, this building became the Freshman Union and later the Barker Center for the Humanities. The original Varsity Club was contiguous, and the "HVC" logo is still visible over the door behind which literary scholars now work.

Harvard's hiring of a professional coach provoked criticism in the outside world as well. The sums of money involved in Harvard's arms race with Yale caused the same kind of public shock a century ago that athletic budgets cause today. *Life* magazine editorialized in 1905, "is it not something of a mistake to think of college football as primarily a game? Has it not come to be primarily a business proposition?"

Eliot's vision of "amateurs amusing themselves" was defeated in a rout. Bowen's hope to "reclaim the game" by returning it to regular students who are just playing for fun will fare no better in the long run. There is nothing to reclaim. There never was such a time as Eliot's and Bowen's purely amateur past when games were played merely for the fun of it.

Eliot wanted to create a purity that never existed in sports, even in the very first rowing and football competitions at Harvard. Racial and economic "purity" did once exist in America, though in days that were drawing to a close. The adoption of amateurism standards in America was an effort to protect the ruling classes, and the rules have had that effect ever since.

Eliot expressed his misgivings about social integration in muted language. In 1874, for example, only five years after he became president, he worried about Harvard students getting mixed up with the wrong sort of people.

> While the Corporation have given the best possible evidence of their desire to foster the manly sports, they have felt compelled to discourage by every means in their power the association of students with the class of persons who make their living by practicing or exhibiting these games; to dissuade students from making athletic sports the main business, instead of one of the incidental pleasures, of their college lives; and to prohibit altogether the taking of money for admission to witness the sports upon the college play-grounds.

The same Eliot who at age twenty-four had penned such irrepressible excitement about his victory over the Irish longshoremen, at age forty would "discourage by every means" the association of students with *the class of persons* who competed professionally. Eliot recognized that he himself might be considered a professional since money had been at stake in his race against the Irish. Yet it wasn't only professionals but anyone in the same "class" who should be avoided. The concept of amateurism, designed to protect the British upper classes from fraternization with manual laborers, had been translated to the social divisions of the New World.

It was Eliot's athletic director, Dudley Allen Sargent, who showed most clearly the thinking behind the amateur myth in America. Sargent was fiercely anticompetitive, a worthy heir to the legacy of gymnastics instructor Charles Follen. "Competition is to-day the archenemy of all true culture," Sargent declared, "mental as well as physical." In his management of Harvard's gymnasium, he avoided "appeal to the spirit of emulation and competition" to attract students to physical exercises, preferring "to appeal to a still higher motive,—the sense of duty which each man owes to himself to improve his physical condition and keep strong and well, that he may be able to bear his burdens in the world, and help to advance the condition of the rest of mankind by improving the stock and raising the average."

Sargent's views of physical education were based on racial theories that were widely accepted at the time. He felt that America's immigrants during the 1800s were not of the "pure stock" of the original settlers from the "higher social strata." The integrity of the American people had been diluted by this "large infusion of foreign blood of an inferior quality," and he thought athletic training would repair the damage. It was in the context of such thinking that Sargent's committees attempted to erect physical and statutory walls around Harvard athletics.

At the end of his presidency, Eliot made explicit his own thoughts on racial questions. "The Whites and the Negroes," he thought, "had better live beside each other in entire amity, but separate, under equal laws." He rejected the presumption, common, he said, among Southern Whites, "that political equality may lead to social admixture, at any rate, to an assertion on the part of Negroes of a right to social intercourse with white people." He further noted, "As to intermarriage between Whites and Blacks, all the best evidence seems to me to show that it is inexpedient." In 1912 Eliot joined many other prominent intellectuals in support of the eugenics movement, serving as vice president of the first International Congress of Eugenics in London.

The separation of the races, of the sexes, of the social classes, and of "amateur" and "professional" athletes were all widely accepted among

the American intelligentsia a century ago. In the early twenty-first century, we have moved past most but not all of these theories.

❧

The humility and grace signified by athletic amateurism are far too
dishonored today. But the amateur standard remains burdened by
the aristocratic baggage with which it was born. Alongside the sin of
competitiveness in the ideology of amateurism stands the sin of extreme proficiency. A second-rate classicist, E. N. Gardiner, built this
theoretical foundation in the early twentieth century. According to
Gardiner, "Before the end of the fifth century, the excessive prominence given to bodily excellence and athletic success had produced
specialization and professionalism," and then "sport, over-developed
and over-specialized, . . . ceased to invigorate the national life." Professionalism was not just the opposite of amateurism; it now meant excellence to excess. As the classicist David C. Young summarized, "*The
amateur philosophy is essentially anti-athletic. . . .* To be good in athletics
is good. To be *very* good in athletics is bad."

The fantastical story about ancient Greek athletics is the ultimate
source of the Standard Theory of College Athletics.* Today Bowen's
books lay claim to the same fictional Greek ideal. The dust jacket of
The Game of Life shows a classical Olympic athlete, a Roman white-marble
copy of the Greek *Discobolos* (discus thrower). The jacket of *Reclaiming
the Game* features a white-plaster female *Torch Bearer* (by Chester Beach,
ca. 1926). She resembles what a classical Greek female athlete would
have looked like, had there been any, and had they, unlike the male
athletes, worn clothes.

The Olympic movement used the amateur standard for exactly the
purposes for which the British aristocracy had created it: to keep out
undesirables. The most famous injustice done in the name of Olympic
amateurism was to the American Indian Jim Thorpe. The toast of the

---

*Among the ironies in the use of ancient Greek athletics to justify the stratification of
athletics by social class in Victorian England is that Greek athletics were a democratiz-
ing, not stratifying, social institution. Because competitors were nude (*gymnos*, as in
"gymnasium"), the wealthy or well-born did not stand out, and victory went to the
speedy or strong rather than to the influential. The classical scholar Stephen G. Miller
attributes the fundamental democratic notion of equality before the law (*isonomia*) to
the preeminence in Greece of the athletic ideal. Miller, *Ancient Greek Athletics* (Yale University Press, 2004), 232–234.

1912 Stockholm Olympics, Thorpe won both the pentathlon and the decathlon and was saluted by King Gustav V as "the greatest athlete in the world." A month later he was charged with being a professional because he had been paid $15 a week by a semiprofessional baseball team in North Carolina while in college. He was stripped of his gold medals, and repeated attempts to have them restored failed until long after his death.

Harvard students recognized early on that application of amateurism standards turned college athletics into an amusement of the well-to-do. In 1878 as a Harvard crew prepared to leave for Henley, the *Crimson* noted with scorn—and more than a little nationalistic provincialism—the British amateurism standard to which American boats might be held.

> That it would be a bitter pill for an English crew, composed possibly of English blue blood, to be defeated by a crew of horny-fisted American carpenters, every one must see; still, as the English sporting motto is supposed to be "Let the best man win," it would seem that our transatlantic cousins might suppress their aristocratic pride in the interest of "fair play," of which we hear so much, but see so little.

And when Harvard adopted the American analogs of the British standards, the student writers exploded in contempt. "The ridiculous ideas of the Harvard faculty about gate-money and fences are well known," wrote the *Crimson*. "Their idea is to cause all expense to be borne by the wealthier students, who can afford to subscribe to the maintenance of athletics. This for sooth brings about a spirit of democracy! Harvard democracy we had better call it." By the 1920s Harvard was trying to enroll students of lesser means, some of whom did not match Harvard's traditional clientele in ethnicity. Then, as now, athletic skill provided a route to a college education for students with neither lineage nor scholarship going for them. When times got tough in 1929, the opportunity to play for money was irresistible. My father-in-law, the son of an Irish fireman, was in exactly that situation. To keep Harvard clean, the dean insisted that Harvard ballplayers sign a pledge that they were not receiving any money, but he knew quite well they were being paid during the summer for playing Cape Cod League baseball.*

---

*Today Cape Cod League baseball operates within NCAA rules limiting the compensation of college players.

Amateurism is a technical concept that carries with it a good deal of conceptual baggage. In everyday usage, the term "amateur" can be merely descriptive ("she is an amateur photographer"), belittling (the great physicist James Clerk Maxwell was surprised that Bell's telephone was "capable of being put together by an amateur"), insulting ("this place is being run by amateurs"), or laudatory, as it is most often meant when applied to athletics. As a term of praise, it has inherited a whole set of favorable secondary meanings from its years of association with gentlemen. Amateurs are good sports, humble in victory and gracious in defeat. Amateurs respect their opponents and behave accordingly. Amateurs take the long view of life and do not let short-term victories and defeats loom too large. Such worthy values, once fundamental to good breeding and reinforced in elite schools, are more elusive today. Popular culture does little to reinforce them, so the athlete, amateur or not, who exhibits these behavioral characteristics is honored as a symbol of human dignity.

"Athletic amateurism," however, is a term with a specific definition, and the definition has to do with none of these values. The definition hinges entirely on the athlete's motivations for playing the game. Amateur athletes don't play for money, and they aren't excessively competitive. The NCAA's "principle of amateurism" is described as follows:

> Student-athletes shall be amateurs in an intercollegiate sport, and their participation should be motivated primarily by education and by the physical, mental and social benefits to be derived. Student participation in intercollegiate athletics is an avocation, and student-athletes should be protected from exploitation by professional and commercial enterprises.

Unfortunately, this affirmative statement is obscured by a great deal of tedious detail about what athletes can't do and by questionable application of principle to practice. The NCAA manual runs to 460 pages and the Ivy League manual adds another 178 pages. An absurd extreme of the NCAA's regulation of amateurism occurred when the U.S. women's hockey team won the 1998 Olympics, and a team photo appeared on a Wheaties box. The players who planned to return to college to play hockey, including five Harvard students, had to be omitted from the photo. Their presence would have been considered a commercial endorsement—even though no money was changing hands—and they would have lost their eligibility.

None of the worthy values associated with amateurism in the popular imagination is out-of-date. They are needed more now than ever, inside and outside the athletic world. Yet the real values that amateurism might represent have been lost in the thickets of Ivy League and NCAA regulations. The ethical ambition of amateurism, as it is commonly understood, is important to preserve in college athletics, but the technical definition of amateurism does not achieve the goal. Instead, it means just two things: Amateurism means not playing for money. And amateurism means playing for the love of the sport and not for the competition. Neither conceit makes sense as an absolute. If they ever did, they do no longer. Certainly extremes should be avoided. Harvard should not hire Shaq for a million dollars to play on its basketball team, and the basketball team needs to know that losing is not the end of the world. But avoiding the extremes should not require putting unreasonable financial burdens on students or denigrating the excitement of competition or the joy of victory gained through training, teamwork, and skill.

The professional-amateur divide as codified in NCAA and Ivy League regulations misses the mark. It serves universities' business interests better than their educational interests, and serves the interests of students aiming to become professional athletes better than the interests of those lifting themselves to success in other arenas.

I have a few proposals for normalizing the experience of college athletes. They pertain to all of college athletics but are aimed particularly at leagues that are already making a strong effort to treat athletes as they do other students—in particular, those leagues that provide financial aid only in proportion to financial need.

For American universities, intercollegiate competitions plainly are, and always have been, commercial activities. The hockey players can't have their photos on the Wheaties box, but their university can feature players' photos on its home page. Almost every intercollegiate sporting venue has commercial advertisements on the boards of college hockey rinks, even in the Ivy League. Students can't accept travel money from a company, but the company can buy a corporate booth at the football stadium and be thanked for it over the loudspeaker at halftime. Students can't make money on the basis of their athletic skills, but their university can put its athletic mascot on credit cards and earn a few cents each time an alum makes a purchase.

The hypocrisy of the dual standard in sports, with colleges trying to raise money however they can while holding the students to a white-as-the-driven-snow standard of financial disinterest, is rationally untenable. Many of the athletes in our colleges, though amateur by NCAA and Ivy standards, are professionals in the ordinary sense of the word. Their parents, if they were financially able, invested tens of thousands of dollars in them by sending them to sports camps every summer and to high schools with excellent coaching. Some college athletes were moved more than once between secondary schools in search of better or more supportive coaches. Some have had personal trainers. The massive level of family investment in development of athletic skill in high school students may be appalling from a public policy standpoint and may be unwise for the children it is supposed to advantage, but it is not against the rules of amateurism, and no rules to circumscribe it could ever be written. Why, then, is the athletically talented student with no such family resources prohibited from accepting modest rewards for athletic achievements? It cannot be because anyone seriously thinks that doing so will keep the preparation and training of all competitors at the same level.

The amateurism principle never made sense in America, but its endurance today is neither a vestige of imported snobbery nor evidence of high ideals for college athletes. Amateurism enables big-time athletic schools to control costs by forming a lawful cartel. Most Division I universities, except for members of the Ivy League, pay athletic grants-in-aid—athletic scholarships that are unrelated to financial need and are discontinued if athletic participation ends. Many students are paid more than is necessary to enable them to attend college. For all practical purposes, athletes receiving athletic scholarships are employees. By agreeing to a common cap on the level of their compensation, however, institutions avoid employment- and tax-law implications of larger payments and also limit their employee costs, albeit at a level far above what athletic revenues would justify if athletic programs were consistently considered as businesses. The limitation on payments to athletes from outside the colleges has no such rational economic justification; it is simply justified by the old idea of amateur purity.

Universities should certainly continue to regulate their athletic activities. In fact, they may be forced to do so more aggressively as it becomes more widely understood that the costs of their programs are being driven more by interinstitutional rivalries than by improvements to the athletic experience of their students or by the opportunity to make a profit. But out of fairness to the students, universities should relax their regulation of athletes. In the Ivy League, athletes in the major sports—football, basketball, ice hockey—are significantly more likely than students at large to be receiving financial aid. Especially as these universities strive to enroll more students of very modest means, the extremely rigid controls of athletes' compensation have discriminatory effects. The amateurism rules are supposed to prevent the unfair competition that would result if some college students were being trained and coached as professionals. But many of the unfair advantages the amateurism rules are supposed to preclude are available to students from wealthy families anyway. In practice, the amateurism rules affect the athletic development only of students whose families have little money.

An effective regulatory apparatus is already in place. Spectacular abuses in a few big-time athletic schools notwithstanding, the system holds athletes in the Ivy League and most other schools to the amateurism standard. To be fair to all students, the rules simply need to be adjusted. The devil would be in the details, of course, but proceeding down this path could reduce hardships, attenuate the endless concern about inconsequential violations of unimportant rules, and restore dignity, credibility, and idealism to the intercollegiate sports world.

There is every reason to let students, under controlled circumstances, earn something on the outside. Musicians who play in a student orchestra can earn pin money from performances outside college; students who form the college computer programming team can earn money from outside employers. There seems to be no intrinsic reason to treat athletes who earn small amounts of money over short time periods in a fundamentally different way. Fear of abuses should be countered by outlawing those abuses, not by preventing large numbers of students from earning small amounts of money in activities they enjoy. To prevent universities from dishonestly padding athletes' scholarships, neither colleges themselves nor their associated alumni should be allowed to pay athletes. Allowable athletic earnings should be capped at a few thousand dollars a year. (There is already a carefully regulated dollar limit of zero.) Students would have to report all their earnings if they wanted to retain eligibility. Schools could also limit the level and duration of professional activity by students who aim to play in college, to lessen concern that college athletes might be receiving significant training or coaching from activities for which they have been paid. To address concerns about professional teams becoming feeders for colleges, or about students' academic seriousness, universities could require students who had played professionally to complete an academic year without playing a sport.

Ivy League colleges rightly award financial aid purely on the basis of financial need. Breaching that line to award scholarships on the basis of either academic or athletic merit would result in a cycle of competition for top students that would shift money from students who need it to students who do not. But if students gain athletic prizes or awards from outside sources, they should be treated as academic prizes and not cause a loss of eligibility for intercollegiate competition.

The Ivy League has a more stringent amateurism standard than the NCAA. In the Ivy League, unlike in the rest of the NCAA, participating professionally in one sport makes a student ineligible to participate as a college athlete in any sport. This regulation does not achieve its intended purpose of maintaining a "level playing field," given the extraordinary levels of private coaching available to students whose families are able to afford it. The Ivy League's stringent standard should therefore be relaxed to conform to the NCAA's. If a student plays a year or two of minor league baseball and wants to play college basketball, he should be allowed to do so. The conditioning the student might receive in A-level baseball would not put him at an unfair advantage over students whose families had paid for years of private trainers and athletic club memberships.

Relaxing such constraints would, of course, create temptations for both families and colleges. Some technical measures such as those already suggested could prevent colleges from enrolling students who had too much truly professional experience. The most important thing to ensure—or restore—is the sense that the athletes representing colleges on the field indeed deserve to be students. Because of their extraordinarily high admission standards, the Ivy League colleges most need to regulate the academic qualifications of their athletes in order to stay true to their mission.

Every athletic league should maintain or increase those controls that truly level the playing field between competing colleges and that express the institutional values in which they take pride. Cynics would doubtless react to a relaxation of the amateurism standard for college athletes by protesting that colleges had become even more sports-crazy than they already are. Critics would likely claim that their suspicions about Ivy colleges having two separate student bodies, athletes and students, had been validated. Schools could refute such suspicions by demonstrating that their athletes were qualified and productive students.

The Ivy League already monitors the "representativeness" of inter-collegiate athletes by means of the "academic index." Coaches hate these "AI" controls, and alumni recall some great player of days gone by who today would be "kept out" by the AI. But admission standards have risen dramatically at all Ivy League colleges, the inevitable consequence of Harvard and Princeton and Yale becoming national institutions. The academic qualifications of Ivy athletes are higher than they once were, just as every part of the college class is now more qualified. Higher academic standards might change the nature of Ivy League sports but not necessarily. The draw of the Ivy League is very strong, and if there are academically talented quarterbacks and shortstops and midfielders anywhere in the world, some will want to enroll at an Ivy college. Likewise, the league's regulations on the length of the competitive season, the intensity of the practice schedule, and time away from classes are more stringent than the NCAA's.

Athletes and alumni sports advocates tend to resent the strictures that already exist. Indeed, some regulations are poorly drafted or imperfectly aimed, but they are not wrong in principle, and they could be maintained or strengthened while relaxing the amateurism rules. The regulations prohibiting athletes from accepting modest prizes from outside the university or being honored by a cereal company have no effect on the "level playing field" objective—they only disadvantage athletes personally, and they most disadvantage those athletes who have the least money.

The Standard Theory provides little rationale for the pursuit of inter-collegiate athletics at a high level. If college sports are for regular students having fun, big stadiums and professional coaches should be unnecessary. Academics resent college athletics, whereas students and alumni enjoy them. Athletic reform movements are launched from the premise that serious athletic competitions are a distraction from the educational mission of universities.

But intercollegiate athletics developed simultaneously with the research university itself. The modern research university with its football team is not a corruption of some earlier temple of the mind where students spent all their time studying. As soon as the principal mission of the university stopped being education of its undergraduates, the undergraduates began taking joy in athletics. The games were from the beginning a humanizing reaction to the large size of the university and to the retreat of the professors into their scholarly academic specialties.

The Harvard writings about athletics in the late nineteenth century almost all tend to one of two extremes. Either they are unrealistic in their indifference to the passion of competition, or they are overstated in their use of athletic victory as a metaphor for success in life or in war. Only the great Harvard philosopher George Santayana, in an 1894 article, managed a realistic assessment of the role of sports in institutions of higher learning that countered Eliot's nascent Standard Theory. When asked why he wasted his time sitting in the bleachers at baseball games, Santayana explained that sports "are a response to a natural impulse and exist only as an end in themselves. That is the reason why they have a kind of nobility which the public is quick to recognize." In athletics as in human intelligence, inequality must exist in order for excellence to exist; he noted that "men have different endowments, and only a few can do each thing as well as it is capable of being done."

Santayana identified a heritage that ties American athletics to English colleges—a heritage far deeper than the artifice of amateurism.

> The English academic tradition, founded upon the clerical life of the middle ages, has always maintained a broad conception of education. . . . [S]chools and colleges . . . contained the student's whole life, and they allowed a free and just development to all his faculties. . . . To this system is due that beauty, individuality, and wealth of associations which make English colleges so beloved and venerable. They have a value which cannot be compensated or represented by any lists of courses or catalogues of libraries,—the value of a rounded and traditional life. But even in England this state of things is disappearing. . . . The real loss would come if a merely scientific and tech-

nical training were to pass for a human one, and a liberal education were conceived to be possible without leisure, or a generous life without any of those fruits of leisure of which athletics are one. . . .

[In athletics there is] a great and continuous endeavor, a representation of all the primitive virtues and fundamental gifts of man. The conditions alone are artificial, and when well combined are even better than any natural conditions for the enacting of this sort of physical drama, a drama in which all moral and emotional interests are in a manner involved.

The ancient Greek *athlon* means more than the game and the victory prize. An *athlon* is any great human struggle, including a struggle against one's own limitations: a struggle for honor, for transcendence, or against mortality itself. Athletic games have been exalted as preparation for the struggles of war and disparaged as distractions from winning the real game of life, but such analogies are too simple and too specific. Athletics are a universal metaphor for the pursuit of excellence. They grip the human spirit with a force that great colleges should inspire in the souls of all their students. A college should teach its students to develop and use their potential to the highest level of which they are capable.

In 1960, at the end of his tenure as Harvard's dean of Admissions and Financial Aid, W. J. Bender wrote a lengthy report distilling the wisdom of years of effort to nationalize the Harvard student body through a vast outreach program. He observed, prophetically, that Harvard was becoming so attractive that it had the prospect of being able to decide exactly what kind of student body it wanted. This power had to be used wisely. A student body composed entirely of the students with the best academic potential could be an unhealthy community, disastrous to the "welfare of the individual student" because of the "total effect on the whole person." Harvard, Bender noted, "can be a bad place for some very promising people at a particular stage in their development." This caution has given rise to the recognition that all students admitted to Harvard, even students unlikely to rank high in the class academically, should have achieved some form of excellence in which they can thrive and take pride—what dean of faculty Henry Rosovsky called "a special talent or spark." Bender's bottom-line question was this:

Should the ultimate goal of Harvard's admission effort be to come as close as possible to a student body all of whom would have outstanding academic ability, all of whom would be . . . in the top 1 per cent, or even better, the top half of 1 per cent, of American college students? . . . Or should we consciously aim for a student body with a somewhat broader range of academic ability, perhaps the top 5 per cent of American college students, a student body deliberately selected within this range of ability to include a variety of personalities, talents, backgrounds and career goals?

In the end, Bender advocated a diverse and pluralistic view of Harvard in which academic excellence was only one of the factors to be considered in choosing the class, specifying that

my prejudice is for a Harvard College with a certain range and mixture and diversity in its student body—a college with some snobs and some Scandinavian farm boys who skate beautifully and some bright Bronx pre-meds, with some students who care passionately if unwisely (but who knows) about editing the *Crimson* or beating Yale, or who have an ambition to run a business and make a million, or to get elected to public office, a college in which not all the students have looked on school just as preparation for college, college as preparation for graduate school and graduate school as preparation for they know not what. Won't even our top-one-percent be better men and better scholars for being part of such a college?

Jerome Karabel, in his recent book *The Chosen*, traces the origins of this kind of rhetoric to President Lowell's overtly anti-Semitic admissions policies. Geographic diversity and athletic preferences—as well as lineage "tips"—were, Karabel argues, ways of holding down the number of Jews at Harvard without resorting to Lowell's explicit Jewish quota. Phrases such as "bright Bronx pre-meds" can be interpreted as thinly disguised codes.

Still, Bender's agenda of diversity served larger goals. It spread the benefits of a Harvard education across society, and it connected Harvard to all of America. "Admissions is a zero-sum game," a review of *The Chosen* summarized, "and any preferences—including affirmative action for African-Americans and other members of minority groups— make admissions criteria more stringent for everyone else." From the

1930s to the 1950s, some Italians and Irish reaped the benefits of incorporating nonacademic criteria into admissions decisions; today the same tensions are fought out around blacks, Hispanics, and Asians.

Even as Harvard continues to shed its history as a college of the moneyed elite, the imperative for academic excellence keeps it at risk of being a college of an intellectual and largely urban elite. The tension between the "Scandinavian farm boys" and the "Bronx pre-meds," the latter group already better educated and with higher test scores, reflects a mistrust between rural and urban America that dates to the nation's founding. When nonacademic criteria figure into the admissions process, they help Harvard look more like America. They provide a passport into a world of learning for young people whose spirit and ambitions are high but whose environment has not nurtured the life of the mind.

Harvard is a college of the best high school students that society can produce, and Harvard will return these students to society when they graduate. We should not be alarmed if our athletes, having distinguished themselves in places where money was short and where athletic excellence was valued more than poetry-writing, wind up being somewhat more interested in making money and somewhat less interested in writing poetry than their classmates. The football team is not going to resemble the Putnam mathematics team anytime soon, because in Texas and western Pennsylvania, the ranching and blue-collar communities instill in children a love of football, not mathematics. We should not be concerned, as Bowen is, when athletes graduate somewhat below where they "should" be in class rank given their objective qualifications. After all, by restricting honors to the top half of the class and making identical all degrees to students in the bottom half, Harvard and several other Ivy universities have signaled in the clearest possible way that it is unimportant whether one graduates in the tenth, twentieth, thirtieth, or fortieth percentile of the class. So long as our athletes meet Harvard's standards of personal probity and of academic achievement—which are not low by society's standards—they deserve our honor, respect, and support.

The reduction in the Standard Theory of athleticism to inborn talent fails to recognize athletes' ethos of self-sacrifice, perseverance, drive, endurance, determined pursuit of distant goals, and passionate ambition for perfection. Nor does the Standard Theory honor the analytical and spatial intelligence, the ability to strategize and to allocate

limited human resources that serious athletes consider essential to winning. These are the same traits that contribute to excellence in other
arenas, even academic and artistic achievement at the highest levels.
Like scholarship or mathematics or music, athletics at their best operate in a glorious parallel universe in which the lucky and the skilled
can temporarily dwell and excel, detached from the banality of ordinary life. Competitive ambitions and financial rewards need corrupt
sports no more than awards debase the value and purpose of learning
or of art. The pursuit of excellence in any area can be more than entertainment—it can be a thing of beauty that brings profound satisfaction to the human spirit.

Conclusion

Harvard strives to be the best at many things, and it often succeeds. But Harvard has protected its reputation for excellence at the expense of its sense of a larger purpose. Harvard's leaders have allowed the school's mission to drift from education to customer satisfaction. For them Harvard is no longer a city upon a hill but merely a brand name.*

Today's Harvard education offers as a common thread nothing like the Puritans' fear that their children would be left without a learned ministry, or Higginson's conviction that "the health and true welfare of our University and our country go hand in hand," or the Red Book's worry that civilization itself might lie in the balance if Harvard did not do its job. The old ideal of a liberal education lives on in name only. No longer does Harvard teach the things that will free the human mind and spirit. In 2005, after a three-year review of its curriculum, it concluded that its students are free agents and for the most part should study what they wish.

A liberal education in the sense Harvard now uses the term is simply an education not meant to make students employable. Undergraduate education should not be too advanced or too specialized, nor should it include courses that would be helpful in the world of business. Harvard's image of the liberally educated graduate mirrors the aristocratic ideal of the amateur athlete. Becoming too skilled at any one thing, so skilled that a graduate could make a living doing it, is distasteful. Students are better off being broadly educated generalists—though not

---

*In late 2005, in the midst of a budget deficit and many unattained educational ambitions, Harvard College prioritized marketing its brand name to its own students. It sought to fill the position of Director of Internal Communications, to "assume leadership of branding efforts for internal communications" and "create a unified brand for Harvard College across publications and websites."

much breadth can be demanded because students would resist any requirement.

Undergraduate education defined in this way allows professors to do as they wish as well. In an effort to persuade me that I should back the newly proposed, requirement-light curriculum, one professor offered that it meant we faculty members would no longer have to teach students who did not want to take our courses. But the courses from which students learn the most are often ones they would be disinclined to take without being pressed to do so. The general education courses I took on Western philosophy stretched and rewarded me in that way, and the Core course I teach on information technology and society plays that role for my students. If professors can define their job as teaching what they wish to those who wish to be taught it, Harvard will not carry the centuries-old ideal of a liberal education forward into the next generation. It will instead indulge students' inclinations to learn more of what they know already, while avoiding unpleasant but enlightening disagreements among professors about the relative importance of different studies. Liberal education will be reduced to an easy compromise among academics rather than a long-term commitment to the welfare of students and the society they will serve.

Even excellence assumes different meanings depending on the circumstances. No more than half the class should graduate with honors, Harvard opines, to preserve the value of the honors degree. The effect may be to make Harvard graduates, in aggregate, less well educated rather than more, but at least the media will no longer deride us for giving too many honors. The very concept of an honors program should be discarded, according to proposals afloat in late 2005. At the same time as Harvard plans to remove incentives to pursue advanced work in a field, it is proposing incentives to dilettantism, in the form of "secondary fields" in which students could earn recognition for a mere smattering of learning. In fact, stimulating Harvard's remarkable students to do excellent work is beyond our ambitions. This lowering of expectations for Harvard graduates may reflect the reluctance of some faculty to educate them. Several departments make it notoriously difficult for undergraduates to find thesis advisors, creating a kind of logic in curricular proposals that will not inspire students to write theses. The limited educational ambitions of faculty and of students reinforce each other. Both groups are happier if left to pursue their own interests.

Harvard teaches students but does not make them wise. They may achieve extraordinary excellence in both academic and extracurricular endeavors, but the whole educational experience does not cohere. Few could give a good answer, five or ten years after graduation day, to the simple question, What was the most important thing Harvard taught you? Parents hope that their children will remember, in later life, lessons greater than how to parallel park or how to balance a checkbook. Like good parents, a good university should help its students understand the complexities of the human condition—or at least what others, men and women of acknowledged wisdom, have thought about the difficulties of living an examined life. A good university challenges its students to ask questions that are both disturbing and deeply important. Part of becoming a responsible adult educated in the best tradition of human thought is to come to grips, personally, with the basic questions of life.

One might argue that the great, sprawling, modern research university must be different things to different people. Perhaps, given the other demands on its faculty, the best it can hope to do educationally is to present a menu from which its multitalented, multiethnic, multicultural, multinational students can pick and choose. This cafeteria theory of education avoids the problem of valuing some things more than others, of judging that the specialties of some professors are more important for educated citizens than the specialties of others. It suggests that character and morality, fundamental standards onto which we hold when some turbulence dislodges the circumstances in our lives, are not the university's business at all.

Some of the forces that have brought universities to incoherence are societal. Universities did not create the consumer culture, but they have been overtaken by it. Universities did not become expensive by themselves, but they are subject to the same economic forces as other institutions. What universities have not done is to resist societal forces where resistance would be right and proper. The greatest universities have fared the best—they are the highest ranked and the most sought after by the customers. Sadly, although their wealth and their desirability have put them in the best position to press back against the forces that have compromised the education they offer, they have instead drifted complacently along with those forces. Harvard, as the best of them all, can push back most easily. Because of its role in graduating many who will be leaders in society, Harvard has unsurpassed leverage to influence society by the lessons it teaches.

The forces controlling Harvard today want it to follow the crowd, to make Harvard like other universities. If most other places have something, be it a simple distribution requirement for graduation or a women's center, the new Harvard thinks they must be right. It is easier to justify doing as others do than to defend the principles behind Harvard's uniqueness, even if those principles have been a source of Harvard's strength. Harvard needs the will to push back where thoughtful consideration should lead it to other choices. That will—and greater willingness to think critically, independently, and coherently—are needed from everyone who is part of the Harvard family.

First, the leadership of the university. Harvard requires strong leadership. Harvard is not a direct democracy, not even a representative democracy. Decisions at Harvard cannot follow the average or the majority sentiment. Harvard needs leaders whom others will follow, not unquestioningly but with confidence and respect. But Harvard is not an autocracy either. In fact, it is more like a volunteer agency. Students at Harvard are volunteers—they would all be welcomed at other good schools if they wanted to leave. Even though they are subject to Harvard rules and regulations while they are enrolled, their power of passive resistance is far stronger than the university's power of coercion. They will study hard and do good work only if they are inspired to do so, only if they believe in the importance of what is asked of them.

Every faculty member is a volunteer too. Leading professors is, admittedly, like herding cats. They could all get jobs elsewhere at the drop of a hat. There are few effective punishments for professors, especially those with tenure, so the president and the deans cannot order them to be obedient. Almost everything professors do, they do because they have come to believe in its importance and rightness, not because someone above their pay grade tells them they should do it.

Even the support staff are volunteers. Those pushing paper can be made to do their jobs in the way that clerks everywhere are kept in line. But when they come in contact with students, they are likely to put on their human faces and to be candid about the way things work. Their loyalty is invaluable. The truth about Harvard's attitudes, motivations, and hypocrisies travels very efficiently by word of mouth in a university, whatever the communications office may say. There is no upstairs and downstairs in a healthy college. Students talk all the time to the police officers, the medical trainers, the financial aid officers, not to mention those with official advising and counseling roles. The employees at the bottom of the organizational tree are the ones who see students the most. They too are educators. They absorb the spirit of the institution and convey its values to students every day.

Most important in articulating and communicating institutional values is Harvard's civil service. Many long-serving educational administrators have inexplicably left Harvard in recent years. The buzzwords of the new approach to such appointments include "professionalizing" the staff, bringing in "fresh ideas," and just "shaking things up." Reorganization is a disruptive and unending process. New organizational trees accompany these reorganizations, with hierarchical, sharply defined reporting structures and new jobs to be filled by newly hired staff. Though touted as making Harvard better, these moves often succeed only in shifting attention away from the big picture. Each new dean or administrator or vice-provost assumes responsibility for some immediate task, which thereby becomes no one else's problem.

The reorganizations have also eliminated many of those who knew how Harvard used to be. Far more significant than any structural effect has been the incalculable loss to Harvard of many administrators who recognized their work as education and saw in it a high calling. They thought rigorously about the goals of a college education and how their part of Harvard might work with others to fulfill those goals. They were reflective about causes and effects, smart about students, and reluctant to risk teaching the wrong larger lesson by a quick decision that might be expedient in the short run. They were self-effacing members of a collective effort, and they provided perspective on deep and enduring problems. They were, in other words, genuine educational professionals. They left Harvard, or were forced to leave, because they did not fit into the new, retail-store university, in which orders are taken, defects are papered over to get the merchandise out the door, and the customers are sent home happy by "student service professionals."

Lawrence Summers was the product, not the source, of the trends that brought Harvard to its present predicament. He is an economist who sees the actions and decisions of men and women as governed by rational choice and power, not by belief and commitment. He was hired by and was answerable to a governing board consisting largely of people from the world of business and finance. As former U.S. Treasury secretary, he understands the power of money to shape society. In his Washington years he learned the ways of politics and the power of the media—and the importance of controlling information and communication, of message over substance.

Summers cultivated a reputation as a provocateur, but he avoided comment on difficult issues, such as banning military recruiters from campus, if stating Harvard's position was likely to excite adverse publicity. The Summers administration cannot even be credited with making the university more businesslike. Summers centralized power in order, he said, to run the university more efficiently. "Academic freedom is wonderful, but it really doesn't have a place in the purchase of cement," he said in explaining his effort to modernize Harvard. But the brilliant economist was a poor business manager. In the five years of his presidency, the balanced budget of the Faculty of Arts and Sciences fell to an annual deficit of $40 million, projected to become $100 million within five years—at the same time as the university endowment rose by more than $8 billion. Summers hired many high-priced consultants to review administrative structures, but the main result of his reorganizations was to swell the bureaucracy of assistant provosts, vice provosts and vice presidents, divisional deans and deputy deans, and assistant deans and associate deans. Much of the daily business of the university now becomes stalled in the bureaucratic thicket.

The vast power Summers held might have enabled him to achieve great successes. But his misfortune arose from the impatience, harshness, thoughtlessness, and lack of candor with which he used that power. Universities must, above all else, be places where reason and truth prevail over irrational exercise of authority. When Summers was installed as president, the Harvard Corporation instructed him of his responsibilities using the words of President Josiah Quincy from the early nineteenth century: to give "a true account of the gift of reason." Instead, describing his method of campus planning, Summers said that "sometimes fear does the work of reason"—a worldview legitimizing authoritarianism and rudeness.

In the Harvard of President Summers, students and Faculty were, like the electorate as seen from Washington, D.C., interest groups, not collections of individuals. Interest groups are given what their spokespersons say the groups want, in proportion to their size and influence. Students were promised fewer requirements; women students were promised a women's center. Educational pros and cons were balanced by political, not intellectual, analysis. The independent thinker could turn conventional populist at the cost of Harvard's uniqueness.

Summers enjoyed his celebrity; the *Crimson* called him a "rock star president." If unhappiness created public relations problems, the president could earmark funds to buy peace. Most retellings of the tale of Summers's remarks at the National Bureau of Economic Development (NBER) about women in science and engineering do not report the real source of the anger it caused. In the speech he belittled the importance of gender discrimination as an explanation for the small number of women scientists and said he thought that "intrinsic aptitude" was a more important factor. Yet three months earlier, when a large group of women professors pointed out to him a dramatic decline in hiring of women faculty, he offered no such theory. The faculty furor came because his NBER speech revealed to what he thought would be a friendly crowd his doubt that ordinary hiring efforts would ever yield many first-class women scientists. He responded by apologizing, creating a new bureaucracy, and committing a large sum of money—large, though only a little larger than the amount the Shleifer affair cost Harvard. The apologies and funds did not, however, erase the memory of his insincerity.

Public controversies and internal dissatisfactions marked Summers's tenure as president, but too much has been made of his personality and his management style in explaining his downfall. Surely he was as much of a bully as a bull in a china shop, and his contempt extended not just to individuals but to entire fields of study, but none of that would have mattered if his ideas had been inspiring. Summers presented no imaginative program, envisioned no educational ideal, carried no flaming torch that students or Faculty wanted to follow. A college needs ideas and goals; it needs an intellectual framework and a purpose. What Harvard offers instead is only a list of ingredients. Because whatever agenda he had was advanced so ineffectively and unconvincingly, Summers will be remembered as a weak president, not a strong one.

The Faculty of Arts and Sciences voted on March 15, 2005, "the Faculty lacks confidence in the leadership of Lawrence H. Summers." This vote came two months after his NBER speech and has often been construed as a rebuke of views he expressed in that talk, but the debate leading up to the vote raised many broader issues of substance, integrity, and governance. Any motion condemning a particular action or opinion probably would have failed.

The lack of confidence of the Harvard Faculty of Arts and Sciences in President Summers was widely caricatured as stemming from a complacent Faculty's resistance to his controversial and innovative ideas, a backlash resulting from his abrasiveness, or more simply an attack by feminist harpies allied with leftist crazies. The reality is that the ideas Summers offered did not meet the Harvard standard. He expressed his "controversial" ideas as one-liners in brief talks, not in essays in which ideas struggle against contrary ideas. There was, in his presidency, a glaring absence of the balanced, thoughtful, and informed analysis that characterizes the academy at its best. Where earlier Harvard presidents, including Summers's immediate predecessors Derek Bok and Neil Rudenstine, wrote eloquent essays about matters they thought worthy of broad attention, Summers avoided using the written word to provide deep analysis of complex issues. He offered no answers to his own challenge "to define what greatness is, what's most important to know and to teach students," and he did not inspire faculty members to do it either.

Summers's willingness to offend made him a hero to some, inside and outside Harvard, even as it insulted others. Anti-affirmative-action pundits lionized the sometime Clinton Democrat for his straight talk. Summers's presidency ended, however, not because of stylistic gaffes but because of disclosures of apparent dishonesty, which tipped the views of professors who supported him during the earlier controversies. When asked in a Faculty meeting on February 7, 2006, if he had any opinion about the university's actions in the Russian scandal, Summers denied knowing enough to make a judgment on the matter. This provoked soft murmurs from the many professors familiar with Harvard's role from a lengthy narrative published in January. A few days later Peter Ellison, the former dean of the Graduate School of Arts and Sciences, reported that in response to a question in an earlier Faculty meeting, the president had misrepresented his plans to change the Faculty's authority over doctoral programs. The issue, said Ellison, had become one of the president's character, not his personality or style. A second no-confidence vote was docketed for February 28; it would certainly have passed by a wide margin, with support from many whose main concerns were the president's integrity and candor. After discussions with the Corporation, Summers resigned on February 21, 2006, rather than face this humiliation. Discredited as a moral leader, he could no longer play the role of academic or executive leader.

Lists of Summers's achievements were quickly posted on the Harvard web site and parroted in major newspapers, both by news reporters and opinion writers. Yet many of the successes claimed for Summers are either not real or not his. To the extent that his agenda had substance, incompetent administration and lack of sustained attention damaged it more than any faculty intransigence.

Ultimately, Summers lacked the skills needed to make significant improvements to undergraduate education. His style was portrayed as hard-nosed and data-driven, but data documenting educational problem areas had been collected and published for years. An expanded seminar program, more study abroad, and an introductory science course are claimed as curricular achievements, but they fit into no big educational picture and may not even be improvements. The Faculty was already discussing the need for a curricular review a year before Summers became president; he deserves the credit for its official launch, but also the blame for its ham-handed management. In spite of the expectations he created when he became president, the undergraduate academic program he leaves behind may be less rigorous than the one he inherited and demand less study of science and of foreign cultures. The new financial aid program amounted to only $2 million in a financial aid budget of almost $85 million—which had grown without fanfare from $54 million over the previous six years. Summers announced the new program in a media blitz, but credited neither William Bowen, who had done extensive research on low-income students' decreasing access to higher education, nor James Engell, who documented the seriousness of the issue for a skeptical Summers many months before the program was announced. In the year preceding his departure, with his academic agenda for the College in tatters, he launched an all-out campaign meant to make students report that they are happier with Harvard but one that is unlikely to help them become more mature.

Planning for Harvard's new campus across the Charles River in Allston, regularly cited as one of Summers's greatest accomplishments, proceeded with the same disorganization as the curricular review—with multiple, poorly coordinated task forces, their work ignored when found to be flawed or unwelcome. The Allston campus would have been inconceivable had President Rudenstine not gradually acquired the real estate on which it will be built, and it would have been better planned under Rudenstine's patient and inclusive leadership than under Summers's chaotic lurching.

All this is to be expected in a university that orients itself toward external markers of prestige and influence. Deliberation and debate, the necessarily gradual processes by which reason prevails over impulse, are not the currency of a university in pursuit of temporal values. Summers is a victim in this drama, not a villain—a victim not of Faculty anger but of his success at the role the Corporation assigned to him.

Lawrence Summers's principal failing was not that he was too strong or too uncongenial, but that the wisdom, knowledge, and judgment he lent to faculty affairs were too feeble. In the end, professors realized that Summers was not offering leadership they could respect. The Harvard Faculty would rather mind its own business than vote down the president; they did not do so for sport. The majority voted against him, and a larger majority was prepared to do it again, because his intellectual contributions as president failed to meet Harvard's high standards and to bring honor to the institution. By failing to distance himself from his most rabid defenders, he legitimized anti-intellectualism and abetted attacks on the research university itself.

What Harvard needs more than anything is ideas and idealism, and those have to be articulated from the top. With the announcement that former president Derek Bok will be acting president, Harvard is already restoring confidence in its leadership. While some media accounts have characterized Harvard professors as inmates eager to run the asylum, the serious question is about the wishes not of the professors, but of the Corporation. In searching for Summers's successor, it runs the risk of being distracted by superficialities—candidates' gender, celebrity, and manners, for example. Yet it also has the opportunity to return to original principles, to think deeply about how a college fits within a research university in the twenty-first century, about how Harvard can do the most good for society, and about how Harvard fits within America and the world.

During most of the Summers years, the Corporation was a leadership vacuum. Its members were rarely heard from in public and rarely spoke to those who make the university run, except the president and his staff. If Harvard were a publicly held corporation in today's climate of intensely scrutinized corporate governance, the shareholders would have been up in arms about the failure of the directors to care responsibly for the institution. In airing their concerns about Summers's leadership, Harvard professors were playing the role of shareholders. In 2005, some Fellows who had joined the Corporation since Summers's selection began to listen to what professors were telling them, and the Corporation ultimately played its proper fiduciary role.

For Harvard to reclaim its soul, the alumni must recognize what has happened to their university. To the extent that controversies at Harvard were portrayed as a struggle between the president and the professors, the alumni stood skeptically on the sideline. They were led to see faculty members as ivory-tower snobs or social radicals, and when President Summers attacked Cornel West, who wears an afro and released a rap album, they gave the president the benefit of the doubt. But alumni who remember Harvard for the lasting values it gave them, and who have been proud when Harvard acted on its principles, should recognize where the economic and market incentives are taking their university. The alumni-elected Board of Overseers, the large if marginalized second body of the Harvard governing boards, was awakened during the Summers presidential crisis. It must not return to functioning as the University's honorees and cheerleaders rather than governors.

The biggest tasks await the Faculty. Every decision concerning undergraduates should be held to an educational standard. Courses, pubs, honors, curricula, maids—no matter what the choice, the question should be asked: If we do this, then over the course of four years, what lessons will Harvard students learn, and will they become better educated? Only if the Faculty is engaged, in small ways and large, in considering the purpose of changes can wise changes be made—changes that will make Harvard graduates both excellent and prepared to serve their roles in society. With good leadership, the Faculty will return to seeing the entire College as an educational enterprise, not a popularity contest.

The next Harvard president must help the Faculty develop a shared sense of educational responsibility for its undergraduates—for the students it actually has, with the backgrounds and ambitions they actually have. There is no better student body anywhere, and we professors are teaching them because they are the promise of the world. We must design a curriculum for these future citizens, professionals, and scholars that we ourselves respect, a course of studies we think will position them to improve the world.

We will never return to the Red Book days when the Faculty imagined that all students might take one course. That kind of unity did not even survive the translation of the Red Book into degree requirements in the 1940s. But there is an enormous difference between that impossible unity and today's total disunity. The Faculty must find a way to set priorities for itself so that it can give some guidance to students about what educated people, civilized people, should know in the twenty-first century.

I urge some great university to try this: Cloister a broadly based faculty committee to design ten general education courses, of which all students would have to take five. The courses could obey the old disciplinary divisions, but they would not have to. There would be no point in a turf battle about how many of the courses should be science courses, because if students did not want to take any of the science courses, they could avoid them. Allow the courses to compete for students, but make sure they did not compete on grades or workload. In case of an angry response from students or faculty that some important subject had been left out of the general education curriculum, a new course could be created, but only if an old course were eliminated. Over time, curricula would shift by an evolutionary process so that the most important subjects were guaranteed always to be available to all students, taught at a level appropriate for the unspecialized undergraduate.

The specifics of this proposal are unimportant. What is important is that it presents a college education as a zero-sum game. The faculty would be forced to select and to prioritize among books, theories, and ideas. If evolutionary theory is more important than gender theory, then the one might be in and the other out, and vice versa. The limited number of courses would force the faculty to make choices rather than pawn the choices off on individual students, while not wholly depriving students of choices. Given the way professors at Harvard and at other research universities are selected, not every professor's research specialty is equally worthwhile for the education of the citizens and the leaders of industry and government that these universities will graduate.

The faculty needs to change too. There is a great deal of goodwill among the faculty for more attention to undergraduates, and a great many disincentives and cultural biases prevent that goodwill from being translated into practice. Some of the change can, with incentives from the university's leaders, happen quickly. Departments that are famously indifferent to undergraduates can, tenure notwithstanding, undergo the same process of reorganization that is applied to other underperforming units. In the longer run, teaching should be a serious component of the faculty-hiring criteria, not simply a peripheral item. Alumni, parents, and students can all take a role in pressing for this change, and properly oriented governing boards can insist on it. Honest means of evaluating teaching will have to be developed, mechanisms that are as scrupulously unbiased as the rigorous system of external reviewers used to evaluate the scholarship of tenure candidates. More fundamentally, "teaching" needs to mean more than skill at lecturing and leading seminars. We must find a way to honor good character in our faculty and to penalize acts that call a professor's character into question. The evaluation of character is easier said than done, given the risks of bias and prejudice. But the present system so discourages any judgment of personal character that a better system would not be difficult to design.

Finally, the counseling and therapeutic services for undergraduates must share the stage with a less clinical treatment of students' hearts and souls. There is no program for this change. Telling students to go to church is not the answer, though church is an answer for some students. Community service is also an answer for some, though it has become so professionalized and technical that many students draw more managerial than spiritual value from volunteering. The opportunity to study under exemplary visitors from the "real world" is a special privilege of Harvard students—many estimable public servants hold study groups at Harvard's Institute of Politics, for example. The teaching of challenging texts, literary or philosophical, can raise in today's students the same important and troubling questions they have raised in other readers for centuries—if they are not taught to elicit "correct" answers that will earn high grades.

None of these proposals is inimical to excellence. Excellence must remain a guiding value, but the pursuit of excellence should no longer be an excuse for ignoring everything else. Faculty searches in very narrow fields should be banned, and faculty should be expected to offer some courses that span large domains of human thought. Excellence, as Lindsay Waters said, should not be confused with uniqueness. Professors, like ideal graduates, should possess knowledge in many things as well as expertise in one. That ideal should inform judgments of faculty excellence. Professors should be able to teach what students need to learn. If faculty members can't teach what needs to be taught, they should be able to learn it so they can teach it.

The restoration of a true core to undergraduate education, an approach to education that will turn dependent adolescents into wise adults, circles back to the question of leadership. The university's leaders must believe in the process of self-discovery, and they must articulate that belief. They must support and praise faculty and coaches and deans and career counselors and therapists who recognize its importance. To this end, the leaders must themselves embody the values of self-understanding, of maturity, of strength of character, and of compassion and empathy for others, as well as scholarly excellence. To lead a university that will turn promising freshmen into graduates who will represent the best of humanity, the leaders themselves must be wise and mature and good people, not merely smart and accomplished and skillful and expert. Everyone in the university family—parents and students and professors and members of the governing boards—should have a say in judging whether that standard is met.

In the spring of 1992, Harvard College experienced a period of unrest over race relations. The trouble had started even earlier, with the hanging of a Confederate flag outside a student room, but articles in student newspapers that year stirred strong emotions. A speech at Harvard by radical black-studies professor Leonard Jeffries and the Rodney King verdict in Los Angeles raised the intensity of the ongoing war of words. Characteristically, Harvard responded by creating a new administrative role, that of race relations czar. It assigned the job to the dean of students, Archie Epps.

Archie C. Epps III came to Harvard from the bayou country of Louisiana and was a graduate of Talladega College in Alabama. He served Harvard for twenty-eight years and by 1992 was as strong a symbol of the traditional values for which generations of alumni have loved Harvard as he was of Harvard's new populations. He led the band at football games, and he dined regularly at Harvard's literary clubs. He was Harvard's most visible minority administrator and also clashed with minority students who thought him insufficiently activist. He was a symbol of Harvard's ability to be new without ceasing to be old.

On issues of race relations, Epps's strategy was, in the apt words of former dean Jeremy Knowles, "tough love, with reason." Part of his response to the swirling controversies of the early 1990s was to require all incoming freshmen to read Ralph Waldo Emerson. For the next decade, the first reading in the first assignment for freshmen was Emerson's 1841 essay "Self-Reliance." Students had to get together in small groups with a faculty member or dean to discuss the text and a few other pieces that varied from year to year.

The Emerson exercise was unlike anything else in any late-twentieth-century university, and yet it was quintessentially Harvard. First, it was hard work. No one thought they were still in high school after arguing about the ambiguous significance of this text to their common lives. Second, everyone had to do it. There are ten classes of Harvard students who read "Self-Reliance" in this way at Harvard. They have no other text in common, nor do they have much else in common. Third, Emerson was *ours,* a member of the Harvard Class of 1821, part of the succession of Harvard graduates Emerson himself called "the long winding train reaching back into eternity," in a phrase now inscribed on a gate freshmen pass every day. By reading Emerson, we could draw on our own traditions in coming to grips with the important questions of life, and connect our traditions to the learning passed down from days long before the Puritans set foot on Massachusetts shores.

Why did Harvard make freshmen read an essay on self-reliance at a moment when it was trying to create community out of diversity? Because the way to free students from the presumptions with which they arrive is to have them believe in themselves as individuals, and not to see themselves first as members of identity groups. Self-understanding and confidence in one's own principles and judgments are key tools of educated citizens and leaders.

The development of self-reliance was not just a solution to the problem of community life. It was a key example of the kind of education that Harvard could offer its students. Archie Epps's introduction to the freshman readings summed up his vision: "The most important goal of a Harvard education is a philosophy of life that brings dignity and honor to human affairs."

Dignity. Honor. Responsibility for oneself. Developing a philosophy of life. Drawing on one's college education for the betterment of humanity. The very idea that a college education would *have* a goa⬛

Remembering that in a university, a lesson is taught and learned at every moment, in every one of the university's decisions and actions, however they are spun. Harvard would be a better place if in planning discussions, in negotiations between deans and departments, in meetings where search committees choose professors or deans or the president, and in speeches at commencement, some voice could remind those assembled that these are the real goals of our mission. It is not a game of strategy for better headlines or more grant money or more prizes for ourselves or for our students, though all those things may accrue if we bear our responsibilities well.

The problems dissected in these pages are but examples of how things go wrong when a college gets lazy. It does not challenge its teachers to decide what is most important to teach, and it does not challenge its students to take the difficult route to educational excellence. Grading becomes an external credential that distracts rather than supports learning. The curriculum becomes a way of keeping students and faculty busy and happy while advancing the university's economic agenda. Students become customers to be placated rather than whole beings challenged to stand on their own. Sports become an alien activity, and athletes become isolated. These are the problems that have troubled Harvard. Most of these problems have troubled the other great research universities as well, and if they are worse at Harvard, it is only because Harvard has most effectively pursued the wrong kind of success.

Harvard can again inspire its students to develop a philosophy of life that brings dignity and honor to human affairs if it signals those values in everything it does. If it fails in that mission, not only Harvard but the nation and civilization will be the poorer.

Notes

Front matter

vi   *Remember that our University: Addresses by Henry Lee Higginson* (The Merrymount Press, 1902), 48.

vi   *the test of a civilization:* A. Lawrence Lowell, Liberty and Discipline: *A Talk to Freshmen,* delivered to the freshmen of Yale College, October 15, 1915, New Haven (Yale University Press, 1916), 15–16.

xiv   *a liberal education:* Jorge Domínguez, Liberal education at Harvard in this century, in *Essays on General Education,* Harvard University Faculty of Arts and Sciences, fall 2004. Domínguez reports that he is paraphrasing Alfred North Whitehead.

Introduction: Hollow Excellence

2   *the dean of the Faculty resigned:* Evan H. Jacobs and Zachary M. Seward, Forced out by president, Kirby resigns, *Harvard Crimson,* February 1, 2006.

3   *"flexibility for intellectual exploration":* Harvard College Curricular Review, Educational Policy Committee Summary Statement on Concentrations, November 22, 2005, 4.

9   *"The demands of productivity":* Lindsay Waters, *Enemies of Promise: Publishing, Perishing, and the Eclipse of Scholarship* (Prickly Paradigm Press, 2004), 22, 36.

10   *top quarter of the class:* Office of Admissions and Financial Aid, Annual Report, Class of 2008, 2003–2004.

13   *A single year's bill:* Census data put median household income in 2003 at $43,300; see http://www.census.gov/hhes/www/img/incpov03/fig05.jpg.

16   *"the broader fabric":* Final Report, Committee to Address Alcohol and Health at Harvard, September 2004, 3.

Chapter 1: Choice and Direction

21   *"ample time, teachers, and oversight":* Josiah Royce, Present ideals of American university life, *Scribner's Magazine* 10, 3 (September 1891), 388.

21   *"I can see of improving":* L. B. R. Briggs, Reports of the President and Treasurer of Harvard College, 1906–07: Faculty of Arts and Sciences, 99. Reports in this series were published under seven slightly different names during the period 1825–1995 and included not only the president's reports but also the reports of treasurers and various deans. For simplicity, all future citations will be to Report of the President, with the name of the university officer who is the author and perhaps the name of the unit that is the subject of the report. All reports are

available through the website of the Harvard University Archives: http://hul.harvard.edu/huarc/refshelf/AnnualReports.htm.

21   *published in a math journal:* William H. Gates and Christos H. Papadimitriou, Bounds for sorting by prefix reversal, *Discrete Mathematics* 27, 1 (1979), 47–57.

23   *"the most comprehensive review":* Lauren A. E. Schuker and William C. Marra, Mixed reviews, *Harvard Crimson,* June 10, 2004.

23   *"How can we give":* Dean William C. Kirby's Letter to Colleagues Re: Undergraduate Education, October 7, 2002.

24   *"guiding philosophy will emerge":* Jeffrey Wolcowitz as quoted by Lauren A. E. Schuker and William C. Marra, Mixed reviews, *Harvard Crimson,* June 10, 2004.

24   *"60 pages of stunningly bland":* J. Hale Russell, Nobody likes a bad review, *Harvard Crimson,* April 29, 2004.

24   *"In the end the committee":* Louis Menand as quoted by Evan H. Jacobs, Committee delays gen. ed. report, *Harvard Crimson,* April 4, 2005.

24   *"frustrated by an endeavor":* Allison A. Frost and Evan H. Jacobs, Faculty to hear review progress, *Harvard Crimson,* April 12, 2005.

25   *"a tangled web":* De-generalizing gen ed, staff editorial, *Harvard Crimson,* May 4, 2005.

25   *"for the advancement":* The Charter of the President and Fellows of Harvard College under the Seal of the Colony of Massachusetts Bay, May 31, 1650, in Samuel Eliot Morison, *The Development of Harvard University Since the Inauguration of President Eliot* (Harvard University Press, 1930), xxv.

26   *"next things we longed for": New England's First Fruits,* 1640, reprinted in Samuel Eliot Morison, *The Founding of Harvard College* (Harvard University Press, 1935 and 1995), 432. Also inscribed on Johnston Gate.

26   *train a literate clergy:* This statement simplifies a complex and somewhat disputed story. According to Morison, Harvard was meant from the beginning to educate a significant number of youth who had no professional ambitions of any kind. Winthrop S. Hudson, calling Morison's explanation a "myth," insisted that preparation of the clergy was the primary purpose of Harvard at its founding; see The Morison myth concerning the founding of Harvard College, *Church History* 8 (1939), 148–159. A "vocational" explanation has also been put forward, though the term must be understood as Luther used it and as it was adapted by English Puritans; see Leonard Buckland Ranson, The vocational basis for the founding of Harvard College, Ph.D. thesis, University of Iowa, 1979, University Microfilms, 1980.

26   *about half the class:* Richard Hofstadter, *Anti-Intellectualism in American Life* (Vintage, 1963), 60.

27   *No graduating class had: Harvard University Quinquennial Catalogue of the Officers and Graduates, 1636–1930* (Harvard University, 1930).

28   *Greenwood presented:* Frederick Rudolph, *Curriculum* (Jossey-Bass, 1978), 42; and Samuel Eliot Morison, *Three Centuries of Harvard* (Belknap Press of Harvard University Press, 1936), 80.

28   *"guilty of various acts": Corporation Records,* vol. 1, p. 246; UAI.5.30.2, Harvard University Archives.

29   *only six instructors had studied:* Morison, *Three Centuries,* 224.

29   *"I am not aware":* Letter from Charles Sumner to Joseph Story, September 24, 1839, quoted by David Herbert Donald, *Charles Sumner* (Da Capo, 1996), part I, 14 (emphasis in original).

29   *"A youth who was regular":* Andrew P. Peabody, *Harvard Reminiscences* (Ticknor and Co., 1888), 202.

29   *"If truth is to be attained":* Quoted by Morison, *Three Centuries,* 226.

29 *"There was an influence"*: Ralph Waldo Emerson, in *The Works of Ralph Waldo Emerson*, vol. 10: Letters and Biographical Sketches (Houghton, Mifflin and Co., 1883), 312.

30 *"We are neither"*: Quoted by Morison, *Three Centuries*, 230.

31 *"separate departments"*: Overseers report of 1825, quoted in Rudolph, *Curriculum*, 77.

32 *"degrade them to the rank"*: Faculty quoted by William R. Thayer, An historical sketch of Harvard University, in *History of Middlesex County, Massachusetts*, vol. 1, D. Hamilton Hurd, ed. (J. W. Lewis, 1890), 94.

32 *unaware of faculty discontent*: Sara Rimer, At Harvard, the bigger concern of the faculty is the president's management style, *New York Times*, January 26, 2005.

32 *"the expression 'Not prepared'"*: Robert Grant, Harvard college in the seventies, *Scribner's Magazine* 21, 5 (May 1897), 560.

32 *"took Harvard College seriously"*: Henry Adams, *The Education of Henry Adams* (Modern Library, paperback edition, 1999), 54.

33 *"Harvard has, of late"*: Daniel Appleton White, The condition and wants of Harvard College: Address delivered before the Society of the Alumni of Harvard University on their anniversary, August 27, 1844, *North American Review* 60 (1845), 40.

33 *"The endless controversies"*: Charles William Eliot, Inaugural Address, in Samuel Eliot Morison, *Development of Harvard University*, 1869–1929, lix.

34 *"going to have new times"*: John Fiske, quoted by Henry James in *Charles W. Eliot* (Houghton Mifflin, 1930), vol. 1, 228.

34 *some thought his impact might rival Eliot's*: Morton Keller, What kind of leader will Harvard's president be? *Boston Globe*, March 13, 2001.

34 *Summers complained of Harvard's parochialism*: Lawrence H. Summers, Letter to the Harvard community, February 21, 2006, http://www.president.harvard.edu/speeches/2006/0221_summers.html.

34 *of which Eliot became president*: Morison, *Development of Harvard University*, xc.

35 *"problem to be solved"* Eliot, Inaugural Address, lx.

35 *"a little of everything"*: A. Lawrence Lowell, Inaugural Address, October 6, 1909, in Morison, *Development of Harvard*, lxxix.

35 *the manifesto "Higher Standard"*: *Harvard Lampoon* 2, 10 (March 1, 1877), 114. Eliot was almost always depicted in left profile because of a large birthmark on the right side of his face. The original caption includes verses from the prologue to Chaucer's *Canterbury Tales*: "A seemly man our hoste was withal, / Bold of his speche and wise and weel y taught, / And of manhode lakkid him naught."

35 *enlarge the faculty*: FAS dean to return to faculty, *Harvard Gazette*, February 14, 2002.

35 *eight new undergraduate houses*: Allston advances, *Harvard Magazine*, July-August, 2004.

36 *"a general acquaintance with"*: Eliot, Inaugural Address, lx.

36 *"the recitation, considered as"*: Eliot, Report of the President, 1879–80, 14.

36 *"become for the teacher"*: Ibid., 14–15.

37 *"school-boy spirit"*: Eliot, Report of the President, 1872–73, 12–13.

37 *"Since no textbooks existed"*: Adams, *Education of Henry Adams*, 303.

37 *"Formerly, the only business"*: James Freeman Clarke as quoted by Morison, *Three Centuries*, 347.

37 *"The whole problem"*: Adams, *Education of Henry Adams*, 302.

37 *"The unusually larger proportion"*: Eliot, Report of the President, 1894–95, 21.

37 *"for inspiration, guidance"*: Eliot, Inaugural Address, lxvi.

37 *"useless expenditure of force"*: Ibid.

38 *"a large admixture"*: Eliot, Report of the President, 1879–80, 15.

38 *"First, and perhaps the most":* Our section, *Harvard Crimson,* December 7, 1877.

39 *a Crimson columnist, oblivious to:* William L. Adams, The people in my section, *Harvard Crimson,* October 27, 2004.

39 *"If the large lecture courses":* L. B. R. Briggs, Report of the President, 1902–03: Faculty of Arts and Sciences, 95.

39 *"made still more efficient":* Eliot, Report of the President, 1903–04, 13.

39 *"increased educational efficiency":* Overseers vote of January 1907, quoted in Report of the President, 1906–07, 98.

39 *"requiring professors to do the work":* L. B. R. Briggs, Report of the President, 1906–07: Faculty of Arts and Sciences, 99.

40 *"that which was desired":* Quoted by Rudolph, *Curriculum,* 102.

40 *"instructors have felt prompted":* Eliot, Report of the President, 1879–80, 13.

41 *"The modern University study":* Josiah Royce, Present ideals of American university life, *Scribner's Magazine* 10, 3 (September 1891), 376–388 (emphasis in original).

42 *"There is nothing remarkable":* Editorial, *Harvard Monthly* 31, 4 (January 1901), 169.

42 *"Will anyone pretend":* William James, The Ph.D. octopus, *Harvard Monthly* 36 (1903), 1–9.

Chapter 2: Meritocracy and Citizenship

45 *Youth is the time:* Plato, *Republic,* quoted on the first page of The Committee on the Objectives of a General Education in a Free Society, *General Education in a Free Society* (Harvard University Press, 1945), 3.

45 *"[O]ur ancestors did not forget":* John Clarke, *Letters to a Student in the University at Cambridge, Massachusetts* (Boston, Samuel Hall, 1796), 13–14.

45 *"We are faced with a diversity":* General Education, 43.

46 *Almost 90 percent of respondents:* 2000 report by Public Agenda, cited by Deborah Wadsworth in Ready or not? Where the public stands on higher education reform, in *Declining by Degrees,* Richard H. Hersh and John Merrow, eds. (Palgrave, 2005), 25.

46 *almost three-quarters of today's:* Carol G. Schneider, Liberal education: Slip-sliding away? in Hersh and Merrow, *Declining by Degrees,* 62.

46 *"the highest development":* Eliot, Inaugural Address, lxv.

48 *"The college of the old type":* A. Lawrence Lowell, Inaugural Address, October 6, 1909, in Morison, *Development of Harvard,* lxxix.

48 *"best type of liberal education":* Ibid., lxxxiv.

49 *areas were (1) Language:* Appendix to Report of the President, 1908–09, 49–50.

49 *between 1901 and 1908:* Rudolph, *Curriculum,* 228.

50 *"a curious mixture":* Daniel Bell, *The Reforming of General Education* (Anchor, 1968), 13.

51 *brief but intense conservative reaction:* See, for example, Stanley Kurtz, Chicago blues: Saving Western civilization at Chicago, *National Review Online,* June 27, 2002; Thomas Bartlett, The smearing of Chicago, *Chronicle of Higher Education,* June 28, 2002; Mourning the fall of Western civ, editorial, *Chicago Sun-Times,* May 3, 2002.

51 *"two aspects of one problem":* James Bryant Conant, Report of the President, 1934–35, 6-8.

52 *Conant "sought to build":* Morton Keller and Phyllis Keller, *Making Harvard Modern* (Oxford University Press, 2001), 23.

53 *"life as a responsible human being":* General Education, 51.

53 *"traits of mind":* General Education, 93.

53 *"The heart of the problem":* James Bryant Conant, Report to Overseers, January, 1943, quoted in *General Education,* viii.

54   *"These two courses": General Education,* 217.

54   *"has become increasingly specialized":* Gen ed has turbulent past, editorial, *Harvard Crimson,* October 17, 1962.

55   *"a hopeless anachronism":* Michael Ryan, Gen ed used to mean something else, *Harvard Crimson,* February 24, 1971.

55   *"chauvinistic and dated":* Gentlemen and gen ed, editorial, *Harvard Crimson,* February 14, 1970.

55   *"For students these days":* Ibid.

55   *"period of confusion and catastrophe":* Quoted in Report of the President, 1945–46, 112.

55   *"some over-all logic": General Education,* 40–41.

55   *"studied in abstraction from values":* Ibid., 73.

56   *"required a staff of instructors":* Rudolph, *Curriculum,* 262 (emphasis in original).

56   *"that part of a student's": General Education,* 51.

57   *"vast changes [that] have occurred":* Henry Rosovsky, Letter to the Faculty on Undergraduate Education, October 1974; Office of the Dean, Faculty of Arts and Sciences, Harvard University, 2–3, 9, http://www.fas.harvard.edu/~secfas/1974Undergraduate.html.

58   *"methods of knowledge": General Education,* 59.

58   *"old-fashioned country-college":* Editorial, *Harvard Crimson,* February 25, 1882.

59   *"direct educational contact":* William C. Kirby, Dean's Annual Letter, 2001–02, February 1, 2003.

60   *"As the 'Red Book'":* Memorandum from William C. Kirby and Benedict H. Gross to the Harvard College Community, December 2003.

61   *"Are we going to teach literature":* Lawrence H. Summers as quoted by Daniel Golden, Shaking up Harvard, *Wall Street Journal,* June 8, 2004.

61   *report on General Education:* Harvard University Faculty of Arts and Sciences, Report on General Education, November 2005.

62   *"benign national ideology":* Report on General Education, 11.

65   *a firestorm erupted:* For example, Pamela Ferdinand, At Harvard, jousting over "jihad": Student's use of word in commencement speech draws controversy, *Washington Post,* May 31, 2002; Matthew Engel, Word association ignites Harvard row as student prepares jihad talk, *The Guardian* (London), June 1, 2002.

65   *jarring thing about the speech:* Zayed M. Yasin, senior English address printed under the title "Of faith and citizenship," *Harvard Magazine,* July-August 2002, 65.

65   *a punchier alternative:* Stephanie M. Skier, "Jihad" struck from title of speech, *Harvard Crimson,* June 3, 2002; also Edward B. Colby, The man behind the "jihad" speech: Senior Zayed Yasin, *Harvard Crimson,* June 6, 2002.

65   *"treat all other members":* Lawrence H. Summers, Letter to Members of the Harvard Community, September 19, 2001, http://www.news.harvard.edu/gazette/2001/09.13/lhs_statement.html.

65   *received a death threat:* See, for example, Free speech: testing, in John Harvard's Journal section, *Harvard Magazine,* July-August 2002. This article also reports humorist Al Franken's revealing joke at a more lighthearted event for seniors the day before Commencement. "I was all set to give a speech today entitled 'American Jihad.' But after receiving several complaints, I've decided instead to give a less controversial speech entitled 'The Case for Profiling Young Arab Men.'"

65   *"Concerns have been raised":* Lawrence H. Summers, Statement regarding Commencement Speech, May 29, 2002, http://www.president.harvard.edu/speeches/2002/commspeech.html.

66   *"I have met the enemy":* Vasugi V. Ganeshananthan, Listening to Zayed, *Harvard Crimson,* June 6, 2002.

66 *"[s]erious and thoughtful people":* Lawrence H. Summers, Address at Morning Prayers, September 17, 2002, http://www.president.harvard.edu/speeches/2002/morningprayers.html.

66 *"We are ultimately stronger":* Statement from President Lawrence H. Summers regarding invitation to Tom Paulin, November 20, 2002, http://www.president.harvard.edu/speeches/2002/poet.html.

67 *"Our intellectual universe":* Beth Potier, "Worldly" education assessed, *Harvard University Gazette,* March 14, 2002.

67 *"Should we not expect":* William C. Kirby, Dean's Letter, 2002–03, 5.

67 *"You know something?":* Lawrence H. Summers, Remarks at 50th Anniversary Celebration of the U.S.-Japan Fulbright Exchange, September 21, 2002, http://www.president.harvard.edu/speeches/2002/fulbright.html.

68 job of *"preparing people":* Lawrence H. Summers, Remarks to Harvard College Fund Assembly, Boston, October 12, 2002, http://www.president.harvard.edu/speeches/2002/collegefund.html.

68 *"As a leading American institution":* William C. Kirby, letter to "Colleagues" accompanying Curricular Review Report of 2004, 2.

68 disavowing any *"assumptions":* Report on General Education, November 2005, 31.

69 engage in extracurricular activities: See, for example, Saritha Komaritreddy, Leaving vs. leading: Debating study abroad, *Harvard Crimson,* December 1, 2003.

69 *"that foolish beginning":* Eliot, Inaugural Address, in Morison, *Development of Harvard,* lix.

69 caelum non animum: Horace, *Epistles* 1.11.27, quoted by Richard Thomas, General education and the fostering of free citizens, *Essays on General Education in Harvard College* (Faculty of Arts and Sciences, 2004), 101.

70 *"If you're going to come to Harvard":* William C. Kirby, quoted in Harvard proposes overhaul of undergrad curriculum, CNN.com, April 27, 2004, http://www.cnn.com/2004/EDUCATION/04/27/harvard.curriculum.ap/.

70 *"the world our students will live and work in":* William C. Kirby, Harvard past and present, at home and abroad, *Harvard Crimson,* June 5, 2003.

70 *"a purposeful mission":* Harvard University, Faculty of Arts and Sciences, A report on the Harvard College Curricular Review, April 2004, 40.

72 *"Since Sept. 11":* Harry R. Lewis, Harvard in America, a year later, *Harvard Crimson,* September 11, 2002.

Chapter 3: Contact, Competition, Cooperation

73 *"The object of the undergraduate":* A. Lawrence Lowell, Inaugural Address, October 6, 1909, *Development of Harvard University,* Samuel Eliot Morison, ed. (Harvard University Press, 1930), lxix.

73 *"The era had not yet come":* Rollo Walter Brown, *Harvard in the Golden Age* (Current Books, 1948), 130.

75 *"Among his other wise sayings":* Lowell, Inaugural Address, October 6, 1909, in Morison, ed., *Development of Harvard University,* lxxvix.

76 *"The personal contact":* A. Lawrence Lowell, Report of the President, 1927–28, 10–11.

76 *"The man of limited means":* A. C. Hanford, Report of the President, 1929–30: The College, 100–101.

77 Lowell also limited: See, for example, Jerome Karabel, *The Chosen* (Houghton Mifflin, 2005).

77 *"Harvard turned out to be"*: Stanley Marcus, *Minding the Store* (University of North Texas Press, 1997), 34–38.

77 *"The House Plan"*: A. Lawrence Lowell, Report of the President, 1928–29, 12.

78 *"People group together"*: Chocolate City Response to RSSC Proposal, http://web.mit.edu/advise/unifiedproposal/CC/RSSC.html.

79 *Harvard announced in fall 2005:* Margaret W. Ho, Plans for women's center solidify, *Harvard Crimson*, September 22, 2005.

79 *"A women's center is"*: Simon W. Vozick-Levinson, Room for improvement, *Harvard Crimson*, October 19, 2005.

79 *comments about the cognitive abilities:* In remarks at a meeting held at the National Bureau of Economic Research on January 14, 2005, Summers speculated that the underrepresentation of women in science and engineering might have little to do with discrimination and more to do with "issues of intrinsic aptitude, and particularly of the variability of aptitude" for these fields and their lifestyle decisions. The comments became national news in spite of Summers's apologies, and they precipitated major internal review at Harvard and significant initiatives aimed at redressing the disproportion at Harvard in these fields. The initiatives did not address the fact that senior women are more underrepresented in Harvard's Economics Department than in many of its science departments. Summers's remarks were posted on the president's website, http://www.president.harvard.edu/speeches/2005/nber.html.

79 *"The integration of Harvard"*: A space for all students, *Harvard Crimson*, September 26, 2005.

80 *"our women students want"*: Vozick-Levinson, Room for improvement.

80 *"distance learning"*: William C. Kirby, Annual Letter, 2001–02.

80 *urged "limiting severely"*: William C. Kirby, Annual Letter, 2002–03, 5.

80 *"Harvard students enjoy learning"*: One of several messages and images displayed cyclically on www.harvard.edu during summer 2004.

81 *"Professor Jardine"*: George Ticknor, *Remarks on Changes Lately Proposed or Adopted in Harvard University* (Cummings, Hilliard and Co., 1825), 7.

82 *"He was the wisest"*: Roger Rosenblatt, *Coming Apart* (Little, Brown, 1997), 70–71.

82 *Given the size of the College:* If every student takes four courses at once, every faculty member teaches two courses at once, and half the courses taught are for graduate students, then the *average* undergraduate course size has to be thirty-two. In fact this average is not achievable because two courses per term or four courses per year is an overestimate of the Harvard teaching load—a significant overestimate for faculty in some fields. I would guess that the average course size couldn't be less than fifty, given the number of small courses and the actual distribution of faculty teaching loads.

83 *the "purpose" stated in the guide:* Harvard University Committee on Undergraduate Education, The CUE Guide, 2004–05, i.

83 *student course evaluations:* Nalini Ambady and Robert Rosenthal, Half a minute: Predicting teacher evaluations from thin slices of nonverbal behavior and physical attractiveness, *Journal of Personality and Social Psychology* 64 (1993), 431–441.

83 *"as original thinkers and authors"*: Charles P. Thwing, *American Colleges: Their Students and Work* (G. P. Putnam's Sons, 1878), 25.

85 *Harvard faculty averaged:* Margaret W. Ho and Joshua P. Rogers, Harvard students less satisfied than peers with undergraduate experience, survey finds, *Harvard Crimson*, March 31, 2005.

85 *"The amount of personal attention"*: Ticknor, *Remarks on Changes*, 7.

85   *"the relations between"*: Andrew P. Peabody, *Harvard Reminiscences* (Ticknor and Co., 1888), 200.

86   *"With [students] it should be"*: White, The condition and wants of Harvard College, 63.

86   *an "increase in the number"*: Robert E. Herzstein, Survey stresses student-faculty contact, *Harvard Crimson,* December 1, 1950.

86   *"You are here to work"*: Nalina Sombuntham, Under the big tent, *Harvard Crimson,* June 5, 2003.

86   *running "Camp Harvard"*: Elisabeth S. Theodore and Jessica E. Vascellaro, Lewis departure may mean shift in college's priorities, *Harvard Crimson,* March 18, 2003.

86   *staff as "camp counselors"*: Anthony S. A. Freinberg, Debunking "Camp Harvard," *Harvard Crimson,* March 21, 2003.

87   *waiting list for meal contracts:* Edward S. Martin, Undergraduate life at Harvard, *Scribner's Magazine* 21, 5 (May 1897), 549. Martin reported that twenty years after Memorial Hall was completed, the student body had so grown that it was serving a third more men than had been intended, and there was a waiting list of six hundred.

87   *lists dozens, everything from: The Harvard Index for 1891–92: A University Directory,* vol. 18 (Alfred Mudge and Son, 1891).

87   *"tie of class"*: Martin, Undergraduate life at Harvard, 537–538.

87   *"The big finding is"*: Richard J. Light, *Making the Most of College* (Harvard University Press, 2001), 26 (emphasis in original).

87   *neutral promise to "examine"*: Kirby, Annual Letter 2001–02.

88   *"activities may enrich the life"*: Sombuntham, Under the big tent.

88   *"how to work effectively with others"*: Derek Bok, quoted in Sombuntham, Under the big tent.

88   *three computer science graduates:* Miguel Helft, Microsoft to buy San Francisco-based Internet advertising firm, *San Jose Mercury News,* November 5, 1998.

89   *Consider the physical activity:* This and the subsequent paragraph are substantially based on an internal memorandum I wrote in 2001.

Chapter 4: The Eternal Enigma: Advising

91   *"[T]here are minor details"*: Charles William Eliot, Report of the President, 1876–77, 24.

91   *"Faculty members have no special"*: Derek Bok, Report of the President, 1976–77, 26–27.

93   *"The relation was intended to be"*: Charles William Eliot, Report of the President, 1888–89, 9.

93   *"may consult his advisor"*: Clement Lawrence Smith, Report of the President: The College, 1888–89, 95.

93   *figure out "the choice of"*: Eliot, Report of the President, 1890–91, 13.

93   *system had "not produced"*: Editorial, *Harvard Monthly* 32, 5 (July 1901), 221–222.

94   *"For a Freshman when he faces"*: L. B. R. Briggs, Report of the President: Faculty of Arts and Sciences, 1901–02, 102.

94   *When the advising committee:* Draft Report of the Committee on Advising and Counseling, May 2005, http://www.fas.harvard.edu/curriculum-review/draft_pdf/report_adv.pdf.

95   *"a top professor who can guide"*: Marcella Bombardieri, Harvard reviews how freshmen are advised, *Boston Globe,* January 2, 2004.

95 *"groove predetermined by"*: James Bryant Conant, Report of the President, 1934–35, 8.

97 *"we remain cognizant of"*: Report on the Harvard College curricular review, April 2004, 22.

97 *"I don't know if we build"*: Fred Hargadon quoted by David Brooks, The organization kid, *Atlantic Monthly*, April 2001.

98 essay *"The Organization Kid"*: Ibid.

100 *"verbalizations of hopelessness"*: What can I do? How to recognize students in distress . . . and how to help, brochure, Harvard University, Student Health Coordinating Board, Office of the Provost, AY 2003–04.

102 *A Massachusetts court*: Marcella Bombardieri, Lawsuit allowed in MIT suicide, *Boston Globe*, July 30, 2005. Cho Hyun Shin et al. v. Massachusetts Institute of Technology et al., Opinion No. 89553, Docket No. 02-0403, Superior Court of Massachusetts, at Middlesex.

102 *"People learn, Dewey insisted"*: Louis Menand, Re-imagining liberal education, in Robert Orrill, executive editor, *Education and Democracy* (College Entrance Examination Board, 1997).

102 *basis of "teaching, scholarship"*: Appointment Handbook, Faculty of Arts and Sciences, Harvard University, 2004.

103 *"a deluge of medium and good men"*: Quoted in Keller and Keller, *Making Harvard Modern*, 155.

104 *"Universities have largely abandoned"*: Bok, Report of the President, 1986–87, 26–27.

104 *only for "grave misconduct"*: Third Statute of Harvard University, http://www .hsph.harvard.edu/facultyhandbook/org&gov4.htm.

104 *"The policy boils down to"*: Education in the Yard, II: Admissions, *Harvard Crimson*, April 27, 1938.

105 *"I have a Harvard office"*: Martin Feldstein quoted by David Leonhardt, Scholarly mentor to Bush's team, *New York Times*, December 1, 2002.

105 *"Fortunately, most faculty"*: Bok, Report of the President, 1986–87, 27.

105 *in the face of a fatwa*: Fatwa feud, *Guardian Unlimited*, August 2, 2005, http://www.guardian.co.uk/elsewhere/journalist/story/0,7792,1541091,00.html.

106 *"drilling holes for dynamite"*: Diana L. Eck, *Encountering God* (Beacon Press, 2003), 7.

106 *"a university can emphasize"*: Bok, Report of the President, 1986–87, 27.

106 *"to help [student athletes]"*: From the job posting for Requisition Number 20076, Assistant Coach, Men's Tennis, posted on jobs.harvard.edu on June 10, 2004.

Chapter 5: Why Grades Go Up

107 *"In the present practice"*: Report of the Committee on Raising the Standard, Harvard University, January 16, 1894, UAIII 5.15, Harvard University Archives.

107 *"Harvard's Quiet Secret"*: Patrick Healy, Matters of honor; Harvard's quiet secret: Rampant grade inflation, *Boston Globe*, October 7, 2001.

107 *"Harvard's Honors Fall"*: Patrick Healy, Matters of honor, second of two parts; Harvard's honors fall to the merely average, *Boston Globe*, October 8, 2001.

107 *"Hilarious"*: Richard Brodhead quoted in ibid.

107 *"In a healthy university"*: Harvey Mansfield, Grade inflation: It's time to face the facts, *Chronicle of Higher Education*, April 6, 2001, 24.

107 *"very concerned about"*: Patrick Healy, Harvard asks faculty to justify grading methods, *Boston Globe*, October 23, 2001.

107 *had lax standards:* Patrick Healy, "Careful review" of grading urged at Harvard, *Boston Globe,* November 14, 2001.

107 *needed "to be sensitive":* Elisabeth S. Theodore, Summers addresses grade inflation, *Harvard Crimson,* January 18, 2002.

108 *"Harvard, long a center":* Why grade inflation is serious, editorial, *New York Times,* December 9, 2001.

108 *"The fact that 50%":* Ivy League grade inflation, editorial, *USA Today,* February 7, 2002.

108 *"the rot of grade inflation":* Jeff Jacoby, Summers's truth-telling, *Boston Globe,* September 26, 2002.

108 *"can't outlaw failure":* Pete DuPont, You can't outlaw failure, *Wall Street Journal,* June 10, 2003.

109 *"committed itself to awarding":* Patrick Healy, Harvard to award more B's, raise honors standards, *Boston Globe,* May 22, 2002.

109 *"to put the excellence back":* Anemona Hartocollis, Harvard faculty votes to put the excellence back in the A, *New York Times,* May 22, 2002.

109 *students on the Dean's List:* The graph and the subsequent discussion are adapted from Harry R. Lewis, The racial theory of grade inflation, *Harvard Crimson,* April 23, 2001. The data are from public reports of the university.

111 *summa degrees to 115 seniors:* Peggy S. Chen, "Worries about summa integrity drive downsizing reform," *Harvard Crimson,* June 5, 1997.

111 *"An A means less":* Lawrence Buell quoted by Andrew S. Chang, "Grade inflation becomes an educational fact of college life," *Harvard Crimson,* June 5, 1997.

111 *"I haven't spent many hours":* Andrew Chang, Grade inflation becomes an educational fact of college life, *Harvard Crimson,* June 5, 1997.

111 *80 percent of the class:* Alice Dembner, Cum laude gets harder to come by, *Boston Globe,* February 11, 1997.

112 *"Academic politics":* Though often attributed to Henry Kissinger, a version of this maxim seems to have originated with the political scientist Wallace Sayre. Sayre is quoted by Charles Philip Issawi, *Issawi's Laws of Social Motion* (Hawthorn Books, 1973), 178: "In any dispute the intensity of feeling is inversely proportional to the value of the stakes at issue—that is why academic politics are so bitter."

112 *"academic life may come to resemble":* George Will, D is for dodo, *Newsweek,* February 9, 1976.

112 *"practices have grown soft":* Lee H. Simowitz, Increase in honors marks prompts study of grading, *Harvard Crimson,* October 13, 1966.

112 *"proportion of the exceptionally bright":* Nathan Marsh Pusey, Report of the President, 1955–56, 19.

113 *"This increase in Honors":* Delmar Leighton, Report of the President, 1952–53: The College, 79.

113 *"It has even been argued":* W. J. Bender, Report of the President, 1951–52: The College, 103.

113 *fact that "the undergraduates took":* Dean A. C. Hanford quoted in Dean's annual report explains higher standard of scholarship, *Harvard Crimson,* January 4, 1933.

114 *"higher than the normal":* A. Lawrence Lowell, letter to I. L. Winter, March 29, 1912, in Lowell Papers, UAI 5.160, 1909–14, folder 1040, Harvard University Archives.

114 *"Does it not appear":* I. L. Winter, letter to A. Lawrence Lowell, November 4, 1914, in Lowell Papers, UAI 5.160, 1909–14, folder 1040, Harvard University Archives.

114 *"tried to maintain":* A. Lawrence Lowell, letter to A. B. Wolfe of the University of Texas, March 27, 1915, in Lowell Papers, UAI 5.160, 1914–17, folder 220, Harvard University Archives.

114 *"Those particular eight":* A. Lawrence Lowell, letter to Professor Mary Augusta Scott of Smith College, December 13, 1910, in Lowell Papers, UAI 5.160, 1909–14, folder 1040, Harvard University Archives.

114 *"in a number of departments":* Report of the Committee Appointed to Consider How Tests for Rank in College may be made a More Generally Recognized Measure of Intellectual Power, Appendix to Reports of the President and the Treasurer of Harvard College, 1908–09, 43. The context makes clear that it is grading, not merely workload, that is thought too lenient.

115 *"[The Committee] believes":* Report of the Committee on Raising the Standard, Harvard University, January 16, 1894, UAIII 5.15, Harvard University Archives.

115 *"everyone knows that C is":* Mansfield, Grade inflation: It's time to face the facts.

115 *That year the average grade:* This is the table of grade distribution at Harvard that was printed in the *Daily Crimson,* April 21, 1890.

1890 *Grades*	%A	%B	%C	%D	%E
Freshmen	15.9	22.7	36.8	21.5	2.9
Sophomores	16.2	26.8	26.4	18.9	1.7
Juniors	17.9	32.8	35.9	13.0	.8
Seniors	22.1	37.6	31.8	7.6	1.2
All Students	17.8	29.7	35.4	15.9	1.6

115 *freshman year, 1949–1950:* Comparison of Distribution of the Grades of Undergraduates for the Fall Term 1949–50, Folder "Course Grading 1946–1950," UAIII 5.33, Box 245, Harvard University Archives.

116 *Mansfield's sophomore year:* Board votes to continue draft grading, *Harvard Crimson,* October 4, 1951.

116 *grade distribution for 2004–2005:* Mailing to all faculty in Arts and Sciences in fall 2004. The appearance of pass-fail grading has made the percentages hard to compare with precision between today and fifty years ago.

116 *It was once possible to buy:* See USDA website, http://www.ams.usda.gov/poultry.

116 *The same dress sizes:* Standardization of women's clothing, NIST website, http://museum.nist.gov/exhibits/apparel.

117 *Favorable evaluations:* See, for example, Valen Johnson, *Grade Inflation* (Springer, 2003).

118 *"Modern students take classes":* Luke Habberstad, Harvard plans to reform grading system, *Yale Herald* 33, 13, April 26, 2002.

119 *became official Harvard policy:* Minutes of the Committee on Educational Policy, November 15, 1950, 416.

121 *consistency is much more important:* Grade inflation is sometimes said to have made grades less informative than they used to be. This claim is amenable to quantitative analysis. The information content of a system is its *entropy,* which depends on the number of categories and the proportions in which they are used. Harvard's grading system today has an entropy of 2.50 bits per grade, down from 2.84 bits per grade in 1987 but up from 1.85 bits per grade in 1950 when pluses and minuses were not used. However, the information content of an A grade has decreased as the number of As has increased. For related calculations carried out at Princeton, see Edward W. Felten, How much information is conveyed by a Princeton grade?, April 22, 2004, http://www.cs.princeton.edu/~felten/grading.pdf, and Jordan Ellenberg: Don't worry about grade inflation, http://slate.msn.com/default.aspx?id=2071759.

121 *"Of the three major":* Laura L. Krug, Faculty express concerns over implications of grade inflation, *Harvard Crimson,* February 13, 2004.

121 *laying "part of the blame":* Patrick Healy, Low, high marks for grade inflation, *Boston Globe,* October 7, 2001.

123 *"motivating students to do":* Letter from Dean Susan Pedersen to members of the Faculty of Arts and Sciences, November 2001.

Chapter 6: Evaluation Is Educational

125 *"[T]he marking system":* Charles William Eliot, Report of the President, 1885–86, 9.

127 *"To the Intent":* Publications of the Colonial Society of Massachusetts, vol. 25, 28, quoted by Samuel Eliot Morison, Harvard College in the Seventeenth Century (Harvard University Press, 1936), part 1, 67.

127 *maximum total possible:* Table showing the comparative power of each department on the scale of comparative merit, Harvard University, Corporation Papers, 2d Series, UAI.5.130, Box 2, 1930, Harvard University Archives.

127 *"the best assurance":* Josiah Quincy, Report of the President, 1830–1831, 3.

128 *"It is difficult for students":* Harvey Mansfield, Grade inflation: It's time to face the facts, *Chronicle of Higher Education,* April 6, 2001.

129 *A student, Mr. Dunkin, refused:* Proceedings of the Overseers of Harvard University relative to the late disturbances in that seminary (James Loring, August 25, 1834).

129 *similar happened at Dartmouth:* David Abel, Aides support accused students, Dartmouth to review facts in cheating case, *Boston Globe,* March 8, 2000; Benjamin Wallace-Wells, Research and its discontents, *Dartmouth Review,* March 13, 2000; David Abel, Dartmouth officials close the book on cheating scandal, most on N.H. campus greet news with relief, *Boston Globe,* March 13, 2000.

129 *"unscholar-like tendency":* Editorial, *Harvard Crimson,* December 3, 1885.

130 *"that spasmodic and unhealthy":* Andrew Preston Peabody, Report of the President, 1868–69, 6.

131 *Eliot graduated second in his class:* Harvard University Quinquennial Catalogue (1930), 252.

131 *a tie for first place:* Peabody, *Harvard Reminiscences,* 31.

132 *"students who are free to":* Charles William Eliot, Report of the President, 1884–85, 4, 39–40.

132 *the "'mark-fiend' who never":* L. B. R. Briggs, Report of the President, 1900–01: The College, 105.

132 *described it in 1869:* Andrew Preston Peabody, Report of the President, 1868–69, 7.

133 *"In such cases, the student":* Harvard University, College Papers, UAI.5.131.10mf, Series 2, vol. 23, 1856, 215, Harvard University Archives.

133 *"honors do not mean as much":* Sara E. Polsky, Honors drop irks Seniors, *Harvard Crimson,* October 19, 2004.

136 *"[Students'] marks in individual courses":* Report of the committee appointed to consider how tests for rank in college may be made a more generally recognized measure of intellectual power, Appendix to Report of the President, 1908–09, 39.

137 *"High attainments in a special":* Charles F. Dunbar, Report of the President, 1878–79: The College, 72.

137 *"encourage effort among":* Ibid., 73.

137 *his book on grade inflation:* Johnson, *Grade Inflation,* 2.

138 *A psychology professor described:* Daniel Gilbert, e-mail to the author.

139 *Harvard Business School until recently:* Harvard Business School, MBA Recruiting Policies and Guidelines, http://www.hbs.edu/mba/recruiting/forms/postagree .html as of December 15, 2005, read: "In support of the academic mission of the

MBA Program and as voted by the student body on January 23, 1998, *individual grades received at HBS shall not be communicated to an HBS recruiter before a job offer is extended.* Likewise, HBS recruiters must agree not to use a student's individual grades as a condition of employment. The award of academic honors is the only standardized measure of academic performance obtained at HBS that can be disclosed during the recruiting process" (emphasis in original).

139 *The Business School rescinded:* Letter from HBS Acting Dean Jay D. Light to HBS students dated 14 December 2005. A memorandum to Light from the HBS Student Association dated 9 December 2005 reported that 87% of 1,559 students polled favored retaining the nondisclosure policy and criticized the decision-making process by which the change was being considered, but Dean Light cited student "liberty" in explaining the decision to make the change. The effect will probably be to make HBS students in the future less likely to use their electives to take courses about things they don't know much about already.

139 *"no large body of writings":* Henry Rosovsky and Matthew Hartley, *Evaluation and the Academy: Are We Doing the Right Thing? Grade Inflation and Letters of Recommendation* (American Academy of Arts and Sciences, 2002), 12.

141 *"students have . . . learned to look":* Eliot, Report of the President, 1885–86, 71–72.

141 *"every student who maintains":* Peabody, Report of the President, 1868–69, 8–9.

141 *"ever the incarnation of":* Charles Franklin Thwing, Peabody and Bowen, *Harvard Graduates Magazine* 40 (1931–32), 258.

142 *"It is well also":* Reports to the Overseers–Harvard, vol. 1885–87; 1886, 2–3. Quoted by Mary Lovett Smallwood, *An Historical Study of Examinations and Grading Systems in Early American Universities* (Harvard University Press, 1935), 84.

143 *differential grading standards:* See, for example, Johnson, *Grade Inflation,* 188–194.

144 *Princeton officials in 2004 adopted:* Robert Strauss, Princeton limits As, *New York Times,* May 2, 2004.

144 *"the existence of conservation":* William Vaughan Jr., An "A" at Princeton, letter to the editor, *New York Times,* April 30, 2004.

Chapter 7: Independence, Responsibility, Rape

148 *"a youth of learning":* Clarke, *Letters to a Student,* 9.

148 *"young men of eighteen":* Eliot, Report of the President, 1871–72, 13.

149 *Some attribute the change:* Sarah Schweitzer, Case of the hovering parents, *Boston Globe,* August 20, 2005.

150 *"had withdrawn from the last":* John Fox, Report of the President, 1983–84: The College, 65–66.

152 *Harvard students were less satisfied:* Marcella Bombardieri, Student life at Harvard lags peer schools, poll finds, *Boston Globe,* March 29, 2005.

152 *"exactly what we've been focusing":* Margaret W. Ho and Joshua P. Rogers, Students less satisfied, *Harvard Crimson,* April 4, 2005.

153 *a Crimson column about love:* Harry R. Lewis, Romance and love at Harvard, *Harvard Crimson,* February 12, 1999.

155 *"Bill Kirby wants a pub":* Joshua P. Rogers and Nicole B. Urken, Administration hopes to buck stereotype, *Harvard Crimson,* April 4, 2005.

155 *disclaimer that only:* Freshman Dean's Office, Calendar of Opening Days for New Students 2005–2006, http://www.fas.harvard.edu/~fdo/publications/calendar0506.

155 *"to take reasonable measures":* Harvard College Freshman Dean's Office, Handbook for Parents 2005–2006.

159 *"To the dean of a large college":* LeBaron Russell Briggs, *School, College, and Character* (Houghton, Mifflin; and Riverside Press, 1903), 6–7.

160 *"an integral part":* John B. Fox Jr., Report of the President, 1980–81: Harvard and Radcliffe Colleges, 55.

161 *"The first is that any student":* Ibid., 57–58.

162 *in 2004 a federal judge:* United States District Court, District of Massachusetts, United States of America v. President and Fellows of Harvard College, Andrei Shleifer, and Jonathan Hay, Defendants, Civil Action No. 00-11977-DPW, Memorandum and Order, June 28, 2004, 87-92. Shleifer was found to have violated 31 U.S. Code §3729(a)(3), which holds a person liable where he or she "conspires to defraud the Government by getting a false or fraudulent claim allowed or paid."

162 *As a trial loomed:* A company owned by Shleifer's wife also paid $1.5 million. See, for example, Russia case (and dust) settle, *Harvard Magazine,* November-December 2005; USAID press release, Harvard defendants pay over $31 million to settle false claims act allegations, August 3, 2005, http://www.usaid.gov/press/releases/2005/pr050803_1.html.

162 *David Warsh tied:* "[A] determined mediation effort by US District Court Judge David Mazzone . . . broke down two weeks after Summers was elected president, in March 2001, and before he recused himself in the matter, apparently at the Corporation's request. . . . The men and women who hired Larry Summers could have hoped that he would settle the matter advantageously as possible for the university, on the terms outlined by the judge. Inexplicably, he did not." David Warsh, The Tick-Tock, *Economic Principals,* January 22, 2006. http://www.economicprincipals.com/issues/06.01.22.html. See also David McClintick, How Harvard lost Russia, *Institutional Investor,* January 2006, 66ff.

162 *reported that Summers had stayed:* Michael M. Grynbaum, A costly case, *Harvard Crimson,* June 9, 2005.

162 *Summers pressed Jeremy Knowles:* United States District Court for the District of Massachusetts, United States of America v. President and Fellows of Harvard College, Andrei Shleifer, Jonathan Hay, Nancy Zimmerman, and Elizabeth Hebert, Civil Action 00 CV 11977-DPW, Deposition of Lawrence Summers, March 13, 2002, 112.

162 *Shleifer was reported to have broken:* Michael M. Grynbaum, Punishing its own, *Harvard Crimson,* June 9, 2005.

163 *"apparent self-dealing":* U.S. v. President and Fellows et al., Memorandum and Order, 73.

163 *"would have, in part, valued":* U.S. v. President and Fellows et al., Deposition of Lawrence Summers, 97.

163 *"there was no aura of wrongness":* Ibid., 128.

163 *"Why not acknowledge":* David Warsh, Andrei and Rafel, economicprincipals.com, August 7, 2005, http://www.economicprincipals.com/issues/05.08.07.html.

163 *For example, Charles Ogletree:* Sara Rimer, When plagiarism's shadow falls on admired scholars, *New York Times,* November 24, 2004; Tribe's tribulation, *Harvard Magazine,* July-August 2005; John Harvard's Journal, *Harvard Magazine,* November-December 2004.

164 *Shleifer has not acknowledged:* In Shleifer's statement, issued after the case was settled, he said that "an individual can fight the unlimited resources of the government for only so long. . . . [And] after eight long years, I have decided to end this now—without any admission of liability on my part. I strongly believe I would have prevailed in the end, but my lawyers told me my legal fees would

exceed the amount that I will be paying the government." Russia case (and dust) settle, John Harvard's Journal, *Harvard Magazine,* November-December 2005.

164 *"take whatever action he":* Faculty of Arts and Sciences, Harvard University, *Principles and Policies that Govern Your Research, Instruction, and Other Professional Activities,* 2002, Section 6: Procedures for Responding to Allegations of Misconduct in Research, http://www.fas.harvard.edu/~research/greybook/misconduct.html.

165 *"If campus authorities are":* Derek Bok, Report of the President, 1986–87, 26.

165 *petty as a student's loud music:* See, for example, Minutes of Faculty Meeting of April 23, 1877, 370, in which the faculty voted that "Mr. Cary, Sophomore, be privately admonished for music out of hours, April 10th," right after it had voted to abolish the Scale of Rank.

165 *"Faculty might delegate":* Eliot, Report of the President, 1889–90, 4.

165 *"subject, however, to the statutory":* Clement Lawrence Smith, Report of the President, 1889–90: The College, 110.

166 *"made a steady effort to attract":* John Fox, Report on Harvard College, 1980–81, 56.

166 *to be "just too much":* Benedict Gross quoted by Katharine A. Kaplan and Rebecca D. O'Brien, Gross finds post overwhelming, *Harvard Crimson,* June 10, 2004.

166 *whose degrees are in business:* Patricia O'Brien named Harvard College deputy dean, *Harvard University Gazette,* June 10, 2004.

166 *A dean of residential life:* Steve Bradt, Student life gets an experienced hand, *Harvard University Gazette,* September 15, 2005.

166 *two long-serving Harvard hands:* Sean Smith, Centering on advisement, *Boston College Chronicle* 14, 5 (November 3, 2005); Joshua P. Rogers, Dean O'Keefe to head for Wellesley, *Harvard Crimson,* July 15, 2005.

166 *Harvard instead hired as:* Robert Mitchell, Rinere appointed advising dean of Harvard College, *Harvard University Gazette,* December 15, 2005.

166 *"issues of wellness":* Professor Judith Ryan quoted by Sara E. Polsky, Senior Tutor reform proposed, *Harvard Crimson,* April 14, 2005.

166 *"the 'Harvard State Fair,' complete":* Welcome back from the dean of Harvard College, September 2005, http://www.college.harvard.edu/deans_office/communications/81.html.

167 *"we will assure more":* Lawrence H. Summers, Inaugural Address, October 12, 2001, http://www.president.harvard.edu/news/inaugurations/summers.html.

169 *"was on 'The Abrams Report'":* MSNBC cable, Abrams Report, August 20, 2002.

170 *Most famously, Antioch College:* Jane Gross, Combating rape on campus in a class on sexual consent, *New York Times,* September 25, 1993.

170 *"The difficulties involved in a common":* Eliot, Inaugural Address, October 19, 1869, Samuel Eliot Morison, ed., *Development of Harvard University,* 1930, lxx.

170 *"It would be a wonder":* Charles William Eliot, address in *A Record of the Exercises Attending the Inauguration of Caroline Hazard, Litt.D., as President of Wellesley College, III October MDCCCXCIX* (Riverside Press, 1899), 16–18.

170 *Carey Thomas, the president:* Helen Lefkowitz Horowitz, The great debate: Charles W. Eliot and M. Carey Thomas, in Laurel Thatcher Ulrich, ed., *Yards and Gates: Gender in Harvard and Radcliffe History* (Palgrave Macmillan, 2004), 133.

172 *"heavily under-reported":* Henry Rosovsky, Report of the President, 1973–74: Faculty of Arts and Sciences, 52.

172 *"to build a society":* A murder, editorial, *Harvard Crimson,* December 4, 1973.

172 *"I shudder to think":* Bernadette Brooten, The meaning of murder, *Harvard Crimson,* November 29, 1973.

172 *Office of Women's Education sponsored:* Paul S. Turner, OWE conference to discuss ways to prevent rape, *Harvard Crimson*, April 17, 1974. Also Matina S. Horner, Radcliffe College, Report of the President, 1972–77: Admissions, Financial Aid and Women's Education, 10.

172 *"Although men have always":* Elisabeth Einaudi and Peggy Mason, Women: Take back the night, *Harvard Crimson*, November 6, 1980.

172 *"she didn't think the march":* Rape protest to proceed without funds, *Harvard Crimson*, October 9, 1980.

173 *"Someone who has been raped":* Melinna I. Weissberg, Harvard seeks wider perceptions of rape: New booklet broadens definitions of the crime, *Harvard Crimson*, October 4, 1983.

173 *"one to two phone calls a night":* Alison L. Jernow, Fighting awareness: Harvard date rape, *Harvard Crimson*, April 17, 1986.

173 *"two students with different interpretations":* Lisa I. Backus and Ellen Porter Honnet quoted in ibid.

174 *"Most of us don't come up with":* Sara O. Vargas, Cornell professor describes potential date rape scenarios, *Harvard Crimson*, October 2, 1986.

174 *"People need to be taught":* Vernon Silver, On campuses, understanding of crime lacking, *Boston Globe*, September 2, 1990.

174 *"A male and a female student":* Ibid.

174 *On October 26, 1990:* Madhavi Sunder, Can the ad board handle date rape? *Harvard Crimson*, October 26, 1990.

175 *"archaic, blame-the-victim":* Editorial, Why the ad board fails: Date rape remarks, *Harvard Crimson*, October 30, 1990.

175 *"any act of sexual intercourse":* Date rape task force proposal quoted in Defining date rape, *Harvard Crimson*, September 14, 1992.

175 *"despite the expressed unwillingness":* Undergraduate council response quoted in ibid.

176 *"The legal definition of rape":* Miller and Dershowitz as quoted by David S. Kurnick, UC date rape terms draw criticism: RUS, Dershowitz voice concerns over council's role; others defend discussion, *Harvard Crimson*, April 17, 1992.

176 *"[T]he bureaucratization of the date rape":* Steven A. Engel, Date rape debate ends, controversy to continue, *Harvard Crimson*, March 8, 1993.

176 *When two students embezzled:* Amit R. Paley, Pudding's Pomey, Gomes plead guilty, *Harvard Crimson*, September 16, 2002.

178 *"What can one say except":* Police describe rape suspect, *Harvard Crimson*, March 7, 1996.

178 *"Calling attention to":* Catherine L. Dunlop, Lewis' comment on safety outrageous, *Harvard Crimson*, March 11, 1996.

178 *came to light in anonymous interviews:* "There is nothing like being able to tell somebody": Two Harvard rape survivors share their stories, *Perspective*, February 1999.

179 *Nor was there any doubt:* Editorial, Warranting expulsion: If the ad board calls it rape, the faculty should expel the perpetrators, *Harvard Crimson*, February 22, 1999.

179 *not everyone found this analogy:* Jenny E. Heller, Sexual assault victims: College action fell short; second student convicted of indecent assault, *Harvard Crimson*, February 19, 1999.

179 *"Lots of issues were":* William E. Paul as quoted by Jenny E. Heller, Faculty to vote on Douglas dismissal Tuesday, *Harvard Crimson*, March 5, 1999.

179 *"Rather it is a category"*: Quoted in editorial opinion, After Douglas, *Harvard Crimson*, March 15, 1999. Two of the five read essentially the same statement to the Faculty during its discussion of the case.

180 *N's assailant was dismissed*: Kate Zernike, Harvard student is ousted, accusation of rape stirred debate at the university, *Boston Globe*, March 10, 1999. A detailed retelling of this case appeared somewhat later as a magazine article, which, however, did not settle some of the important uncertainties; Lisa Gerson, Rape at Harvard, *Boston Magazine*, August 1999, 104ff.

180 *Later in the year*: Tara L. Colon, Elster dismissed by full faculty in quick vote, *Harvard Crimson*, April 14, 1999.

180 *voiced by Harvard counselors*: Nadja Burns Gould and Veronica Reed Ryback, Misconceptions about date rape, *Boston Globe*, March 12, 1999; Azell Murphy Cavaan, Universities struggle with date-rape cases, *Boston Herald*, March 14, 1999; Ben Gose, Harvard expels student in controversial date-rape case, *Chronicle of Higher Education*, March 19, 1999.

180 *either couple was dating*: Jenny E. Heller, Records show no consent in Douglas case: Concerns over communication seem unfounded, *Harvard Crimson*, March 11, 1999.

180 *"Harvard was not taking"*: Beverly Ford and Tom Farmer, Student ousted for sex assault; Harvard demonstrators cheer faculty vote, *Boston Herald*, March 10, 1999.

180 *account said that he had written*: Ibid.

180 *"deans will now take"*: Rosalind S. Helderman, Sr. tutors gain new role in discipline, *Harvard Crimson*, May 26, 1999.

183 *I explained the problem*: Harry R. Lewis, Annual Report on Harvard College, 2000–2001, http://www.college.harvard.edu/deans_office/dean_lewis/annual report2001/annual_report_2001.html.

183 *"presents the type of evidence"*: Report of the Ad Hoc Faculty Committee on the Administrative Board, January 18, 2002, http://www.fas.harvard.edu/~secfas/Ad-Bopard/AdBoardAdHoc.pdf.

183 *"Starting in September, the Board"*: Anne K. Kofol, Lewis requests changes in sex assault policy; ad board to limit investigations into "he-said-she-said" cases, *Harvard Crimson*, February 11, 2002.

183 *"Harvard to Require More Proof"*: Patrick Healy, Harvard to require more proof in sex cases, *Boston Globe*, May 8, 2002.

184 *"Alert: Disturbing Evidence"*: Kathleen Parker, Alert: Disturbing evidence of common sense found at Harvard, *Orlando Sentinel*, May 12, 2002.

184 *"Blatant disregard for the rights"*: Cathy Young, A turning tide on date rape, *Boston Globe*, May 13, 2002.

184 *"Crimes are the jurisdiction"*: Eileen McNamara, Arrogance at Harvard, *Boston Globe*, May 19, 2002.

184 *faculty members ended their threats*: Adjudicating sexual-assault cases, John Harvard's journal, *Harvard Magazine*, July-August 2002.

184 *complaint with the U.S. Department*: Patrick Healy, U.S. probe expected of Harvard policy on sexual assault, *Boston Globe*, August 6, 2002.

185 *"first school to put in writing"*: Elizabeth Mehren, Harvard is sued for its new sex assault policy, Women's eNews, December 8, 2002, http://www.feminist.com/news/news130.html.

185 *"OCR found that, as currently described"*: Letter from Thomas J. Hibino to Lawrence H. Summers dated April 1, 2003, http://www.thefire.org/issue.php?doc=harvard-hibino_040103.inc.

185 *a way to announce victory:* Jenna Russell, U.S. review finds no bias in Harvard's revised policy on sex assault, *Boston Globe,* April 2, 2003.

185 *a national cover-up effort:* Gretchen Cook, Campuses may be developing tactics to hide rapes, Women's eNews, May 25, 2003, http://www.womensenews.org/article.cfm/dyn/aid/1342/context/archive.

185 *sexual-assault study committee:* Committee to Address Sexual Assault at Harvard: Public Report, April 2003, www.fas.harvard.edu/~casah/FinalReport.html.

185 *"a complete review of [Harvard's]:* Associated Press, Harvard panel urges changes in abuse policy, *Washington Post,* April 18, 2003.

186 *virtually every allegation of date rape:* National data are cited in the Report of the Committee to Address Sexual Assault at Harvard, 22.

186 *"There are many misconceptions":* Nadja Burns Gould and Veronica Reed Ryback, Misconceptions about date rape, *Boston Globe,* March 12, 1999.

187 *"Any offense—rape, assault":* Daniel Gilbert as quoted by Ben Gose, Harvard expels student for role in controversial date-rape case, *Chronicle of Higher Education,* March 19, 1999.

187 *"express confusion about":* Committee to Address Sexual Assault at Harvard, Public Report, 34.

187 *"nearly as well-adjusted":* Richard J. McNally, *Remembering Trauma* (Belknap Press of Harvard University Press, 2003), 22.

188 *"Rather than interpreting the article":* Ibid., 23.

189 *"be trained to recognize symptoms":* Title IX complaint questionable: Moral, not legal arguments needed against university's new sexual assault policy, editorial, *Harvard Crimson,* September 18, 2002.

189 *"Forensic psychologists have sounded":* McNally, *Remembering Trauma,* 281.

189 *In addition, only a minority:* Ibid., 89.

189 *remember their trauma as having been worse:* Ibid., 82.

190 *"The College Faculty is not a body":* C. C. Felton, Report of the President, 1859–60, 34.

191 *"as Harvard's rules once provided":* The 1816 rules stated that "the Government [of the College] may inflict any of the College censures" on a student for "any offense, for which, by the laws of the land, he might be punished by fine, imprisonment, or otherwise." *Laws of Harvard College,* for the use of the students, with preliminary notices and an appendix (Cambridge, printed at the university press by Hilliard and Metcalf, 1816), 14.

191 *"Whoever has sexual intercourse":* General Laws of Massachusetts, ch. 265, §22(b) (2003).

191 *prosecution needs to establish separately:* For example, Commonwealth v. Lopez, 433 Mass. 7222, 745 N.E.2d 961 (2001): "We have construed the element, 'by force and against his will,' as truly encompassing two separate elements each of which must independently be satisfied. See generally Commonwealth v. Caracciola, 409 Mass. 648, 653-654, 569 N.E.2d 774 (1991) (stating elements of 'force' and 'against his will' not superfluous, but instead must be read together)."

192 *Schaer v. Brandeis University:* 716 N.E. 2d 1055, 48 Mass. App. Ct. 23, Schaer v. Brandeis University (Mass. App. Ct. 1999). Citations in the decision have been omitted.

193 *discussed at length and noted:* Faculty Council notice for Feb. 6, On campus, *Harvard University Gazette,* February 7, 2002.

Chapter 8: Students and Money

195 *"The student in a polytechnic":* Charles William Eliot, The new education: Its organization, part 1, *Atlantic Monthly* 23 (February 1869), 214.

195 *"More than ever before":* James Engell and Anthony Dangerfield, The market-model university: Humanities in the age of money, *Harvard Magazine,* May-June 1998.

195 *Kirp's* Shakespeare, Einstein: David L. Kirp, *Shakespeare, Einstein, and the Bottom Line: The Marketing of Higher Education* (Harvard University Press, 2003).

195 *Washburn's* University: Jennifer Washburn, *University Inc.: The Corporate Corruption of Higher Education* (Basic Books, 2005).

195 *Engell and Dangerfield's:* James Engell and Anthony Dangerfield, *Saving Higher Education in the Age of Money* (University of Virginia Press, 2005).

196 *major speech delivered February 29:* Higher education and the American dream, speech to 86th Annual Meeting of the American Council on Education, February 29, 2004, http://www.president.harvard.edu/speeches/2004/ace.html.

197 *Harvard's initiative prompted stories:* Karen W. Arenson, Harvard says poor parents won't have to pay, *New York Times,* February 29, 2004; Mary Beth Marklein, Harvard to boost aid to needy students, *USA Today,* March 1, 2004.

197 *who in his Jefferson Lectures:* William G. Bowen, Jefferson Lectures, April 6, 2004, http://www.mellon.org/pursuitofexcellence.pdf.

197 *"Sounds to me like":* Louise Story, Following Princeton, Harvard beefs up aid, *Yale Daily News,* February 22, 2001.

197 *"We had not hoped for":* Harold Shapiro quoted by Bill Beaver, New financial aid policy may pressure other universities to follow, *Dailyprincetonian.com,* February 5, 2001.

198 *"I wanted a college experience":* Pamela Burdman, Dollars&sense, *Princeton Alumni Weekly,* April 23, 2003.

198 *increased by 22 percent, to 360:* Class of 2009 chosen from record 22,796, *Harvard University Gazette,* April 7, 2005.

198 *maid dubbed "Olde Mary":* quoted in Maids are a College institution, but time may bring changes, *Harvard Crimson,* November 22, 1950.

198 *student riots in 1817:* Lee P. Howard, *The Story of the Yard, 1638–1932* (Andover Press, 1932), 14.

198 *invokes the Goody as muse: The Rebelliad,* (Welch, Bigelow, and Co., 1863), 11–12, 71.

199 *Harvard eliminated bed-making:* Stephen L. Seftenberg, Lowell House and Yard will lose maids in fall, *Harvard Crimson,* February 20, 1954.

199 *"I object to the twentieth":* Perkins deplores maid loss; would fight for them, *Harvard Crimson,* February 25, 1954.

199 *"one of the few remaining":* Room rents, *Harvard Crimson,* October 10, 1963.

200 *"By creating yet another differential":* Staff editorial, Maid for Harvard? *Harvard Crimson,* March 10, 2005.

200 *"There's so many ways":* Pam Belluck, At Harvard, an unseemly display of wealth or merely a clean room? *New York Times,* March 22, 2005.

200 *"Somehow our eyes remained dry":* James Taranto, WSJ.com Opinion Journal from the *Wall Street Journal* editorial page, March 14, 2005.

205 *"In the college, the desire":* Eliot, The new education, part 1, 214.

206 *"What can I do with my boy?":* Ibid., 203.

206 *of "quiet and seclusion":* Eliot, The new education, part 2, *Atlantic Monthly* 23 (March 1869), 364.

206 *"spirit proper to a polytechnic":* Eliot, The new education, part 1, 214–215.

206 *Three times he tried:* Morison, *Three Centuries,* 372.

207 *precipitating a challenge in:* Supreme Judicial Court of Massachusetts, November 27, 1917, 228 Mass. 396; 117 N.E. 903; 1917 Mass. LEXIS 1277.

207 *"The lamb is always inside":* Letter from Adelaide Sherman Blackman to the president of MIT, May 25, 1905, MIT Archives, AC 13:19.

207 *granting degrees to women:* Letter to the editor, *The Nation*, February 26, 1914, 209.
207 *"training in schools of that kind":* N. S. Shaler, Gordon McKay, *Harvard Graduates' Magazine* 13, 52 (June 1905), 573–574.
207 *court ruled against Harvard's effort:* President and Fellows of Harvard College v. Attorney General et al., Supreme Judicial Court of Massachusetts, Suffolk, 228 Mass. 396; 117 N.E. 903, November 27, 1917.
207 *responsible for Harvard having an applied:* Gordon McKay was born in 1821 and died in 1903. Though he had pledged his vast estate to Harvard more than a decade before his death, the final payments were not made to Harvard until 1949, by which time the legacy amounted to $16 million, the largest gift Harvard had ever received up to that time. The full amount was slow in coming to Harvard because his will and codicils provided for various annuities to be paid for the lifetime of their recipients. Twenty-three annuitants are listed in the printed form of his will, including two who had died by the time of publication and several whose annuities were either created or revoked in six codicils to the original will. McKay enjoyed female company; the twenty-three annuitants were his divorced wife, "her two children" surnamed McKay, her mother and sister, and eighteen women apparently unrelated to him. William Bentinck-Smith, *Harvard University: History of Named Chairs: Sketches of Donors and Donations*, Secretary to the University, 1991–1995, vol. 1, 338–341; *Will and Codicils of Gordon McKay*, 1902(?), Harvard University Archives, HUB 2562.
208 *"The motive of earning":* Eliot, Report of the President, 1892–93, 10–11.
208 *"old-fashioned college":* Ibid., 12. Harvard College's spirit of resistance to the engines of material progress is captured beautifully in an anecdote in *The Late George Apley*, the great satirical novel of Harvard and Boston. Apley, a fictional Harvard College graduate of the class of 1887, in the 1920s is so offended by the Business School that he must look away when driving by it. John P. Marquand, *The Late George Apley* (Little Brown, 1937), 330.
208 *At Harvard University this movement:* Eliot, Report of the President, 1877–78, 10.
208 *Students on financial aid:* Data supplied by the Harvard College Registrar's Office for the Class of 2005.
209 *"In an era of increasing":* Faculty of Arts and Sciences, Curricular Review (2004), 6.
209 *"mastery of a field":* Ibid.
209 *"For some students, work in the field":* Ibid., 23.
210 *"to educate students as independent":* Ibid.
212 *"freedom from the isolation":* Frank H. T. Rhodes, *The Creation of the Future* (Cornell University Press, 2001), 112. For another eloquent modern defense of a liberal education, see James O. Freedman, *Idealism and Liberal Education* (University of Michigan Press, 2000).
212 *"must provide a broad introduction":* Report of the Committee on General Education, November 2005, 1.
212 *"what that breadth of knowledge":* Ibid.

Chapter 9: College Athletes and Money

213 *"The War of Secession":* Francis A. Walker, College athletics, (Phi Beta Kappa oration, June 29, 1893), *Harvard Graduates' Magazine*, September 1893, no. 5, 6–7.
213 *"When I hear, therefore":* George Santayana, Philosophy in the bleachers, *Harvard Monthly* 18 (July 1894), 190.

218 *two detailed studies:* James L. Shulman and William G. Bowen, *The Game of Life* (Princeton University Press, 2001); and William G. Bowen and Sarah A. Levin, *Reclaiming the Game* (Princeton University Press, 2003).

218 *books received widespread praise:* For example, in The *New Yorker* (January 22, 2001), Louis Menand said *The Game of Life* might be "one of the most important books on higher education published in the last twenty years."

218 *Two critical reviews of The Game:* Hal S. Scott, What game are they playing? A review of *The Game of Life* by James L. Shulman and William G. Bowen, *Journal of College and University Law* 28 (2002), 719–755; and J. Douglas Toma and Thomas Kecskemethy, College sports, the collegiate ideal, and the values of the American university, A review of *The Game of Life*, ibid., 697–718.

218 *the facts of college athletics:* The books are based on an extensive database about students in many colleges. Law professor Hal Scott raised a question as to whether it was lawful for any of the Institutions to have supplied the Mellon Foundation with the data, since they include what the Family Educational Rights and Privacy Act (FERPA) calls "personally identifiable information." That is, the data are sufficiently detailed that legally protected privacy rights of individual students might have been violated by communicating the information to parties outside the university. Scott did not suggest that the Mellon Foundation improperly disclosed this information to others. But a layman's reading of FERPA indicates that the universities should not have disclosed the information to the Mellon Foundation unless the study had the objective to "improve instruction," which seems a bit of a stretch. 34 Code of Federal Regulations 99.31(a)(6)(i)(C).

218 *"by competing one learns 'life lessons'":* Reclaiming the Game, 243.

218 *"for regular students":* Ibid., 325.

218 *"With intellectual capital":* James L. Shulman and William G. Bowen, Playing their way in, *New York Times*, February 22, 2001, A-25.

220 *"Students who excel in sports":* Reclaiming the Game, 12.

220 *"Each recruited athlete who attends":* Ibid., 250.

221 *"In an ideal world, we":* Game of Life, 275. The data on which this caution rests do not imply that there is no diversity in the dimensions it mentions. The data simply show that some groups are somewhat more likely than others to enter certain fields, for example.

222 *calculates the lifetime earnings:* Stephen G. Miller, *Ancient Greek Athletics* (Yale University Press, 2004), 213–214.

222 *After the runner Astylos placed:* David C. Young, *The Olympic Myth of Greek Amateur Athletics* (Ares Publishers, 1985), 141.

223 *"nearly all the members":* Letter to *Athletic Record and Monthly Journal*, June 1876, quoted in Peter Bailey, *Leisure and Class in Victorian England* (University of Toronto Press, 1978), 136 (emphasis in original).

223 *"Any person who has never competed":* H. F. Wilkinson, ed., *The Athletic Almanack* (1868) as quoted in ibid., 131.

223 *may not "Use your athletics skill":* NCAA website, http://www.ncaa.org/eligibility/cbsa/index1.html. The full set of regulations provides a number of exceptions to these broad strictures; for example, it is possible for an athlete to earn limited amounts of money giving athletic lessons without losing eligibility, and to accept prize money under restricted conditions to meet the expenses incurred in competing.

224 *"The question of purifying athletics":* Athletics: The undergraduate rule, *Harvard Graduates' Magazine*, April 1893, 470.

224 *"recreate your Self a little"*: Thomas Shepard Jr., A letter from the Revd Mr Thos Shepard to His Son [at] His Admission into the College, circa 1670, in Publications of the Colonial Society of Massachusetts, vol. 14, *Transactions 1911–1913* (Colonial Society of Massachusetts, 1913), 104; reprinted in Thomas L. Altherr, ed., *Sports in North America: A Documentary History,* vol. 1, part 1: Sports in the Colonial Era, 1618–1783 (Academic International Press, 1997), 14.

224 *"we suppose there are Diversions"*: Mather, circa 1726, A serious address to those who unnecessarily frequent the tavern, 10, quoted in Altherr, *Sports in North America,* 15.

224 *"The Freshmen shall furnish"*: President, Professors, and Tutor's Book, vol. IV, 1781, 259–260, Harvard University Archives, UAIII.5.5.2. (The buttery was a sort of supply room, not just for butter.)

224 *"teaching a System of Gymnasticks"*: John Thornton Kirkland, Report of the President, 1825–26, 52.

225 *Mr. Follen should be regarded*: Morison, *Three Centuries,* 207.

225 *"no student was allowed to keep"*: F. O. Vaille and H. A. Clark, eds., *The Harvard Book: A Series of Historical, Biographical, and Descriptive Sketches,* vol. 2 (Welch, Bigelow, and Co., 1875), 188.

225 *"toward the close of 1850"*: Ibid., 194.

225 *calls "jock culture"*: Game of Life, 150. Oddly, when challenged on this inflammatory language, the authors denied having used it. James L. Shulman and William G. Bowen, Authors respond to Hal Scott's and Douglas Toma and Thomas Kecskemethy's reviews of *The Game of Life, Journal of College and University Law* 29, 1 (2002), 191.

225 *"shins unnumbered bruised"*: James Cook Richmond, The battle of the Delta, *Harvard Register,* October 1827; reprinted in Larry K. Menna, ed., *Sports in North America: A Documentary History,* vol. 2: The Origins of Modern Sports, 1820–1840 (Academic International Press, 1995), 156.

225 *"growing custom of scholars"*: C. C. Felton, Report of the President, 1859–60, 32.

225 *"annual game of football had degenerated"*: Ibid., 31.

226 *on July 2 the Faculty banned*: Vote of the Faculty, July 2, 1860, quoted by Morton Prince, History of football at Harvard, 1800–1875 (June), in *The H Book of Harvard Athletics,* John A. Blanchard, ed. (Harvard Varsity Club, 1923), 334.

226 *"Exult, ye Freshmen"*: Sibley's Private Journal, September 3, 1860, http://hul.harvard.edu/huarc/refshelf/Sibley.htm#1860.

226 *"the eight grim reapers"*: Michael R. James, King James Bible: Council Hurting Ivies, *Harvard Crimson,* May 7, 2004; and James, Presidents need to drop the grudge, *Harvard Crimson,* November 2, 2004.

226 *James Elkins, superintendent*: Robert F. Herrick, *Red Top: Reminiscences of Harvard Rowing* (Harvard University Press, 1948), 71; Thomas C. Mendenhall, *The Harvard-Yale Boat Race 1852–1924* (Mystic Seaport Museum, 1993), 15–16.

227 *"bringing home members"*: Charles William Eliot, Rowing in the fifties, in *H Book of Harvard Athletics,* 10.

227 *"Are we to regain"*: The boating reputation of Harvard, *Harvard Magazine* 4, 5 (June 1858), 194. Widener Library's copy indicates in pen that the authors are E. L. Motte and F. C. Hopkinson of the Class of 1859.

227 *"without aspiring to any great"*: Eliot, Rowing in the fifties, 12. The description of the 1858 race follows this article.

228 *"row just as hard as"*: Letters from Charles William Eliot to Ellen Peabody, June 19 and 20, 1858, reprinted in Henry James, *Charles W. Eliot,* vol. 1 (Houghton Mifflin Co., 1930), 81–83.

228 *"making or being present":* Laws of Harvard University, Relative to Undergraduates (Metcalf and Co., 1845), 25.
228 *"great stout Irishmen":* Letter from Eliot to Peabody, June 20, 1858, in James, *Charles W. Eliot,* vol. 1, 82.
228 *"Saints and Their Bodies":* Thomas Wentworth Higginson, Saints and their bodies, *Atlantic Monthly* 1 (1858), 582-595.
229 *"Only keep a boy a pure":* Ibid.
229 *feminization of religion:* See, for example, Clifford Putney, *Muscular Christianity* (Harvard University Press, 2001), 3.
229 *"for an average American man":* Thomas Wentworth Higginson, Gymnastics, in *Out-Door Papers* (Lee and Shepard, 1886), 134.
229 *"a new model for manhood":* Putney, *Muscular Christianity,* 5.
230 *"general tendency among people":* Theodore Roosevelt, Machine politics in New York City, *Century Magazine* 23 (1886), 76, quoted in Putney, *Muscular Christianity,* 26.
230 *"the most glorious of all games":* Higginson, Saints and their bodies.
230 *"There is, or ought to be":* Higginson, Gymnastics, 137-139.
230 *"For the late-Victorian":* T. J. Jackson Lears, *No Place of Grace* (Pantheon Books, 1981), 48, 300.
230 *action, a "primitivist hero":* Richard Hofstadter, *Anti-Intellectualism in American Life* (Vintage Books, 1962 and 1963), 159.
231 *"The aspiring politician":* Ibid., 196.
231 *"Will the same marketing":* Game of Life, 112.
232 *"ask permission to play":* William R. Tyler, quoted in Morris A. Bealle, *The History of Football at Harvard, 1874–1948* (Columbia Publishing, 1848), 17.
232 *drank the gate receipts:* H Book of Harvard Athletics, 358–364.
233 *gave rise to the basic parameters:* The story of the Harvard-McGill contests is detailed by Robert Grant, Harvard College in the seventies, *Scribner's Magazine* 21, 5 (May 1897), 562–563. Only eleven students played on each team, fewer than the usual number for rugby, because at the last minute some McGill players were unable to make the trip from Montreal. The convention of eleven to a side was not settled for several years. The first Harvard-Yale match, in 1875, was played with fifteen to a side, the next one, in 1876, with eleven to a side, and there was no match in 1877 because the two schools could not agree on the number!
234 *to know "whether the members":* John Williams White, The constitution, authority, and policy of the committee on the regulation of athletic sports, *Harvard Graduates' Magazine* 1, 2 (January 1893), 209–210. This article is, in general, a candy-coated history of the committee's stormy early history.
234 *"assumed for the first time":* Charles William Eliot, Report of the President, 1881–82, 16–19.
234 *"professional standard of excellence":* Ibid., 18.
234 *"protect the grounds and exclude":* Harvard Athletic Committee, minutes of June 15, 1882, quoted in Ronald A. Smith, *Sports and Freedom* (Oxford University Press, 1988), 127.
235 *"It is agreed on all hands":* Eliot, Report of the President, 1881–82, 19.
235 *"There are still many excesses":* Eliot, Report of the President, 1887–88, 10.
235 *more in the breach than:* William Shakespeare, *Hamlet,* I.iv.14.
235 *It paid its crew and baseball:* Ronald A. Smith, Introduction to *Big-Time Football at Harvard 1905: The Diary of Coach Bill Reid* (University of Illinois Press, 1994), xxxiv.
235 *"other manly sports in which":* Eliot, Report of the President, 1892–93, 15.

235 *"To pitch a curved ball":* James, *Eliot,* vol. 2, 69. James noted that he was reporting L. B. R. Briggs's account of this incident (*Atlantic Monthly,* November 1929, 600).

236 *"Three cheers for Harvard":* Ibid., 69–70.

236 *"the beauty and the holiness":* The Soldier's Field, Henry Lee Higginson, June 10, 1890 (brochure recording the events at the dedication of the field).

237 *"the students do not meet":* Report of the Committee of Five (Charles Francis Adams, Wm. Roscoe Thayer, Henry E. Warner, Thomas C. Thacher, William Endicott 3d, *Harvard Graduates' Magazine,* 4, 15 (March 1896), 455.

237 *largest ever to witness:* Harvard's great stadium, *New York Times,* November 22, 1903; Yale's football team defeated Harvard, *New York Times,* November 22, 1903.

237 *the committee offered $3,500:* Smith, *Sports and Freedom,* 156.

238 *"is it not something of a mistake":* Life 45, 1159 (January 12, 1905), 40.

238 *"While the Corporation have given":* Eliot, Report of the President, 1873–74, 22–23.

238 *Eliot recognized that he himself:* James, *Eliot,* vol. 1, 85.

239 *"Competition is to-day the arch-enemy":* Dudley A. Sargent, The physique of scholars, athletes, and the average student, *Harvard Graduates' Magazine* 16 (June 1908), 611–613.

239 *"to appeal to a still higher motive":* Dudley A. Sargent, The Hemenway Gymnasium: An educational experiment, *Harvard Graduates' Magazine,* December 1894, 172.

239 *"large infusion of foreign blood":* Dudley A. Sargent, *Physical Education* (Ginn and Co., 1906), 21–23.

239 *"had better live beside each other":* Letter from Eliot to unnamed correspondent, April 30 and May 5, 1909, in James, *Eliot,* vol. 2, 166–168.

239 *joined many other prominent:* Carl N. Degler, *In Search of Human Nature* (Oxford University Press, 1991), 43. Eliot's rationale for the separation of the social classes extended to his stance against coeducation. In 1874 the wife of a Johns Hopkins University trustee reported Eliot's view "that coeducation does very well in communities where persons are more on an equality, but in a large city where persons of all classes are thrown together it works badly, unpleasant associations are formed, and disastrous marriages are often the result." Letter from Mary Whitall Thomas to M. Carey Thomas, June 10, 1874, quoted by Horowitz, The great debate, 130.

240 *"Before the end of the fifth":* E. Norman Gardiner, *Greek Athletic Sports and Festivals* (London, 1910), 4, as quoted by Young, *The Olympic Myth,* 78.

240 *"The amateur philosophy is essentially":* Young, *The Olympic Myth,* 78 (emphasis in original).

241 *"That it would be a bitter pill":* Our sporting column, *Harvard Crimson,* May 17, 1878.

241 *"The ridiculous ideas":* Letters to the editor, *Harvard Crimson,* February 22, 1884.

242 *"put together by an amateur":* James Clerk Maxwell, as quoted by Hofstadter, *Anti-Intellectualism,* 31.

245 *In the Ivy League: Reclaiming the Game,* 109.

248 *assessment of the role of sports:* Santayana, Philosophy on the bleachers, 181–190.

249 *"a special talent or spark":* Henry Rosovsky, Report of the President, 1975–76: Faculty of Arts and Sciences, 66.

250 *"my prejudice is for a Harvard":* W. J. Bender, Final Report, excerpts reprinted from the Report of the President of Harvard College and the Reports of Departments, 1959–60, 1–38.

250 *recent book The Chosen:* Jerome Karabel, *The Chosen* (Houghton Mifflin, 2005). Karabel also attacks the supposed "happy bottom quarter" policy he attributes to Bender's successor, Fred Glimp. In fact, reflection on the welfare of the bottom

of the class dates at least to 1869. President Andrew Preston Peabody wrote of the "positive benefit to a college class to have a certain proportion of members of the kind now under discussion. Their defect of memory will always keep them near the foot of the class; and by occupying that position they sustain the self-respect and ambition of those next above them. The ninetieth scholar in a class of a hundred has an appreciable rank, which he will endeavor at least to maintain, if possible to improve. But if the ten below him be dismissed or degraded, so that he finds himself at the foot of his class, the depressing influence of this position will almost inevitably check his industry and quench his ambition, so that he will sink to the lower grade on which the hundredth scholar stood. This process, if repeated, might bring the eightieth scholar down to the same level, and so on indefinitely." Peabody, Report of the President, 1868–69, 9.

250 *"Admissions is a zero-sum game":* Julia M. Klein, Merit's demerits, *Chronicle of Higher Education,* November 4, 2005.

251 *somewhat below where they "should":* The Game of Life, 65–68.

Conclusion

254 *incentives to dilettantism:* Harvard College Curricular Review, Educational Policy Committee Summary Statement on Concentrations, November 22, 2005, 8.

259 *The independent thinker could turn conventional populist:* For example, Summers said he thought Harvard should have a student center, as the student government demanded, because most other colleges had one. Lawrence H. Summers, Remarks to the Harvard College fund assembly, October 29, 2005, http://www.president.harvard.edu/speeches/2005/1029_hcf.html.

259 *"rock star president":* Alexander D. Blankfein, Nina L. Vizcarrondo, and Ying Wang, To students, a rock star president, Harvard Crimson, February 22, 2006.

259 *Summers's remarks at the National Bureau of Economic Development:* Lawrence H. Summers, Remarks at NBER conference on diversifying the science and engineering workforce, January 14, 2005, http://www.president.harvard.edu/speeches/2005/nber.html.

259 *a large group of women professors pointed out:* Stephen M. Marks, Female faculty discuss tenure, *Harvard Crimson,* October 8, 2004.

260 *tipped the views of professors who supported him:* Sara Ivry, Did an exposé help sink Harvard's president?, *New York Times,* February 27, 2006.

260 *a lengthy narrative published in January:* David McClintick, How Harvard Lost Russia, *Institutional Investor,* January 2006, 62ff.

260 *misrepresented the truth about plans to change:* Marcella Bombardieri, Summers should go, ex-Harvard dean says, *Boston Globe,* February 16, 2006.

261 *posted on the Harvard web site and parroted:* Summers to step down as president at end of academic year, *Harvard University Gazette,* February 23, 2006; Scott S. Greenberger, Bold style brought firm Allston plans, larger public role, *Boston Globe,* February 22, 2006; John Tierney, The faculty club, *New York Times,* February 25, 2006.

261 *data documenting educational problem areas had been collected and published:* David C. Newman, Survey says advising lags, *Harvard Crimson,* December 10, 2001.

261 *only $2 million in a financial aid budget:* Michael M. Grynbaum, A year after Harvard, Yale expands aid, *Harvard Crimson,* March 4, 2005; College's yield rises to nearly 80 percent, *Harvard University Gazette,* May 12, 2005.

262 *inmates eager to run the asylum:* See, for example, Faculty 1, Summers 0, editorial, Boston Herald, February 22, 2006.

263 *the Corporation ultimately played:* In a welcome signal of changing attitudes, a
     few days after the resignation one of the Fellows publicly stated that she knew
     the Faculty did not want to take over the university. Maria Sacchetti and Kath-
     leen Burge, At Harvard, faculty push for openness, Boston Globe, February
     24, 2006.

265 *Excellence, as Lindsay Waters said:* Waters, *Enemies of Promise*, 39, 87.

267 *"tough love, with reason":* Jeremy Knowles quoted by Anthony Flint, Harvard's
     Archie Epps is dead at 66, *Boston Globe*, August 23, 2003.

Index